Young People, Employment and Work Psychology

GW00778421

Youth unemployment and underemployment is a serious issue in most developed countries in the world. Having few young people in the workplace has serious and lasting consequences for generations of young people, their families, businesses and society as a whole. Dr Carter explores these important issues from multiple (and international) perspectives, offering research evidence and guiding frameworks from social and work psychology, to get more young people into good work.

Young People, Employment and Work Psychology brings together educators, researchers, occupational psychologists and government agencies responding to young people struggling to gain and sustain employment. Theoretically based and evidence-driven, this book explores the consequences of unemployment, suggests ways in which businesses can enable young people's first steps into employment and gives practical advice to young people and employers to prepare for and gain entry-level roles and develop more diverse workplaces. From the reasons why organizations are often reluctant to employ young people, to issues of motivation and confidence which often affect young people's perspective in looking for work, the book covers several interventions within both the public and private sector.

This book is an invaluable resource for employers, policy makers and professionals working with young people, as well as for students and researchers in work and organizational psychology, HRM, business management and social policy.

Angela J Carter is an Occupational Psychologist with over 20 years' experience of working with individuals, groups and organizations. She is passionate about applying the knowledge of work and organizational psychology to our daily work.

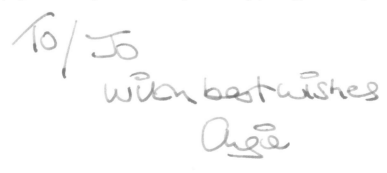

Young People, Employment and Work Psychology

Interventions and Solutions

Edited by Angela J Carter

Routledge
Taylor & Francis Group

LONDON AND NEW YORK

First published 2019
by Routledge
2 Park Square, Milton Park, Abingdon, Oxon OX14 4RN

and by Routledge
711 Third Avenue, New York, NY 10017

Routledge is an imprint of the Taylor & Francis Group, an informa business

British Library Cataloguing-in-Publication Data
A catalogue record for this book is available from the British Library

Library of Congress Cataloging-in-Publication Data
A catalog record has been requested for this book

ISBN: 978-1-138-93779-6 (hbk)
ISBN: 978-1-138-93780-2 (pbk)
ISBN: 978-1-315-67612-8 (ebk)

Typeset in Goudy
by Swales & Willis Ltd, Exeter, Devon, UK

MIX
Paper from
responsible sources
FSC
www.fsc.org   FSC® C013056

Printed and bound in Great Britain by
TJ International Ltd, Padstow, Cornwall

Contents

Author biographies

David Carew is an Occupational Psychologist. He joined the Department for Work and Pensions in 2006 and he is currently Chief Psychologist. David has worked in different employment sectors spanning public, private and non-governmental organizations. His work includes organizational development and change, culture redesign, development of health, work and well-being interventions and design of learning and development interventions.

He has also worked in the field of employment, disability and work rehabilitation for over 25 years where he has contributed to frontline services, staff development and policy work with the UK and Scottish Governments and he has worked extensively in Europe and the US.

His areas of special interest are the role of work psychology and psychosocial factors in workplace health, the psychological contract, job-seeking behaviour, customer engagement, head injury, mental health, ex-offenders and the application of work psychology to the needs of people who experience unemployment. David has published in the field of employment rehabilitation and head injury and has lectured in organizational and work psychology. He is a past Chair of both the British Psychological Society Division of Occupational Psychology and Qualification in Occupational Psychology Board, and is the current Deputy Chair of the BPS Qualifications Committee.

Angela J Carter is an Occupational Psychologist with a passion for applying the knowledge of work and organizational psychology to practice. Angela has just celebrated 50 years of working as a scientist and an educator, first in the health care sector, then in higher education and consultancy (with her company Just Development). Leaving school with ordinary level qualifications Angela gained part-time qualifications of ONC, diploma, higher and teaching diploma in Radiography and NVQ qualifications before achieving a BSc Psychology and MSc Occupational Psychology from London University and a PhD from the University of Sheffield. At the Institute of Work Psychology her research spanned teamwork, well-being, management style and performance appraisal.

Angela has many years of experience in voluntary working for professional bodies. She was the Chair of the Division of Occupational Psychology and

Trustee of the British Psychological Society (BPS) in times of change and regulation with the Health and Care Professions Council (HCPC). She has worked extensively for the European Association of Work and Organizational Psychology (EAWOP) developing practitioner education programmes (the WorkLab), an applied journal (*InPractice*), and professionalising Work and Organizational Psychology across Europe. She received EAWOP's life-time achievement award for her work in 2017 and the BPS Division of Occupational Psychology award for Lifetime Contribution to Occupational Psychology in 2019.

Her most recent research has focussed on youth employment after being struck by how few organizations employ young people under the age of 24 years. She shares these concerns with the authors of this book who are all active in championing better work opportunities for young people.

Dawn Gosden is an Occupational Psychologist and Associate Fellow of the British Psychological Society. Employed by the Department for Work and Pensions (DWP), she has 20 years' experience of organizational consulting at individual, team and organizational levels. Dawn also has considerable experience of working as a Human Resource (HR) Business Partner in large multi-site areas of the business within DWP. Balancing practical experience of working as an Occupational Psychologist Consultant and HR Specialist, Dawn's focus has been on selection and assessment, including programmes designed to identify and develop high potential talent and graduate recruitment programmes. She has valuable experience of the design and delivery of leadership development and organizational change initiatives. A qualified and experienced cognitive behavioural/executive coach, Dawn has coached a range of people from school students and graduate trainees through to senior managers. Applying her experience as a Talent Consultant, one of Dawn's recent work assignments entailed designing the DWP Coaching Strategy, aimed at enabling the organization to create a coaching culture. She continues work on implementing this strategy in her present HR Business Partner role. Throughout her career, Dawn has demonstrated a passion and commitment to working with individuals and groups to help them raise their self-awareness, either to identify ways of working together more effectively, cope with organizational change, or realise their potential by overcoming barriers to their career development.

Sue Gould is an Occupational Psychologist who works as a Senior Work Psychology Leader within the Department for Work and Pensions. She has experience of working across both public- and private-sector organizations. Sue has also worked in the educational sector, both as a teacher and Senior Research Officer, undertaking educational research and evaluation of education and training programmes.

Sue's interest in youth employment includes membership of the Division of Occupational Psychology Youth Employment Working Group where she has presented papers as part of a symposium on the importance of employment assessment interventions to facilitate employment outcomes in young people. Sue has presented papers at both the Division of Occupational Psychology annual conference and the European Association of Work and Organizational Psychology Congress.

Sue has worked within the area of employment and disability for over 20 years, with specialist interest in the areas of mental health, job-seeking behaviour, specific learning difficulties, workplace job design, coaching and application of occupational psychology to support individuals to obtain and remain in work.

Yeşim Guner is an Occupational Psychologist and Associate Fellow of the British Psychological Society, with over 13 years of experience working with young people. She was born in London to hard-working parents who immigrated to the UK from North Cyprus in the 1960s, telling her to "put your back into anything, you shall succeed". Her father, who trained as an electrical engineer, was her main inspiration to entering her pursuit to becoming an Occupational Psychologist.

Yeşim completed her Master's degree at the Institute of Work Psychology (University of Sheffield) in 2004 and qualified as an Occupational Psychologist in 2008, which was also when she embarked on her journey as a local government employee. Here she utilised past and current knowledge, skills and abilities to provide young people living in the borough with the support they needed. She soon became a strong advocate for these young people, ready to support them in breaking down barriers and "fighting" for their success.

Yeşim has stated she is hopeful that the 2020 Government initiatives for "more unified working amongst all professionals to support vulnerable young people and their families to the highest standards" will be a true success. She says

> it is fair to say that my husband and I wish for nothing more for our daughter than to grow up to be a well-rounded member of society with a strong foundation and good employment opportunities when (if she decides to take that route) she graduates and becomes ready to embark on her own professional career, whatever that may be.

Afreen Hussain completed her BSc Psychology (Counselling) in 2014 followed by her MSc in Occupational Psychology in 2015. Whilst studying for her Master's degree Afreen had the opportunity to conduct community research to encourage disadvantaged young people to share the personal nature of their unemployment. Afreen is passionate about guiding young people to flourish in society, to lift barriers and hurdles, thus inspiring self-confidence.

Afreen's personal journey of hardship made it possible to relate to young people not in employment, education and training (NEET) from rural areas, and so consequently aid an understanding of a diverse range of adverse experiences. This skill has enabled the study and collection of relevant information in turn adding value to the field of work psychology around young people.

Rebecca Levi has worked in Human Resources for over 20 years, following the completion of degrees in Marketing and French including an 18-month placement in France. Her varied roles have included Graduate Recruitment Manager for large blue chip organizations, developing the ASPIRE Programme at Axe Valley Community College and, currently, as a People Development Specialist for a large energy company. Rebecca has recently designed and launched a Work Insight Programme for the energy company, providing students from low-income backgrounds with the opportunity to gain an in-depth insight into the world of work through work experience opportunities, development centres and a 1–1 mentor during their two years in Sixth Form.

Rebecca is a strong believer in developing employability skills from a young age and, eight years ago, she designed and ran Dramakids workshops for pre-school children in East Devon, developing their self-esteem, confidence and communication skills. She also managed a local pre-school for three years.

Hannah Matta is an Occupational Psychologist and coach, passionate about applying the science of psychology at work. Based in Dubai for the past four years, currently she is the Head of Talent, Learning and Culture at a young, dynamic and fast-moving start-up in the ride-hailing industry where the purpose is to "simplify and improve the lives of people and build an awesome organization that inspires. My part in that is to revolutionize the colleague experience". Prior to this Hannah was based in the UK with a mix of in-house and external consulting roles held over the past 13 years in a variety of sectors.

Rosalind H Searle holds the chair in HRM and Organizational Psychology at the Adam Smith Business School at the University of Glasgow. She is an Occupational Psychologist and a Fellow of the British Psychological Society (BPS). Her research focusses on organizational trust and HRM, trust and controls, change and counterproductive work behaviours. Her previous academic positions include those at Coventry University, where she co-founded the Centre for Trust, Peace and Social Relations, and at the Open University and Aston University. She is co-editor of the *Routledge Companion to Trust* (2018) and serves on the editorial boards of the *Journal of Management*, the *Journal of Trust Research* and *International Perspectives in Psychology: Research, Practice, Consultation* (IPP). Her research appears in leading international journals (e.g., *Human Resource Management*, *Journal of Organizational Behavior*, *International Journal of HRM* and *Long Range Planning*) and in commissioned research for regulators (e.g., Professional Standards Authority), government (e.g., Welsh Audit, Scottish and English Governments) and private organizations (e.g., energy sector). She was lead author for the Alliances of Organizational Psychology White Paper on youth employment.

Eva Selenko is a senior lecturer in Work Psychology at Loughborough University, UK. Her research centres on precarious employment situations and how these affect well-being, performance and non-work-related behaviour. She is particularly interested in the relationship between work and identity, and how atypical work situations undermine and affect people's professional identity. Her research has been well published in numerous world-leading academic journals and is well cited. She also acts as associate editor for the journal *Applied Psychology: An International Review*. Eva holds an MSc in Social and Organizational Psychology from the University of Groningen, the Netherlands, a doctorate in Psychology from the University of Graz and has recently gained Habitation at the University of Linz (both in Austria). Prior to joining Loughborough in July 2016, Eva was a lecturer at the Institute of Work Psychology at the University of Sheffield.

Glossary of terms

ABC Work psychologists and work coaches use the ABC model of skills, values, interests and work goals. Self- or peer-assessed measures allow people to appreciate their longer-term goals for a job, a better job and their career. Young people develop action plans using the ABC to judge their progress towards these goals and to see what they have been able to achieve (for more detail see Chapter 8).

ACEVO Association of Chief Executives of Voluntary Organizations is a UK network for charity and social enterprise leaders. For more information see: www.acevo.org.uk/about-us.

Apprentice National Minimum Wage The minimum hourly rate of pay set by the UK Government for apprentices. The amount varies with age (under and over 19 years) and accounts for costs of training in their job role. For more information see: www.gov.uk/national-minimum-wage-rates. Rates may be set higher than minimum (see discussion in Chapter 7).

Apprenticeship Training Provider (ATP) Organizations that are eligible to receive government funding (in England) to train apprentices.

Atypical work Work with irregular contracts (e.g., zero hours) or no contract of employment. Evidence suggests that atypical work is increasing across Europe, with the youngest workers most affected by these insecure types of work. This work is often described as part of the gig economy.

British Psychological Society (BPS) The representative body for psychology and psychologists in the UK, responsible for the development, promotion and application of psychology for the public good. See: www.bps.org.uk.

CAMHs Child and Adolescent Mental Health services are specialist NHS children and young people's mental health services.

Claimant Commitment (CC) Agreement made by those claiming Universal Credit describing their availability for work and job-search activities aimed at securing work.

Coach or mentor An adult selected to work with young people to talk through their work aspirations and associated decisions with education and work to help achieve their goals. Coaches may be chosen by schools (see Chapter 6), being carefully vetted to take this role. Various models of coaching or mentorship may be used when working with young people.

Confederation of British Industry (CBI)   Britain's biggest business lobby group providing a voice for firms to policymakers at a regional, national and international level. The CBI represents over 190,000 businesses and 140 trade organizations employing over one third of the UK's private sector workforce (over seven million people). Their purpose is helping business create a more prosperous society.

Connexions   Connexions was a UK governmental information, advice, guidance and support service for young people aged 13 to 19 years (and up to 25 years for young people with learning difficulties and/or disabilities), created in 2000 following the Learning and Skills Act. Connexions is no longer a coherent national service following the announcement of changes to the delivery of careers in England in 2008.

Contingency work   Temporary or part-time work with precarious contracts such as zero-hours. See also **Atypical work**.

Convention on the Organization for Economic Co-operation and Development (OECD)   The OECD was set up in 1960 and 34 countries are members. See: www.oecd.org/about/membersandpartners/list-oecd-member-countries.htm.

Coping strategies   Coping strategies are psychological patterns that individuals use to manage thoughts, feelings and actions encountered during various stages of ill health and treatments. Various coping strategies are advocated to deal with the stress and anxiety associated with looking for work. For example, see **ABC**.

Department for Work and Pensions (DWP)   UK employment service responsible for welfare, labour market policy, pensions and child maintenance policy. The biggest UK public service department, which administers the state pension and a range of working age, disability and ill-health benefits to over 22 million people.

Departmental psychologists   Psychologists working at the DWP.

Detached youth work   Youth work provides targeted social education opportunities for young people in a variety of settings. Detached youth work (sometimes called outreach work) aims to identify and provide support to vulnerable young people in their own 'territory' such as streets, cafés and parks. This work is aimed particularly at reducing youth-related anti-social behaviour (see Chapter 5).

Development Centre (DC) and Assessment Centre (AC)   Places that assess (an Assessment Centre) and provide feedback (a Development Centre) on the skills and competencies of individuals. Often assessment includes a number of individual and group exercises (e.g., a mock interview) collecting evidence against a set of competencies judged sufficient to perform a job role or task. Provision of feedback as part of the event is the main difference between ACs and DCs, with individual development plans formulated to focus on key personal development needs. Strengths-based exercises, such as making a presentation, are often used with young people (see Chapter 6). There are professional standards for assessment centres, see: www1.bps.org.uk/networks-and-communities/member-microsite/division-occupational-psychology/assessment-centre-standards.

Emotional Intelligence (EI) A popular concept describing an individual's capability to recognise their own emotions and those of others, to discern between different feelings and label them appropriately, to use emotional information to guide thinking and behaviour, and to manage and/or adjust emotions to adapt to environments or achieve one's goal (see Chapter 6).

Employee Assistance Programmes (EAPs) Employer-funded benefit offering employees confidential counselling and advice on work and personal issues. Providers may be recognised by the UK EAP Association that promotes standards of employee assistance, psychological health and well-being.

Employment Assessment (EA) Technique exploring the attributes of the individual, the environment, and the individual–environment interaction as a dynamic process; assisting job seekers to make informed decisions about an appropriate and specific job. Employment assessment involves interviews, feedback and action planning, using, for example, aptitude tests, work samples and job trials in order to contribute to predicting potential job performance. This process helps the job seeker to build the belief that they can perform in the job role (see Chapter 8).

Employment assets Evidence demonstrating the employability or employment potential of an individual (see Chapter 8).

Eudaimonic well-being Well-being is about optimal psychological functioning and experience. Current research focusses on two different perspectives: the eudaimonic approach focussing on meaning and self-realisation and examining how we function; and the hedonic approach focussing on the experience of happiness. (See Ryan, R.M. & Deci, E.L. 2001. On happiness and human potentials: a review of research on hedonic and eudaimonic well-being. *Annual Review of Psychology, 52*(1), 141–166).

Focus groups A research or consultation method in which a group of people are asked a series of questions that they discuss and their conversations are recorded and analysed. A useful method of gaining opinions or views where others' opinions can be heard, unlike in a one-to-one interview.

General Certificate of Secondary Education (GCSE) Academic qualification generally taken in a number of subjects by pupils in secondary education in England, Wales and Northern Ireland. Each GCSE qualification is in a particular subject and stands alone, but a suite of such qualifications (or their equivalents) is generally accepted as the record of achievement at the age of 16 years in place of a leaving certificate or baccalaureate qualification in other countries. Introduced in 1988 to replace O-Level (GCE Ordinary Level) and CSE (Certificate of Secondary Education) qualifications.

Generation Y Term to describe a group of people born between 1979 and 1991.

Gig economy Contemporary phrase referring to a labour market that is characterised by short-term contracts and unregulated working. Contingency work and atypical work that many young people have to take on in order to get a job is described as part of this work sector.

Good work   It is not just important to find a job, but to find one that is stable and will lead to growth and development. But many young people do not find these job roles. (Chapters 1 and 9 describe characteristics of good work.)

Health and Care Professions Council (HCPC)   The UK governmental body regulating people working in various professions including psychologists. Its role is to protect the public by keeping an open register of health and care professionals who meet the standards of training, professional skills, behaviour and health. See: http://hpc-uk.org/aboutus.

Hedonic well-being   Well-being is about the experience of happiness and optimal psychological functioning. Current research focusses on two different perspectives: the hedonic approach focussing on the experience of happiness (and the avoidance of unhappiness); and the eudaimonic approach focussing on meaning and self-realisation, examining how we function. (See Ryan, R.M. & Deci, E.L. 2001. On happiness and human potentials: a review of research on hedonic and eudaimonic well-being. *Annual Review of Psychology*, *52*(1), 141–166.)

Human capital   Defined by the Office for National Statistics (ONS) as "the knowledge, skills, competencies and attributes embodied in individuals that facilitate the creation of personal, social and economic well-being". It sees education and training as investment into individuals' value and how much potential they gain. The stock of human capital is measured in order to understand the economic growth and performance of the educational sector. Looking at changes over time provides important information on the long-term sustainability of economies (for more detail see Chapter 9).

International Labour Organization (ILO)   Formed in 1919, the ILO is a United Nations agency dealing with labour issues, particularly international labour standards, social protection and work opportunities for all. The International Labour Office is the administration office of the ILO.

Jobcentre Plus (JCP)   The DWP department providing a range of job broking and financial assistance programmes to individuals who are unemployed. Young people looking for work and wishing to claim benefits can contact the department through a number of channels in order to speak with an advisor or to make a job search. Jobcentre Plus employs work coaches, work psychologists and disability employment advisers to help individuals to find employment.

Key Skills   In the 1990s employers were concerned that apprenticeships were not developing young peoples' essential skills in English, Mathematics and Information and Communication Technology. This led to the development of Key Skills qualifications as an important component of 14–19 year olds' education in England, Northern Ireland and Wales. Such qualifications are now described as Functional Skills.

KSAs   Abbreviation referring to an individual's knowledge, skills and attributes that they bring to a job role. When recruiting young people with little experience of work it is important to consider their potential (rather than actual) KSAs.

MENA countries   A grouping of countries from the Middle East, North Africa and Asia.

Mentor or coach   A mentor gives a younger or less-experienced person help and advice over a period of time, especially at work or school. Coaching is a form of development where a coach supports a learner to achieve specific personal or professional goals by providing guidance. Coaching could be an informal relationship between two people, where one has more experience and expertise offering guidance as the other learns; or co-coaching is where both people provide guidance and learn. Some differentiate the processes of mentoring and coaching, but in this book both are used in relation to support and guidance.

Millennials (Generation Y)   Those born after 1980.

Moderator   Statistical term offering evidence that a specific variable has an influence on a particular relationship. For example, age influences the experience of unemployment with younger and older people being more likely to experience negative effects of unemployment than those in middle age (for more detail see Chapter 4).

NEETs   A group of people who are not in education, employment or training.

Occupational Psychology   The application of the science of psychology to work. Occupational psychologists use psychological theories and approaches to deliver tangible benefits by enhancing the effectiveness of organizations and developing the performance, motivation and well-being of people in the workplace. Occupational psychologists are regulated by the HCPC in the UK, and may be known as Work and Organizational Psychologists in Europe and Industrial and Organizational Psychologists in the USA.

Office for National Statistics (ONS)   The ONS is the UK's largest independent producer of official statistics and its recognised national statistical institute. The ONS is responsible for collecting and publishing statistics related to the economy, population and society at national, regional and local levels.

Pupil Referral Unit (PRU)   A Pupil Referral Unit is a multi-agency centre providing short-term educational support for young people suffering from severe mental health issues. These pupils have been previously assessed as being unfit for mainstream school provision.

Secondary school (UK)   A secondary school is both an organization that provides secondary education and the building where this takes place. Some secondary schools can provide both lower secondary education and upper secondary education, but these can also be provided in separate schools, as in the American middle-school and high-school system. Secondary schools typically follow on from primary schools and lead into vocational and tertiary education.

Sector-based academies   A government initiative to help young people get into work with programmes lasting for six weeks.

SEND   A classification of Special Educational Needs and Disabilities where an individual's disabilities are graded mild, moderate or severe.

Snowball sampling   A technique used by researchers when it is difficult to gain participants to take on a study. Contributing participants are asked to recommend others fitting the study criteria.

Social capital   Social capital is a complex concept looking at how social groups function. This includes interpersonal relationships where there is a shared sense of identity, values, trust, and co-operation. Social capital can be used to explain the improved performance of diverse groups and the development of communities (for more detail see Chapters 4 and 9).

Statementing   This refers to a statement of special needs, which is a formal document detailing a child's learning difficulties and the help that they will be given. Only around 2 per cent of children need a statement; not every child with special learning needs necessarily needs a statement but it is required if a school is unable to meet a child's needs without external assistance.

STWT   School to Work Transition and its associated study.

Supply chains   Organizations do not work in isolation and goods and services are supplied from one organization to another to produce end products (such as clothes or cars). Many components travel between countries in a pattern called a supply chain. The notion of globalisation of production implies that the local supply of materials has been extended world-wide to provide the cheapest and most accessible resources.

Support for Schools Initiative   An initiative supported by the DWP enabling young people to make effective transitions from school to work, training or further study. Young people in secondary schools are provided with information and advice about the labour market, employer expectations, vocational routes into employment and work experience, allowing them to make well-informed decisions about their future career paths.

Tertiary education   The third stage of education, following completion of school providing a secondary education; also described as post-secondary education. Tertiary education generally culminates in the receipt of certificates, diplomas or academic degrees.

Universal Credit (UC)   Universal Credit was introduced in the UK in 2012 to help those without work to make the transition to employment, and for those in work to increase their prospects to earn more (described as an in- and out-of-work credit). Jobcentre Plus work coach support aligns with UC and is designed to support the Government's welfare reform agenda to reduce poverty by making work pay. For more information see Chapter 8.

Visioning   A method used by psychologists to explore future work roles and identities to enable decision-making and goal-setting.

Work Psychology   The practice of Occupational Psychology is often described by the easier to understand term of Work Psychology. In essence this is the science of people at work.

Work Skills Pilots   The 18–21 Work Skills Pilot Scheme is designed to assist 18 to 21 year olds to improve their chances of obtaining employment by supporting them to develop English and Mathematics proficiency (or both), or to undertake skills training or work-related activity such as a period of work experience.

Work solution   A term used in the DWP to identify a disparity between the job and a person related to a labour market constraint. When resolved, the solution enables the individual to perform the job successfully.

Youth Employment Initiative (YEI)   The YEI provides training, support and voluntary activities to complement existing government programmes aimed at reducing NEETs.

Youth Engagement Fund Social Impact (YEFSI) Bond   The YEFSI Bond is investment targeted at specific groups of young people who may require additional and specific support to access the job market (such as lone parents, looked-after children and care givers, carers, ex-offenders, those involved in gangs and those with learning difficulties and disabilities), (see Chapter 8).

Youth Guarantee scheme   The Youth Guarantee is a number of plans by the European Union to target youth unemployment (see Chapter 4).

Youth Obligation   Commencing in the UK in April 2017, this policy provides for young people to remain in school (or other mandatory participation) up until they reach 18 years of age. A three-week programme of support is provided to young people to help them find work, an apprenticeship or a training position within a period of six months (see Chapter 8).

Youth Unemployment Innovation Fund   The Youth Unemployment Innovation Fund employs social investment partnerships to work with disadvantaged young people aged 14 years and over to improve their chances of gaining employment.

Preface

Angela J Carter

Behind every book there is a story and this one is about a group of people coming together over a period of six years determined to improve the employment prospects for young people. I first became aware that there were nearly one million young people unemployed in the UK in 2012. This was a stark contrast to my own easy transition from education to employment decades before. Being involved in higher education I was aware of the talent and energy young people could bring to the workplace and I was really aghast to read that only one in four UK organizations employed young people under the age of 24 years (SKOPE, 2012). As a practicing Occupational Psychologist assisting companies in their employment decision-making, I felt the application of work psychology could open up more job opportunities for young people. The starting point was to make more people (not just psychologists but business owners and employers) aware of the issues facing young people transitioning into employment and how few job opportunities were available for them.

As my own awareness of young people's employment issues was developing I had the pleasure of working with two young and inspiring trainee Occupational Psychologists who were involved in supporting young people from youth work and organizational development perspectives. However, what was missing from their research was the voices of the young people themselves describing what it was like to leave education and to try and find work. At this time, I was invited to work with a Metropolitan University in the north of England along with an employer. This offered the opportunity to bring together young people and the Department for Work and Pensions (DWP) to explore experiences of the transition from education to work and to offer feedback to the DWP about how they could make their services more accessible for young people.

Thus, our group of work psychologists formed and we captured our research and interventions in a symposium (Carter et al., 2013a) at the British Psychological Society (BPS) Division of Occupational Psychology (DOP) Conference in January 2013. Presenting this material, we met two other like-minded professionals working with a community college in the south-west of England and they quickly joined our group. Two important stakeholders were impressed by these presentations. The DOP Executive agreed to fund a working party to explore the issues young people were facing and the Youth Employment Working Group immediately formed. Second, the volume editor of this publication invited the group to write an edited book on this topic, but this approach was initially declined as we felt our thoughts and ideas had yet to mature.

The Youth Employment Working Group carried out a series of awareness-raising events with psychologists, employers and students over the next year (e.g., Carter 2013b), culminating in a second DOP symposium highlighting what can be done to sustain communities of good work (Carter et al., 2014). Here the conference delegates heard more about the work being done in London Local Authorities to engage young apprentices (see Chapter 7); how many psychometric screening processes worked against young people's employment selection and how a forward-thinking college was preparing young people for future employment (see Chapter 6). This time the approach from the volume editor was accepted by the group and ideas for this publication started to take shape.

In 2015 a position paper outlining the group's purpose was presented in the *Psychologist* (Carter, 2015a) and the youth employment situation was explored in other European countries and from a global perspective (Carter et al., 2015). The bulk of the book was written between 2015 and 2016 adding further young people's voices (Chapters 3 and 5), European (Chapter 4) and international perspectives (Chapter 2). A further step forward was achieved when funding was gained from the University of Sheffield for doctoral study of the transition from education to work commencing in 2016.

We felt that awareness raising was gaining ground when I was invited to give a paper about (the lack of) workplace diversity (Carter, 2015b) at the annual Health and Well-being at Work conference. A further international awareness-raising symposium was given in Dubai highlighting the very high incidence of youth unemployment in the Middle East (Carter, Choumar & Morshed, 2016).

The book was taking shape in 2016 when a series of events highlighted the challenges of bringing a publication on such an important topic to fruition. As two of the chapters are written by authors working for DWP, a government department, there is a requirement for a review process to take place before their work can be released for publication. Additional contextual factors including the introduction of new regulations and legislation on youth employment meant that any description of this work had to be accurate and up to date if it was to be published. Then, there was an unexpected UK General Election suspending all government decision-making during the pre-election period (a period known as Purdah (n.d.)). Thus Chapter 8 in this book takes a slightly more recent approach to the UK provision to support young people.

The work of the Youth Employment Working Group continues today, and we thank the DOP for their on-going support. Awareness raising continues with a European symposium held in 2017 (Carter, Parry & Gould, 2017) exploring young people's transitions from education to work and an international symposium in June 2018 (Parry, Bal, Jameson & Dean, 2018). Further events are planned for 2019 bringing employers and young people together to highlight opportunities for the co-creation of entry-level roles, supported by this publication.

This book is dedicated to increasing our understanding of the problems young people are facing as they leave education and attempt to enter the work place. We examine these issues principally from a work psychology perspective, suggesting models and theories that will inform research and intervention with the aim of assisting young people in their education-to-work transitions.

References

Carter, A.J. (Chair), Richmond, P., Walker, A., Guner, Y., Gould, S., Lewis, H. & Matta, H. (2013a). Supporting young society. Symposium given at the BPS Division of Occupational Psychology Conference, 9–11 January, Chester.

Carter, A.J. (2013b, July). Supporting young society: what can psychologists do to help youth employment? Paper given to the BPS South West Branch 'Psychology in the Pub', Exeter.

Carter, A.J. (Chair), Levi, R., Gosden, D., Matta, H., Palermo, G., Bourne, A., Gould, S. & Carew, D. (2014). Sustaining communities of good work. Symposium given at DOP conference, 8–10 January, Brighton.

Carter, A.J. (2015a). Youth employment – the missing facts. *The Psychologist*, 28(6), 462–465.

Carter, A.J. (2015b, March). The challenge of youth employment. Health and Well-being at Work conference, Birmingham, UK.

Carter, A.J. (Chair), Peiró, J.M., Vakola, M., Nickolaou, I., Kyriakou, O., Searle, R.H., Gabrielsen, S. & Brøgger, B. (2015). We need to tackle youth employment in other ways. Symposium given at the EAWOP Congress, 20–23 May 2015, Oslo, Norway.

Carter, A., Choumar, S. & Morshed, A. (2016, October). Youth employment: a global dilemma. International Psychology Conference, Dubai, UEA.

Carter, A.J., Parry, E. & Gould, S. (2017, May). Supporting young peoples' journey from education to work. Symposium given at the 18th EAWOP Congress, Dublin, Ireland.

Parry, E., Bal, E., Jameson, A. & Dean, L. (2018, June). Young people's transitions from education to employment: organizational and individual perspectives from Turkey, Ireland and the UK. Symposium presented at the International Conference of the Institute of Work Psychology, held in Sheffield, 19–21 June.

Purdah (n.d.). Purdah [definition]. *See* https://en.wikipedia.org/wiki/Purdah (pre-election period).

SKOPE: ESRC Centre on Skills, Knowledge and Organizational Performance (2012, May). Youth transitions, the labour market and entry into employment: some reflections and questions. Research Paper no. 108, SKOPE: ESRC Centre on Skills, Knowledge and Organizational Performance. Oxford: University of Oxford.

1 Youth employment

Unpacking different perspectives

Angela J Carter

Issues facing young people leaving education

As we begin our enquiry there are 625,000 young people (aged between 16 and 24 years) unemployed (ONS December, 2015) and 848,000 not in education, employment or training (NEET) (ONS November, 2015). While this figure has dropped from nearly one million young people in 2012 (IPPR, 2014), youth unemployment in the UK remains at an alarmingly high rate (3.74 times that of the adult population (Eurostat, 2013)), almost double that of most of our European neighbours. A recent report by the Joseph Rowntree Foundation (George, Metcalf, Tufekci & Wilkinson, 2015) describes young people under the age of 25 years having the greatest disadvantage in the labour market, with the current generation of job seekers being more affected by unemployment than the previous generation, despite overall employment having risen.

The UK is not alone with this issue. Youth unemployment (aged 18–25 years) is a major issue in European countries (Eurostat, 2013), the United States of America (Symonds, Schwartz & Ferguson, 2011) and other developed countries (Chand & Tung, 2014). Unemployment rates differ between countries, with almost half of the under 25 year olds in Greece, Spain and Croatia being unemployed (IIEA, 2014) in comparison with 14% in the UK, 11% across the European Union (Eurostat, 2013), 7.2% in the USA and 4.9% in Japan (Akkermans, Nykänen & Vuori, 2015).

However, young people in the UK are exceptional within the EU, with higher percentages entering the labour market aged 16 years and fewer participating in post-compulsory education (OECD, 1998, cited in Canny, 2001). However, while trends in youth employment in Europe seem to be associated with the most recent economic crisis, employment of young people in the UK is decreasing (George et al., 2015, p. 17) and has been declining for 15 years (Low Pay Commission, 2015; SKOPE, 2012) or even longer (Canny, 2001; Manpower Services Commission, 1978). In the previous recession it was noted that school leavers were experiencing greater difficultly in gaining employment than other job seekers (Manpower Services Commission, 1978), particularly if they had few or no qualifications. This suggests young people in the UK have been disadvantaged in the job market for many years before our current focus and little has been done to address the lack of job opportunities available for young people.

With so many young people seeking work it is perverse to hear recruiters and managers lamenting the poor quality of applicants they receive for new and existing roles. But, with fewer than one in four organizations in the UK actually employing those under 24 years of age (SKOPE, 2012) and as few as 6% of organizations employing school leavers of 16 years (UKCES, 2011), few employers have experience of working with young people transitioning from education. Further, a dichotomy exists with employers reporting ageing workforces (CIPD, 2015; UKCES, 2011, 2012) and being concerned about future skills shortages. So why are the majority of UK employers not recruiting young people and investing in their skills development?

The exclusion of young people from the workplace affects everyone in our society. Young people themselves are going to extraordinary lengths to be seen as credible employees. However, with their efforts being rarely acknowledged by employers, young people's enthusiasm for work decreases along with their self-esteem and confidence. Parents are only too aware of these issues and many families are struggling to support young people, both psychologically and financially, through extended adolescence, with young people often not finding independence until their late 20s or 30s. Among these problems are poor mental health, alcohol and drug abuse, affecting both young people and their family's futures. Further, these issues cost local and national government millions of pounds each year to provide health and welfare support. Society notices the impact of young people's behaviour, frustrated by their lack of independence and denying them a true sense of identity (Brown, 2011). Young people can be drawn into antisocial and criminal behaviour, sometimes encouraged by their peers who are similarly disaffected.

Models of education differ widely, across countries and between regions within countries, particularly in relation to the emphasis placed on higher or vocational education. However, in the 21st century most educational providers have increased their efforts to assist school, college and university leavers with employability advice, aided by a host of publications (e.g., Cottrell, 2015) offering support and advice. The UK Government strives for solutions to youth unemployment favouring developing and supporting apprenticeship schemes. Unfortunately, many employers and members of the public misinterpret these schemes as narrowly focussed on science subjects (such as engineering) rather than the broad array of possible apprenticeships. But, despite these efforts, young people are still struggling to find employment that offers them a decent wage and stimulating work.

Youth employment is a sensitive political issue and the school leaving age in the UK was increased to 18 years in 2016. Compared with other European countries the UK has appeared slow to support the Youth Guarantee scheme (European Commission: Employment, Social Affairs & Inclusion, 2013) taken on by most other European Union (EU) countries. However, these facts, along with few job opportunities available to young people, are rarely discussed by the general public or employing organizations. Yet, youth unemployment is a real problem for the future of the UK economy. The Working Futures projects (e.g., Wilson, Beaven, May-Gillings, Hay & Stevens, 2014) examine employment trends every ten years (most recently from 2012 to 2022) to understand industry demands and enable planning for skills and qualifications for the future. Employment in the highest status occupations (scientists, research and development managers, Higher Education teaching professionals and associate professionals) is projected to increase by 1.8 million new jobs by 2022. Therefore, it is critical that young people have early access to these occupations in order to build their skills and experience to progress in order to sustain the UK economy.

In summary, the lack of youth employment opportunities is a major social problem of our time and has been a growing issue for several decades. Faced with high fees for education, young people are fast becoming dissatisfied and frustrated, feeling forgotten by our society (cf, Howker & Malik, 2010). Clearly this a complex issue and this chapter will explore some of the many factors contributing to the UK's low rates of youth employment and will suggest a model to enable research and develop solutions.

Contemporary nature of work

If you were born before the 1970s you probably walked into a paid job as soon as you left education and those with reasonable school-leaving qualifications often chose between several work roles. So, what has happened in the 21st century to make the situation so different for young people today? To answer this question, we need to explore the changing nature of employment.

Social arrangements for work have changed significantly in the last 50 years (Savickas et al., 2009). The industrialization of the 20th century led to growth in jobs and stable working conditions. The growing complexity of work required skilled and experienced workers and supervisory (or senior) roles became available, enabling workers' opportunities to transition upwards through organizational tiers. The familiar phrase 'moving up the ladder' was an integral part of career development and it was others' upward progression that generated the entry-level roles for young people to begin their experience of work. Sadly, this is no longer the description of organizational life in the 21st century.

More recent working arrangements have had to adapt to a labour market that is reducing in size due to several economic recessions in the last 50 years. To remain competitive organizations have had to become smaller, reducing the number of hierarchical levels to lower the cost of human resources. Companies previously enjoying dominance in local marketplaces have been undercut by organizations with lower costs in an increasingly global marketplace. Supported by developments in travel and communication these changes have happened quickly, resulting in a less stable and quickly changing job market that is open to a wider range of job applicants than before. Full-time job roles have been lost or reduced to part-time or contract working, and upwards movement in organizations has become rarer. Workers have had to respond to these changes by adapting to different ways of working, such as home or tele-working, and by taking on a number of part-time roles or self-employment to generate sufficient income. Thus, there is little room in the labour market for the young person seeking their first job.

Crowded market place for work

One of the features of the contemporary workplace is that many different people are looking for work. The declining manufacturing industry in the UK has meant the loss of many jobs, including entry-level roles for young men. The removal of these full-time roles means people are taking lower-paid, part-time, or self-employed work to compensate for their loss in income. Further, there are increasingly larger numbers of women working in full-time roles and staying in those roles as they are taking fewer breaks to bring up children or care for older family members.

Work is changing, with fewer entry or casual roles being available. For example, intensification of production, particularly in the food sector, has seen casual farm workers' jobs being undertaken by gangs of workers doing 14-hour shifts, seven days a week. Globalization has changed the nature of work with many lower-paid or entry-level roles being offshored to other countries at lower costs to the employer. In the UK, as in other European countries, there are many non-UK nationals and migrant workers seeking employment and prepared to take on low-paid work.

Adapting to these changes are an increasing number of self-employed workers (up to 28% of the working population, (ONS, 2015, January)). However, while a small proportion of professional workers earn a good wage from their endeavours, many self-employed people are trapped in low-paid work with minimal contracts (e.g., zero-hours). Self-employed workers in these conditions are often underemployed, seeking better quality work or extra hours to improve their incomes. Among this group are retired people who find their pension arrangements insufficient to maintain themselves without work and so they too are looking for work. The final group of workers are students, working as well as taking full- or part-time education programmes, seeking part-time roles (often in retail or service sectors) to supplement the cost of their education.

Consider the crowded job market as a mosaic of potential workers all willing to take on the entry-level roles previously available to young people. Those aged between 25 and 49 years typically have better labour market outcomes (George et al., 2015), with young people having the greatest challenges both in entering and in progressing within the labour market. Those leaving full-time education with few or no qualifications are at the greatest risk of 'being left behind' (George et al., 2015, p. 7).

A major difference between job seekers is workplace experience, with younger applicants having little actual work experience. Employers, being mindful of bottom-line costs of goods and services, feel more confident employing experienced workers who they feel are able to transfer their knowledge, skills and abilities (KSAs) directly to a new job role without the expense of training. As one London business owner told me, "There is no business case to employ young people; they will just cost me money".

So where do young people find work? Labour market surveys tell us young people take on part-time work, temporary contracts or low-paid employment (in trade, accommodation and transport sectors), and work in low-status occupations (caring, leisure, sales, customer service, process, plant and machine operatives). Therefore, it is important to differentiate between the availability of work (or job quantity, upon which most unemployment statistics are based) and job quality (work that engages the young person's KSAs). Underemployment (wanting to do more hours of work) is common for young people and is an increasing issue for this age group (15% of Generation Y report underemployment compared with 12% of the older Generation X, (George et al., 2015, pp. 22–23)). These trends paint a bleak picture for young job seekers and highlight significant changes that will need to be made to enable young people to gain the experience to fill the projected increase in high-status occupations of 2022.

Developing work identity

Much of our personal identity is gained from the work we do, giving us a place in society. When asked "what do you do?" giving our job title indicates our KSAs, values and our incomes. However, with less stable working conditions in the 21st century, a growing number of people have multiple jobs, making the answer to "what do you do?" much less clear. Multifaceted working patterns are less about what you do and more about how you use work opportunities and your influence. So how can young people develop their personal identity during the long transition between education, work and independent living?

In the past many young people were introduced to work as teenagers, having part-time or Saturday jobs whilst still at school. For example, in the 1990s between 67 to 75% of 15–24 year olds were employed in part-time work in Austria, Sweden and Denmark (United Nations, 1996, cited in Loughlin & Barling, 2001). Responsibility came early in these young people's lives; their identities developing as they examined various aspects of work and education at first hand. Young people noticed differences in autonomy between work and education encouraging them to positively associate with a work role identity (Loscocco, 1989). Early exposure to work helps young people to examine others' work roles, assisting them to make decisions about the work identity they wish to seek in the future. Following the stage models of adult development (e.g., Super, 1957, 1990), ideas and motivation for young people's futures are based on aspirations developed by observing others or developing a "dream" (Levinson, 1976) of the work identity they would like to assume. When work opportunities offer variety, interest and skill development, work identity is likely to strengthen (Caplan, 1985). The plentiful job opportunities of this time helped young people to try out several work identities before settling on a path designed to achieve a particular status (or career) along with an income that allowed choice and independence.

Personal identity encompasses aspects of our self-concept that reflect us as individuals, differentiate us from others, even from those in the same social group (Arnold et al., 2010, p. 707). Young people with a clear concept of their chosen job role have a self-concept differentiated from others in their educational cohort. Being the first person from a family to go to university would have a strong impact on a young person's self-identity, and if they are successful in their studies this will strengthen their self-esteem. As we mature we become increasingly aware of our social identity (i.e., aspects of our self-concept that reflect the general characteristics of people in the same social groups as we are, and that differentiate ourselves from members of other groups, (Arnold et al., 2010, p. 712)). Getting a job or entering specialist training develops young people's social identity as they see themselves being part of a social group, such as being a psychologist or a nurse. Membership of professional associations through the achievement of specific qualifications serves to strengthen and deepen work-related social identities boosting individual self-esteem. However, developing a strong work-role identity requires access to secure and stable work roles, particularly entry-level roles that are often scarce in today's crowded labour market.

However, childhood in the late 1990s that today's young job seekers have experienced was different. Decreasing birth rates, smaller families and working parents often meant more resources were available to secure what was thought to be a better childhood for these young people. Freed of the responsibilities of early working experiences (noted as a decline in labour market activity for this generation (George et al., 2015)), an extended childhood was encouraged. With awareness of a more difficult and differentiated job market many parents placed their emphasis on prolonged education to protect their children against future unemployment. However, these aspirations may have removed opportunities for young people to develop their work-role identities through temporary work. Erickson (1956) views adolescence as a stage where the young person is resolving their identity confusion and, if the transition from education to work is long, identity confusion may remain.

Increased time within education, reduced childhood experiences of work and continued family dependence can lower young people's self-esteem. Many young people are now in their mid-20s before interacting with the job market for the first time. They have little experience of work to offer employers and their personal identities are based on educational experiences, creating an immediate mismatch of outlook between employers and young people. Sabine Sonnentag (2012), examining the temporal aspects of our lives, explains that we become aware of our place in the world (or our 'fit' of what we can offer and what is needed) by looking back at what we have done in the past. Reflecting on the notion of fit enables us to look ahead and consider where we see ourselves in the future. Without opportunities to develop work-role identities today's young people are struggling to relate their educational experiences to the workplace, leaving them lacking in confidence and self-esteem.

Examine this example to illustrate the differences of fit between a hiring manager and the young person they are interviewing for a job. The manager comes from a meeting about future company income. Having joined the company five years ago, the manager has progressed from a shop-floor role and has introduced cost savings and innovated new products. The job is going well and the manager is hoping to gain a senior role in the future. She feels part of the company (*she fits*) and she is actively contributing to company growth. Thinking back to her first job, the manager wants to put the young person at his ease and asks him "So, where do you see yourself in five years' time?" The young person was not expecting such a complex question so early in the interview. Startled he looks back at his time in education and thinks, well I don't know, the next stage of my life is to find a job, but I don't know where that will be. The young person answers "I would like to find a job" because he is unsure whether what he has to offer will fit the company's needs. Immediately the manager thinks the young person has little ambition to work and no knowledge and experience to offer the company. Further, it is difficult for the young person to see any fit with the company unless he understands what he has to offer in terms of the KSAs required by the company. The young person lacks a developing work-role identity that would help him to translate his past educational experiences into recognisable attributes in the workplace.

What can research tell us about youth employment?

While there has been research interest in career development and transitions from education to work since the 1940s (Akkermans et al., 2015), much work has focussed on people's adaptation to the labour market throughout their career. Little emphasis has been placed on the issues young people face getting a foothold into work and the barriers they face trying to meet employers' demands for labour. Reviewing the literature offers several useful strands to develop our understanding.

When do young people become aware of work?

Studies suggest awareness of parents' work and economic circumstances develops between the ages of four and 11 years (Berti & Bombi, 1988), with children accurately reporting their parents' job satisfaction from age seven years (Abramovitch & Johnson, 1992). Family influences were thought to be the main stimulus for young people's attitudes and behaviours towards work (Barling, 1990).

Many students have their first encounters with work in part-time roles while studying (e.g., 80% of high-school students in North America (Barling & Kelloway, 1999), 37% students in the UK (ONS, 2015, December)). There was concern that more than 20 hours of work per week would be detrimental to educational attainment, and likely to be associated with distress, increased drug and alcohol use and delinquency (Bachman & Schulenburg, 1993; Steinberg, 1982). To examine these concerns researchers explored the quality of young people's early work experiences (Loughlin & Barling, 1999) to see if features known to be beneficial to adult work experiences, such as variety, autonomy and support

(Hackman & Oldham, 1980; Karasek & Theorell, 1990; Warr, 1987), were generalizable to younger workers. Work offering young people the opportunity to use their skills, particularly those useful for future work, were found to be psychologically beneficial (O'Brien & Feather, 1990) along with opportunities for social interaction and autonomy (Loughlin & Barling, 2001). Therefore, good quality part-time work has benefits for young workers.

Young people (Millennials) entering the workforce after 2000 are aware of the instability of work, having seen family members losing their jobs or making great sacrifices as companies struggled to adjust to the economic downturns of the 1980s and 1990s. Millennials are said to be lacking in trust about work, they are unimpressed by authority and are self-reliant about what they want from work (Jurkiewicz, 2000). While much generational research is rather broad brush, Barling and colleagues (Barling, Dupre & Hepburn, 1998) suggest young people's perceptions of job insecurity are likely to predict their own work attitudes (such as cynicism) and beliefs (e.g., feelings of separation from the work environment).

Unemployment studies

Interest in unemployment studies in the UK was prompted by the early 1980s' economic recession and in particular by the loss of manufacturing and mining jobs and the resulting unemployment in the North of England. Several detailed studies (e.g., Jackson et al., 1983) consistently found that psychological strain (Goldberg & Hillier, 1979) was associated with unemployment, with levels of strain deceasing with subsequent re-employment. Further, if people were strongly committed to finding employment they were more likely to report increased psychological strain when unemployed compared with those less committed to finding work (Warr & Jackson, 1985).

Several studies focussed on school leavers' experiences of gaining work. A detailed interview study of 647 school leavers (Stafford, Jackson & Banks, 1980) found young people had a strong desire to be in work. Those that were unemployed were likely to have few or no qualifications, a father that was unemployed and a low preference for work involvement. Crucially this study demonstrated that those young people with higher work involvement were more likely to be strained by unemployment than those with lower work involvement (as in previous research with adults). Unusually, this study recognized the critical role employers played in young people's successful transitions into work. Employers preferred young people to have some qualifications rather than none, and they noted that the job-seeking style of those with unemployed fathers was ineffective, possibly due to limited informal work networks.

Another study interviewed over 900 young people in their last year at school, and twice over the next two years. Those gaining employment were more likely to report increased well-being than when they were at school, with those who were unemployed experiencing decreased well-being. The longitudinal nature of this study confirmed it was the experience of unemployment that affected well-being and not solely the loss of work (Banks & Jackson, 1982). Similar findings were reported in a study conducted in the south-east of England (Donovan, Oddy, Pardoe & Ades, 1986). Further, a study from Australia (Feather & O'Brien, 1986) found that school leavers unable to find work reported lower self-esteem, less peer and family support, felt less competent, saw themselves as being less pleasant, less active and reporting greater strain, increased anxiety and reduced life-satisfaction when compared with their working peers. A subsequent meta-analysis (a study of studies) looking at the experience of psychological well-being during unemployment (McKee-Ryan, Song, Wanberg & Kinicki, 2005) confirms a causal effect of unemployment on psychological well-being with the detrimental effects of job loss being higher with the longer duration of job loss. Of particular concern was the finding that unemployed school leavers reported lower well-being than unemployed adults. The authors note: "School leavers face the extra burden of establishing their occupational identity when faced with early career unemployment" (p. 67). Further, a Swedish study following school leavers from the ages of 16 to 30 years (Hammarström & Janlert, 2002) found early career unemployment was associated with reduced well-being and further experiences of unemployment over time. These studies suggest that unemployment at a young age can cause "scaring effects" in later working life.

A study of the rapid increase in unemployment in Europe (Noll, 2002, cited in Vansteenkiste, Lens, De Witte, De Witte & Feather, 2005) found the experience of unemployment particularly distressing to those who valued work, while others found unemployment gave opportunities to undertake other activities such as caring for their home, family and enjoying hobbies (Vansteenkiste et al., 2005). By exploring the strength and quality of motivation associated with job search (e.g., Vansteenkiste, Lens, De Witte, De Witte & Deci, 2004; Vansteenkiste et al., 2005), researchers found that people who *wanted to find* (rather than feeling they *had to find*) work were more persistent in their job search. Participants of both these studies were from welfare programmes held in Belgium and a third of the participants were under the age of 26 years, indicating these findings were likely to be applicable to a younger age group. We explore the voice of young unemployed people and specific difficulties some young people face in their education-to-work transition in Chapters 3 and 4 of this book.

Why do young people find the experience of unemployment so detrimental?

Well-known psychologists Marie Jahoda and Peter Warr describe the positive psychological and physical benefits of work. Work provides daily time structure, opportunities for activity and socialisation, a sense of purpose and increased status (Jahoda, 1979). Warr (1987; Warr & Clapperton, 2010) describes the "needed nine" features of happiness (and unhappiness): opportunity for control, skill use and goal achievement, variety, environmental clarity, money, physical security, opportunity for social contact and a valued social position. If these features are not provided by work then benefits can be found from other activities such as studying, voluntary work or activities with family and friends. While different people's experience of unemployment varies (McKee-Ryan et al., 2005), it is easy to see how many young people will struggle to exert control, use their skills, gain variety and goal achievement without work, let alone achieve some level of independence without financial resources. Further, work experiences enable a young person to resolve their identity confusion, enabling development of work and social identities beyond those gained in education. These are important milestones in the transition from education to work.

The transition from education to work

Several UK government and industry reports describe the difficulty young people experience in the transition between education and work (IPPR, 2014; SKOPE, 2012). Work by the Institute for Public Policy and Research (IPPR, 2014, January) notes "Young people face increasing difficult and protracted transitions from school to work" (p. 2), citing poor links between schools and businesses and failing careers services. Specifically, this study followed school pupils visiting UK car manufacturers and receiving career talks, after which they completed a survey. Two hundred and twelve pupils identified workplace experience as a priority for them to make decisions about their futures, along with the need for more information about local employment opportunities.

The ESRC Centre on Skills, Knowledge and Organizational Performance (SKOPE, 2012) describes extended and risky transitions from education to the labour market involving few jobs, poor quality jobs (e.g., lacking in working hours), skill-mismatches, over-qualification and jobs that lack of subsequent progression (p. 4) as the experiences of many young people. Their report notes that research in this area tends to focus on educational matters (rather than employment), evaluating small-scale projects often of short duration offering few generalizable conclusions. Crucially, the availability of work opportunities and their quality, geographic and sectoral distribution was ignored. Sadly, there is growing evidence that poor quality work that is dull, routinised and repetitive, with few opportunities for training and development, is increasing (Lawton, 2009).

Employers' views of young job seekers

Several reports suggest that employers "constantly complain about the standards of those leaving education" (Pring, Hayward, Hodgson et al., 2012, p. 3), concluding that young people have inappropriate work skills and attitudes (Spoonley, 2008) and are ill-prepared for the contemporary economy (Taylor, 2005). However, research by the UK Commission for Employment & Skills (UKCES, 2011) states the emphasis on employability skills is over-stated (p. 17) with most problems focussing on lack of work experience and maturity. Both reports (UKCES, 2011, p. 3; SKOPE, 2012, p. 15) call for employer action to work with education to build young people's work experience (p. 3) and to provide feedback (at local and national levels) on necessary training requirements.

Interventions using a joined-up model of educational and employer-led inputs will be described in more detail in Chapters 5, 6 and 7 of this book.

Summary

Examining research about young unemployed populations we can conclude there is less research examining the early steps into employment. Thus we can question the attitudes ascribed to young workers by generational researchers, suggesting that cynical views of work may be a response to the experience of low-quality work. Much research focusses on the young people themselves, suggesting a deficit model of what may be lacking rather than considering what young people could contribute to the workplace or acknowledging that organizations are playing a role in constructing unemployment (Salognon, 2007). Therefore, new frameworks are required to guide research in order to develop more balanced interventions to increase work opportunities for young people.

A new model to guide understanding of youth employment

Current psychological research offers some explanation of the difficulties young people are facing finding work but we have little insight into the organizational influences on youth employment. With few entry-level jobs being available to young people, a simple model of supply (the young people) and demand (jobs) would help to focus on particular issues and opportunities associated with youth employment (see Figure 1.1; Carter et al., 2013). To explain, imagine a plank weighed down on one side by nearly a million young people looking for work, out of balance with the other end of the plank representing the jobs provided by organizations.

ISSUES IDENTIFIED ABOUT YOUNG PEOPLE SEEKING WORK:

- Lack of work experience & maturity (UKCES, 2011);
- Lack of readiness for work environment;
- Long, difficult transitions from education to the workplace.

SUPPLY ISSUES OF MANY YOUNG PEOPLE SEEKING WORK

ARE COMPANIES OFFERING WORK TO YOUNG PEOPLE?

- Only 25% of UK organizations employ young people and less than 6% employ school leavers;
- Trend to employ young people is decreasing, even before the recession;
- Lack of quantity, quality, geographic and sectoral work opportunities available (SKOPE, 2012).

LACK OF DEMAND WITH FEW JOBS FOR YOUNG PEOPLE

Figure 1.1 See-saw model of supply and demand issues of youth employment.

This see-saw model demonstrates insufficient demand from organizations unable to balance the number of young people seeking employment. Therefore, it is at the demand end of the model that research and innovation is needed to produce employment opportunities for young people (Carter, 2015).

This model is incomplete as many factors will influence the pivoting of the see-saw (e.g., economic climate, availability of experienced workers; societal, political and educational influences). However, our understanding of these influences is in its infancy requiring guidance from models and theories to understand how these factors influence the employment of young people.

What theories could influence youth employment?

Youth unemployment is a complex concept that can be explored from many different perspectives. Further, underemployment is seen as "lurking in the shadows" of unemployment (McKee-Ryan & Harvey, 2011, p. 963) and insights from this area of study are enlightening. Feldman (1996) describes four sectors of research examining different aspects of underemployment: management science, sociology, economy and community psychology. While this classification reflects US educational traditions, it highlights the value of taking a work psychology approach to bridge different perspectives and gain clarity in youth employment.

Importantly, Human Capital Theory (HCT) (Becker, 1993, cited in McKee-Ryan & Harvey, 2011) is an integrating concept. Young people make choices of how to develop their human capital by investing in education, skills development and experience. Organizations make their recruitment decisions based on their assessment of job seekers' human capital (Lepak & Snell, 1999). Further, people decide how to invest their capital with expectations of rewards provided by those obtaining their capital. Thus, HCT is the underpinning concept of the see-saw model of youth employment, being applicable to both young people and organizations. Developing a supply and demand understanding of HCT has the potential to pivot employment decisions by building understanding of capital expectations. Further, HCT offers some explanation of the negative outcomes young people experience when they are unable to find work as a result of the unmet expectations of reward after many years invested in education.

Identity concepts

Understanding how young people develop their sense of identity and what experiences enrich their self-concept are fundamental to understanding what will bridge the gap between employers and young people. Social Identity Theory (SIT) (Tajfel, 1978; Tajfel & Turner, 1985) suggests we define ourselves largely in terms of our membership of social groups, often valuing our group more than others (Arnold et al., 2010, p. 712). Therefore, when hiring managers meet young job seekers their personalities, experiences and identities are very different and they may perceive they are communicating with a minority group (Bandura, 1977). The SIT enables us to understand these differences, suggesting that activities undertaken with the minority group (young people) will help to build self-esteem thus informing work and communication with other group members (employers). Young people can gain more experience of the work environment in activities such as work experience, and employers can broaden their understanding of what young people have to offer by engaging in mentoring relationships (see Chapter 6). However, while young people frequently engage in work experience, it is less usual for employers to take part in activities with young people, resulting in a lack of understanding of their capabilities.

Importantly, young people don't want to be seen as different to others in the workforce and this will challenge 75% of UK companies not employing those under 24 years of age. The absence of young people in these organizations will affect both minority and majority groups. Young people may not be attracted to organizations where they perceive themselves as a minority. Similarly, the majority group may feel that they have too much to lose by engaging a younger workforce. Such feelings and attitudes may activate age stereotypes (Steele, 1997) causing members of the stereotyped group to monitor their environment for any signs of being evaluated like their group's negative stereotype (Walton, Murphy & Ryan, 2015). This process is known as *stereotype threat* and dealing with negative feelings reduces resources that are available in the workplace. Indeed, evidence suggests that such perceptions will disrupt work performance and negatively impact on an individual's motivation and engagement (Kulik, Perera & Cregan, 2016; Robertson & Kulik, 2007). Managerial and organizational practices limiting negative stereotyping and encouraging identity affirmation will reduce the stereotype threat, encouraging the minority group members to feel valued in the workplace. In Chapter 7 we examine workplace activities such as workplace forums (with managers and apprentices) as ways of bridging identity barriers across different social groups.

Imagining yourself in a specific work role (such as being a psychologist or a teacher) helps young people to make decisions that will help them to achieve their goal. The notion of *a dream* as the driver of career development is fundamental to career theories (e.g., Levinson, 1976) and has been further developed into the concept of *possible selves* (Markus & Nurius, 1986) and more recently the concept of *future work self*. The future work self is an "Explicitly future focused, idealistic image of the self within the context of work" (Strauss, Griffin & Parker, 2012, p. 5). Those who can describe elaborate images of their hoped-for futures are likely to undertake proactive career behaviours such as exploring a range of career options and setting career-related goals to develop skills and abilities and accumulate work experience (Claes & Ruiz-Quintanilla, 1998; Strauss et al., 2012). While the notion of a future work self is an intuitive concept that can assist conversations and actions around career development, it does depend on the availability of work opportunities to develop skills and experience in order to achieve an imagined work self. Appreciation that employers can realistically shape the future aspirations of young people will deepen employers' understanding of young job seekers. But, without employers' support, set-backs in planned actions and unhelpful feedback will damage the young person's self-esteem and ego. Unfortunately, there is evidence this is already happening with a Prince's Trust (2015) report stating 67% of young people report being anxious about finding work.

Finding a fit in the workplace

Person–Environment Fit (P–E Fit) is an influential theory highlighting the value of human resource within organizations (Ferris & Judge, 1991). Fit is the compatibility between an individual and the work environment that occurs when their characteristics are matched (Kristof-Brown, Zimmerman & Johnston, 2005, p. 281) and the resulting fit is satisfying. Person–Environment Fit has been used to explore many relationships including students' notions of fit with their college environment (Pervin & Rubin, 1967). Lack of fit is also informative where there is a mismatch between students' need for autonomy and the autonomy afforded by the college environment, which led to students leaving.

There are several sources of fit. Person–Job Fit (P–J Fit) encourages attention to specific aspects of the job itself, such as the knowledge, skills and attitudes (KSAs) required; being the traditional focus of selection processes. Once in the job, if there is good fit then that person is likely to experience job satisfaction (Kristof-Brown et al., 2005). In addition to P–J Fit there is the fit between person and organization (P–O Fit). Person–Organization Fit is a broader concept considering the match between the individual's values, personality traits and the organization's attributes (e.g., the company's values and aspirations; Ferris & Judge, 1991). Person–Organization Fit is less specific than P–J Fit and is important when the nature of work is more complex and flexible (e.g., working across several job roles), and is more important in contemporary work. Evidence suggests that when P–O Fit is experienced individuals are likely to be more committed to an organization and less likely to leave (Kristof-Brown et al., 2005).

However, P–E Fit is complex, particularly when it is examined within the context of the employment interview influenced by social and situational factors (Howard & Ferris, 1996). This study is of particular interest as videotapes of young men in their "early-twenties" were reviewed and rated by a range of experienced interviewers (of average age 35 years). If the interviewer felt the job seeker was similar to them this affected their perceptions of the job seekers' competence and suitability for the job role. Job seekers were seen as competent and suitable for the job if they used positive non-verbal behaviours (smiling, direct eye contact) and were able to promote themselves. However, exploration of recruiters' perceptions of job seekers' P–O Fit were found to have little connection with reality (Kristof-Brown et al., 2005, p. 319) and were more likely to resemble the "similar to me" bias than a true fit to an organization's culture (Howard & Ferris, 1996). Thus P–E Fit usefully allows exploration of differing perceptions of job and organization held by hiring managers and young job seekers, particularly if there is awareness of potential bias. Again, examination of both demand and supply attitudes will lead to more equitable processes of assessment for young people, or encourage simple solutions such as including a young person in the panel of interviewers (see Chapter 7) enabling differing notions of fit to be explored. Continuing the focus on the increased complexity of work, we now look at the career choices young people are making.

Flexible notion of careers

Work in the 21st century is complex and rarely based around a single employer as traditional stage models of career development assume (for an excellent review see Savickas et al., 2009). Therefore, dynamic career models are required to assist decision-making. Work Role Transitions is one such model, referring to any change in employment status (Nicholson, 1984, p. 173) including employment, unemployment and re-employment (Carter, 1993). Transition begins when the role holder encounters the realities of a new position and is concerned about how to handle the challenges. They can either adapt themselves to the new role by developing new KSAs and building experience, or proactively change the role (role innovation) to benefit from their KSAs and experience. The cycle completes when the role holder is competently performing in the role and is ready for another sequence of change. Appreciating this cycle and the options available to cope with change can be helpful but it requires opportunity or autonomy to change the way things are done. Further, understanding how we adapt to new role challenges can be useful for employers; appreciating that role innovation can be creative and valuable rather than assuming there is one best way to do things. Application of work-role transitions can lead to mentorship and discussion forums as facilitators of adaptation and these methods will be described in more detail in Chapters 6 and 7.

Contemporary career planning needs to be both flexible and responsive to available opportunities and driven by the individual's search for meaning at work (Duarte, 2004). This idea, known as the "new career" (Akkermans, Brenninkmeijer, et al., 2013), is proactively managed by the individual as they steer their work experience between different work roles within and across various organizations. To do this people need to develop both *career adaptability* and *career competencies*. Career adaptability (Savickas & Porfeli, 2012) is "the readiness to cope with the predictable tasks of preparing for and participating in the work role and with the unpredictable adjustments prompted by the changes in work and work conditions" (p. 254). Four resources are needed: looking ahead and planning (career concern); knowing what path to pursue and making responsible decisions (career control); exploring alternative roles and strategies (career curiosity); and having confidence to take on activities and overcome obstacles (career confidence). These are valuable resources to develop as they are associated with more stable employment patterns, with fewer transitions to unemployment (Germeijs & Verschueren, 2007) and more re-employment (Koen, Klehe, Van Vianen, Zikic & Nauta, 2010). Career adaptability is also positively related to job quantity (Zikic & Klehe, 2006), job quality (Koen et al., 2010), well-being and career success (Hirschi, 2010).

Career competencies are the skills and abilities required to plan ahead, to recognise opportunities, and to learn from experience. A framework of three competencies has been developed specifically to assist young people with their decision-making (Akkermans, Brenninkmeijer, et al., 2013): *reflective competencies* to aid the development of values, motivation, strengths and skills; *communicative competencies* to develop and expand contacts with whom to communicate work KSAs; and *behavioural competencies* to achieve active exploration of work opportunities, setting career goals and taking active steps towards their achievement. Developing career competencies has been found to enhance perceived employability and work engagement (Akkermans, Schaufeli, et al., 2013) and to enable career success (Eby, Butts & Lockwood, 2003).

Activities enhancing both career adaptability and career competencies enable young people to make smoother transitions from education to work and to cope with the demands of changing work roles. However, the role employers play in these transitions is rarely explored. Reflecting on the way young people approach tasks and acquire resources could also encourage innovation in goods and service provision in industry. Some organizations get this concept and actively recruit young people (e.g., in telecommunications), while others miss opportunities for innovation and change.

Setting the right goals

An influential theory of motivation-associated performance or learning is Goal Setting (e.g., Locke, Shaw, Saari & Latham, 1981), suggesting higher levels of attainment can be achieved by setting specific and difficult goals compared with less precise or vague goals. Specific difficult goals are likely to focus attention on task, increase and maintain effort, and encourage varied ways to achieve the goal. Goal setting can be applied to job searching as it is a self-regulated management process (Kanfer, Wanberg & Kantrowitz, 2001, p. 849), finding job search effort and intensity to be associated with employment success. Sadly, goal setting was less strongly related to success for new job entrants when compared with those previously employed, suggesting motivational effort is only one of the many factors associated with successfully finding work.

Feedback on progress towards goal attainment enables people to adjust strategies that lead to success (Latham & Pinder, 2005). Feedback is critical in job seeking as it encourages focus, perseverance and the use of different ways to find work. Employer feedback is vital to assist young job seekers, particularly those who have been rejected, enabling adjustment of their job-seeking strategies. Less appreciated by employers is that interactions with job seekers will help them to adjust their recruitment and selection strategies, thus maintaining a high quality pool of applicants. Again, some organizations like the energy companies are aware of the need for feedback on their recruitment processes and invest in resources specifically to employ young people in order to maintain the KSAs of their future workforce.

Young people need to believe they will be able to get work (self-efficacy) and need to develop skills of job searching. However, persevering with job searching in areas of high unemployment is difficult, particularly if there are few role models. Chapter 3 hears the voices of young unemployed people as they seek work, often getting little feedback about their efforts to sustain their job search. Further, Chapter 8 will look at how UK government policy and resources can be used to assist job seekers and employment opportunities for young people.

Building youth-friendly organizational cultures

Some companies easily attract young job applicants (e.g., Google, Accenture) as they have an organizational culture and climate that favours and encourages young people. *Organizational culture* refers to the values and beliefs of people working in the company and the common behaviours that get things done in the organization (Eldridge & Crombie, 1974). Charles Handy (1979) describes four main types of behaviour reflecting how things get done: power, role, task and people. While this is a simple classification, it does suggest that culture is not always a result of managerial choice and that workers' values and beliefs influence the ways things get done. Young people, as new employees or prospective starters in the workplace, will be strongly influenced by organizational culture, hoping it will match with their own values and beliefs. Particularly they look for the presence of other young workers so that they will not be a minority group. This may be a challenging task for organizations with an older age profile (e.g., local and national government). Chapter 7 will describe how a London Local Authority took on the challenge of changing its culture to develop apprenticeships and the employment for young people.

What about the work itself?

Finally, we need to consider the type of work young people will perform in organizations. Decades of research in work psychology points to the need for well-designed work involving autonomy, variety of task and skill use, task significance and feedback, factors of the Job Characteristics Model (JCM) (Hackman & Oldham, 1976, 1980) that are important for motivation, job satisfaction and job performance (e.g., Fried & Ferris, 1987). Research continues to highlight the value of the JCM in job redesign (e.g., Parker & Wall, 1998) while broadening the job characteristics specified by the model (to include, for example, physical security, interpersonal contact, valued social position) (Warr, 1987). Further, the work we do provides structure to our daily life, strongly influencing our well-being (Warr, 1987; Warr & Clapperton, 2010). For example, variety of work, freedom to choose the way we work and feedback about our work are important factors for people to enjoy work, and the absence of such factors will affect people's well-being. Peter Warr describes aspects of working life that are positively associated with well-being as the "needed nine" (Warr, 1987; p. 11).

This framework is also known as the Vitamin Model as the positive association with aspects such as task variety will only continue to be positive up to a certain threshold, beyond which the individual perceives, for example, there is "too much" variety and the benefit is lost.

The JCM and the Vitamin Model offer useful frameworks to understand the characteristics of a good job (often called the concept of *good work* (Hall & Las Haras, 2010)) enabling people to develop and thrive in the workplace. Unfortunately, evidence suggests that many jobs young people are taking to gain entry to the workplace do not live up to these ideals, being repetitive, lacking autonomy, providing low feedback and little engagement (Lloyd, Mason & Mayhew, 2008), and offering little chance of progression or development. Therefore, these models both help us to understand the work that young people aspire to and offer an explanation of the negative attitudes expressed by young people about job roles that do not embody these characteristics. These models also identify the characteristics of work needed to maintain employee well-being. However, in a crowded labour market, it is probable that many people stay in poor work roles from necessity rather than choice.

This section has described some theories and models associated with work psychology that can assist in the exploration of the supply and demand of youth employment. Appreciating the balance of these perspectives may act as a pivot to tilt the model, thereby increasing the employment of young people in organizations (see Figure 1.2 below). These theories are not discrete and many work

PIVOTAL THEORIES OF WORK PSYCHOLOGY
Underpinned by *Human Capital Theory*

> Identity Concepts: Social Identity Theory, Stereotype Threat, Future Work Self
> Person–Environment Fit
> Role Transition, Career Adaptability, Career Competencies
> Goal Setting
> Organizational Culture
> Job Characteristics Model
> Vitamin Model.

Figure 1.2 Pivotal theories of the see-saw model of supply and demand issues of youth employment.

together in the complex interactions of the workplace. We will review these theories throughout this book, examining the value they offer in developing our understanding of youth employment.

Chapter summary

This chapter has introduced some of the many issues affecting youth employment in the 21st century. Much of the research describes a deficit model of young people's knowledge, skills and abilities while not recognising that employers play a part in constructing unemployment (and underemployment). In order to balance these perspectives a demand and supply model of youth employment is proposed underpinned by theories and models used in work psychology. In the next chapters various authors will explore different aspects of youth employment, offering depth and understanding to the issues facing young people and suggesting interventions and solutions. Chapter 9 will offer a summary and focus on ways to improve young people's working futures.

References

Abramovitch, R. & Johnson, L.C. (1992). Children's perceptions of parental work. *Canadian Journal of Behavioural Science*, 24(3), 319–332.

Akkermans, J., Brenninkmeijer, V., Huibers, M. & Blonk, R.W.B. (2013). Competencies for the contemporary career: development and preliminary validation of the career competencies questionnaire. *Journal of Career Development*, 40(3), 245–267.

Akkermans, J., Nykänen, M. & Vuori, J. (2015). Practice makes perfect? Antecedents and consequences of an adaptive school-to-work transition. In J. Vuori, R. Blonk & R.H. Price (Eds), *Sustainable working lives: managing work transitions and health throughout the life course*. New York, NY: Springer.

Akkermans, J., Schaufeli, W.B., Brenninkmeijer, V. & Blonk, R.W.B. (2013). The role of career competencies in the job demands-resources model. *Journal of Vocational Behavior*, 83(3), 356–366.

Arnold, J., Randall, R., Patterson, F., Silvester, J., Robertson, I., Cooper, C., Burnes, B., Swailes, S., Harris, D., Axtell, C. & Den Hartog, D. (2010). *Work psychology: understanding human behaviour in the workplace* (5th Ed). Harlow: Pearson Education Ltd.

Bachman, J.G. & Schulenburg, J. (1993). How part-time work intensity relates to drug use, problem behavior, time use, and satisfaction among high school seniors: are these consequences or merely correlates? *Developmental Psychology*, 29(2), 220–235.

Bandura, A. (1977). Self-efficacy: toward a unifying theory of behavioral change. *Psychological Review*, 84(2), 191–215.

Banks, M.H. & Jackson, P.R. (1982). Unemployment and the risk of minor psychiatric disorder in young people: cross sectional and longitudinal evidence. *Psychological Medicine*, 12(4), 789–798.

Barling, J. (1990). *Employment, stress and family functioning*. Chichester, UK: Wiley.

Barling, J., Dupre, K.F. & Hepburn, C.G. (1998). Effects of parents' job insecurity on children's work beliefs and attitudes. *Journal of Applied Psychology*, 83(1), 112–118.

Barling, J. & Kelloway, F.K. (Eds) (1999). *Young workers: varieties of experiences*. Washington, DC: American Psychology Association.

Berti, A.F. & Bombi, A.S. (1988). *The child's construction of economics*. Cambridge: Cambridge University Press.

Brown, R. (2011). *Prejudice: its social psychology* (2nd Ed.). Chichester, UK: John Wiley & Sons.

Canny, A. (2001). The transition from school to work: an Irish and English comparison. *Journal of Youth Studies*, 4(2), 133–154.

Caplan, R.D. (1985). Psychosocial stress at work. *Work Management and Labour Studies*, 10(2), 63–76.

Carter, A.J. (1993). An empirical investigation of the experience of job change of Health Service employees. Unpublished MSc thesis, London University: Birkbeck College.

Carter, A.J. (Chair), Richmond, P., Walker, A., Guner, Y., Gould, S., Lewis, H. & Matta, H. (2013). Supporting young society. Symposium given at the BPS Division of Occupational Psychology Conference, 9–11 January, Chester.

Carter, A.J. (2015). Youth employment – the missing facts. *The Psychologist*, 28(6), 462–465.

Chand, M. & Tung, R.L. (2014). The aging of the world's population and its effects on global business. *Academy of Management Perspectives*, 28(4), 409–429.

Chartered Institute of Personnel and Development (CIPD) (2015). *Resourcing and talent planning: Survey report*. London: Chartered Institute of Personnel and Development. www.cipd.co.uk/hr-resources/survey-reports/resourcing-talent-planning-2015.aspx, downloaded 02/08/2016.

Claes, R. & Ruiz-Quintanilla, S.A. (1998). Influences of early career experiences, occupational group, and national culture on proactive career behavior. *Journal of Vocational Behavior*, 52(3), 357–378.

Cottrell, S. (2015). *Skills for success: personal development and employability*, 3rd Ed. London: Palgrave Macmillan.

Donovan, A., Oddy, M., Pardoe, R. & Ades, A. (1986). Employment status and psychological well-being: a longitudinal study of 16-year-old school leavers. *Journal of Child Psychology and Psychiatry*, 27(1), 65–76.

Duarte, M.E. (2004). O indivíduo e a organização: Perspectivas de desenvolvimento. [The individual and the organization: perspectives of development]. *Psychologica (Extra-Série)*, 549–557.

Eby, L.Y., Butts, M. & Lockwood A. (2003). Predictors of career success in the era of the boundaryless career. *Journal of Organizational Behavior*, 24(6), 689–708.

Eldridge, J.E.T. & Crombie, A.D. (1974). *A sociology of organizations*. London: George Allen and Unwin.

Erickson, E.H. (1956). The problem of ego identity. *Journal of American Psychoanalytic Association*, 4(1), 56–121.

Eurostat; European Commission for Employment, Social Affairs and Inclusion (2013). *Youth Employment*. http://europa.eu/social/main.jsp?catld=1036, downloaded 20/01/2013.

Feather, N.T. & O'Brien, G.E. (1986). A longitudinal study of the effects on employment and unemployment on school-leavers. *Journal of Occupational Psychology*, 41(2), 422–436.

Feldman, D.C. (1996). The nature, antecedents and consequences of underemployment. *Journal of Management*, 22(3), 385–407.

Ferris, G.R. & Judge, T.A. (1991). Personnel/human resources management: a political influence perspective. *Journal of Management*, 17(2), 447–488.

Fried, Y. & Ferris, G.R. (1987). The validity of the job characteristics model: a review and metaanalysis. *Personnel Psychology, 40*(2), 287–322.

George, A., Metcalf, H., Tufekci, L. & Wilkinson, D. (2015, June). *Understanding age and the labour market.* Report from the Joseph Rowntree Foundation (JRF), p. 17. www.jrf.org.uk/work/labour-markets, downloaded 10/08/2014.

Germeijs, V. & Verschueren, K. (2007). High school students' career decision-making: consequence for choice implementation in higher education. *Journal of Vocational Behavior, 70*(2), 223–241.

Goldberg, D.P. & Hillier, V.F. (1979). A scaled version of the General Health Questionnaire. *Psychological Medicine, 9*(1), 139–145.

Hackman, J.R. & Oldham, G.R. (1976). Motivation through the design of work: test of a theory. *Organizational Behavior and Human Performance, 16*(2), 250–279.

Hackman, J.R. & Oldham, G.R. (1980). *Work redesign.* Reading, MA: Addison-Wesley.

Hall, D.T. & Las Haras, M. (2010). Reintegrating job design and career theory: creating not just good jobs but smart jobs. *Journal of Organizational Behavior, 31*(2–3), 448–462.

Hammarström, A. & Janlert, U. (2002). Early unemployment can contribute to adult health problems. Results from a longitudinal study of school leavers. *Journal of Epidemiology and Community Health,* 56, 624–630, doi.org/10.1136/jech.56.8.624.

Handy, C. (1979). *Gods of management.* London: Pan.

Hirschi, A. (2010). The role of chance events in the school-to-work transition: the influence of demographic, personality and career development variables. *Journal of Vocational Behavior, 77*(1), 39–49.

Howard, J.L. & Ferris, G.R. (1996). The employment interview context: social and situational influences on interviewer decisions. *Journal of Applied Social Psychology, 26*(2), 112–136.

Howker, E. & Malik, S. (2010). *Jilted generations: how Britain has bankrupted its youth.* London: Icon Books.

Institute of International and European Affairs (IIEA) (2014, March). *EU's unemployment puzzle.* www.iiea.com/blogosphere/youth-unemployment-mind-the-gap---eus-unemployment-puzzle-infographic, downloaded 12/02/2016.

Institute of Public Policy and Research (IPPR) (2014). *Youth unemployment in Europe: lessons for the UK.* www.ippr.org, downloaded 20/02/2014.

Jackson, P.R., Stafford, E.M., Banks, M.H. & Warr, P.B. (1983). Unemployment and psychological distress in young people: the moderating role of employment commitment. *Journal of Applied Psychology, 68*(3), 525–535.

Jahoda, M. (1979). The impact of unemployment in the 1930s and the 1970s. *Bulletin of the British Psychological Society, 32,* 309–314.

Judge, J.A. & Ferris, G.R. (1992). The elusive criterion of fit in human resources staffing decisions. *Human Resource Planning, 15*(4), 47–67.

Jurkiewicz, C.L. (2000). Generation X and the public employee. *Public Personnel Management, 29*(1), 55–74.

Kanfer, R., Wanberg, C.R. & Kantrowitz, T.M. (2001). Job search and employment: a personality-motivation analysis and meta-analytic review. *Journal of Applied Psychology, 86*(5), 837–855.

Kaplan, J.D. (1950). *Dialogues of Plato.* New York, NY: Washington Square Press.

Karasek, R. & Theorell, T. (1990). *Health work: stress, productivity, and the reconstruction of working life.* New York, NY: Basic Books.

Koen, J., Klehe, U.C., Van Vianen, A.E.M., Zikic, J. & Nauta, A. (2010). Job search strategies and reemployment quality: the impact of career adaptability. *Journal of Vocational Behavior*, *71*(1), 126–139.

Kristof-Brown, A.L., Zimmerman, R.D. & Johnston, E.C. (2005). Consequences of individuals' fit at work: a meta-analysis of person-job, person-organization, person-group and person-supervisor fit. *Personnel Psychology*, *58*(2), 281–324.

Kulik, C.T., Perera, S. & Cregan, C. (2016). Engage me: the mature-age worker and stereotype threat. *Academy of Management Journal*, *59*(6), 2132–2156.

Latham, G.P. & Pinder, C.C. (2005). Work motivation theory and research at the dawn of the twenty-first century. *Annual Review of Psychology*, 56, 485–516.

Lawton, K. (2009). *Nice work if you can get it: achieving sustainable solutions to low pay and in-work poverty*. London: Institute for Public Policy Research (IPPR). www.ippr.org/publications/nice-work-if-you-can-get-it-achieving-a-sustainable-solution-to-low-pay-and-in-work-poverty, downloaded 21/01/2017.

Lepak, D. & Snell, S. (1999). The human resource architecture: towards a theory of human capital allocation and development. *Academy of Management Review*, *24*(1), 31–48.

Levinson, H. (1976). *Psychological Man*. Cambridge, MA: Levinson Institute.

Lloyd, C.L., Mason, G. & Mayhew, K. (2008). *Low-wage work in the United Kingdom*. New York, NY: Russell Sage Foundation.

Locke, E.A., Shaw, K.N., Saari, L.M. & Latham, G.P. (1981). Goal setting and task performance 1969–1980. *Psychological Bulletin*, *90*(1), 125–152.

Loscocco, K. (1989). The interplay of personal and job characteristics in determining work commitment. *Social Science Research*, *18*(4), 370–394.

Loughlin, C. & Barling, J. (1999). The nature of youth employment. In J. Barling & F.K. Kelloway (Eds) *Young workers: varieties of experiences*, pp. 17–36. Washington, DC: American Psychology Association.

Loughlin, C. & Barling, J. (2001). Young workers' work values, attitudes and behaviours. *Journal of Occupational and Organizational Psychology*, *74*(4), 543–558.

Low Pay Commission (2015). *National Minimum Wage*, p. 125 and p. 134. www.gov.uk/government/organisations/low-pay-commission, downloaded 02/02/2016.

Manpower Services Commission (1978). *Young people and work*. London: HMSO.

Markus, H.R. & Nurius, P. (1986). Possible selves. *American Psychologist*, *41*(9), 954–969.

McKee-Ryan, F.M. & Harvey, J. (2011). "I have a job, but . . . .": a review of underemployment. *Journal of Management*, *37*(4), 962–996.

McKee-Ryan, F.M., Song, Z., Wanberg, C.R. & Kinicki, A.J. (2005). Psychological and physical well-being during unemployment: a meta-analytic study. *Journal of Applied Psychology*, *90*(1), 53–76.

Nicholson, N. (1984). A theory of work role transitions. *Administrative Science Quarterly*, *29*(2), 172–191.

O'Brien, G.E. & Feather, N.T. (1990). The relative effects of unemployment and quality of employment on the affect, work values and personal control of adolescents. *Journal of Occupational Psychology*, *63*(2), 151–163.

Office for National Statistics (ONS) (2015, January). *Labour force survey*. www.ons.gov.uk/employmentandlabourmarket/peopleinwork/employmentandemployeetypes/adhocs/fulltimestudentsaged1824inlondonandrestofukbyemploymentstatusjulsep2014, downloaded 31/01/2017.

Office for National Statistics (ONS) (2015, November). *Young people Not in Education, Employment or Training (NEET)*. www.ons.gov.uk/ons/rel/lms/young-people-not-in-education--employment-or-training--neets-/november-2015/index.html, downloaded 01/02/2016.

Office for National Statistics (ONS) (2015, December). *Statistical bulletin, UK labour market, section 12, young people in the labour market.* www.ons.gov.uk/ons/rel/lms/labour-market-statistics/december-2015/statistical-bulletin.html-1/02/2016, downloaded 01/02/2016.

Parker, S.K. & Wall, T.D. (1998). *Job and work design.* San Francisco, CA: Sage.

Pervin, L.A. & Rubin, D.B. (1967). Student dissatisfaction with college and college dropout: a transactional approach. *Journal of Social Psychology, 72*(2), 285–295.

Prince's Trust (2015). *Youth index.* www.princes-trust.org.uk/about-the-trust/research-policies-reports, downloaded 16/02/2016.

Pring, R., Hayward, G., Hodgson, A. et al. (2012). *Education for all: the future of education and training for14–19 year olds.* Abingdon, UK: Routledge.

Robertson, L. & Kulik, C.T. (2007). Stereotypes threat at work. *The Academy of Management Perspectives, 21*(2), 24–40.

Salognon, M. (2007). Reorienting companies hiring behaviour: an innovative 'back-to-work' method in France. *Work, Employment and Society, 21*(4), 713–730.

Savickas, M.L., Nota, L., Rossier, J., Dauwalder, J.-P., Duarte, M.E., Guichard, J., Soresi, S., Van Esbroeck, R. & van Vianen, A.E.M. (2009). Life designing: a paradigm for career construction in the 21st century. *Journal of Vocational Behavior, 75*(3), 239–250.

Savickas, M.L. & Porfeli, E.J. (2012). Career adapt-abilities scale: construction, reliability, and measurement equivalence across 13 countries. *Journal of Vocational Behavior, 75*(3), 661–673.

SKOPE: ESRC Centre on Skills, Knowledge and Organizational Performance (2012, May). *Youth transitions, the labour market and entry into employment: some reflections and questions.* Research Paper no. 108, SKOPE: ESRC Centre on Skills, Knowledge and Organizational Performance. Oxford: University of Oxford.

Sonnentag, S. (2012). Psychological detachment from work during leisure time: the benefits of mentally disengaging from work. *Current Directions in Psychological Science, 21*(2), 114–118.

Spoonley, P. (2008). Utilizing a demand-led approach in a local labour market. *Local Economy, 23*(1), 19–30.

Stafford, E.M., Jackson, P.R. & Banks, M.H. (1980). Employment, work involvement and mental health in less qualified young people. *Journal of Occupational Psychology, 53*(4), 291–304.

Steele, C.M. (1997). A threat in the air: how stereotypes shape intellectual identity and performance. *The American Psychologist, 52*, 613–629.

Steinberg, L. (1982). Jumping off the work experience bandwagon. *Journal of Youth and Adolescence, 11*(3), 183–205.

Strauss, K., Griffin, M.A. & Parker, S.K. (2012). Future work selves: how salient hoped-for identities motivate career behaviors. *Journal of Applied Psychology, 97*(3), 580–598.

Super, D.E. (1957). *The psychology of careers: an introduction to vocational development.* New York, NY: HarperCollins.

Super, D.E. (1990). A life-span, life-space approach to careers. In D. Brown & L. Brooks (Eds), *Career choice and development* (2nd Ed.), pp. 197–261. San Francisco, CA: Jossey-Bass.

Symonds, W.C., Schwartz, R.B. & Ferguson, R. (2011, July 28). *Pathways to prosperity: meeting the challenge of preparing young Americans for the 21st century.* Pathways to Prosperity Project, Harvard Graduate School of Education, Industry Trade Federation Conference, Auckland, New Zealand.

Tajfel, H. (1978). The achievement of group differentiation. In H. Tajfel (Ed.) *Differentiation between social groups. Studies in the social psychology of intergroup relations*, pp. 77–98. London: Academic Press.

Tajfel, H. & Turner, J.C. (1985). The social identity theory of intergroup behavior. In S. Worchel & W.G. Austin (Eds), *Psychology of intergroup relations* (2nd Ed.), pp. 7–240. Chicago, IL: Nelson-Hall.

Taylor, A. (2005). What employers look for: the skills debate and the fit with youth perceptions. *Journal of Education and Work*, 18(2), 201–218.

UK Commission for Employment and Skills (UKCES) (2011). *The youth enquiry: employers' perspectives on tacking youth unemployment.* Wath-upon-Dearne: UKCES.

UK Commission for Employment and Skills (UKCES) (2012, July). *The youth employment challenge.* Wath-upon-Dearne: UKCES.

Vansteenkiste, M., Lens, W., De Witte, S., De Witte, H. & Deci, E.L. (2004). The 'why' and 'why not' of job search behaviour: their relation to searching, unemployment experience and well-being. *European Journal of Social Psychology*, 34(3), 345–363.

Vansteenkiste, M., Lens, W., De Witte, S., De Witte, H. & Feather, N.T. (2005). Understanding unemployed people's job search behaviour, unemployment experience and well-being: a comparison of expectancy-value theory and self-determination theory. *British Journal of Social Psychology*, 44(2), 269–287.

Walton, G.M., Murphy, M.C. & Ryan, A.M. (2015). Stereotype threat in organizations: implications for equity and performance. *Annual Review of Organizational Psychology and Organizational Behavior,* 2(2), 523–550.

Warr, P.B. (1987). *Work, unemployment and mental health.* Oxford: Oxford University Press.

Warr, P. & Clapperton, G. (2010). *The joy of work? Jobs, happiness and you.* Abingdon, UK: Routledge.

Warr, P.B. & Jackson, P.R. (1985). Factors influencing the psychological impact of prolonged unemployment and of re-employment. *Psychological Medicine*, 15(4), 795–807.

Wilson, R., Beaven, R., May-Gillings, M., Hay, G. & Stevens, J. (2014). *Working Futures, 2012 to 2022.* UK Commission for Employment and Skills. Evidence Report No. 83, March. Wrath-upon-Dearne: UK Commission for Employment and Skills.

Zikic, J. & Klehe, U.C. (2006). Job loss as a blessing in disguise: the role of career exploration and career planning in predicting reemployment quality. *Journal of Vocational Behavior*, 62(3), 390–410.

2 Youth unemployment and underemployment

A global problem of our time

Rosalind H Searle

Introduction

Work plays several significant functions in a person's life and fulfils important needs, not only in economic terms but also at a social, health and psychological level. Across the world, young people's access to the labour market is an important route to maturity in becoming an adult, and yet evidence at a global level is revealing that, endemically, their journeys to employment are becoming increasingly complex and difficult to navigate. The International Labour Office (ILO, 2017) has reported a slight rise to 70 million or 13.1% of young people worldwide are currently unemployed. However, investigating this situation is hindered by the lack of available or comparable data, making generalisation difficult. In addition, labour markets themselves can vary due to distinct and different macro and micro contexts.

This chapter considers evidence from national and international studies and reports to reveal the insidious rise in youth unemployment, marking it out as a global phenomenon to which more attention should be given. While there is longstanding knowledge of the consequences of unemployment for individuals, youth unemployment is a distinct issue having important spill-over consequences extending beyond the individual into young people's families and communities, but that may also have unanticipated regional and national implications (Searle, Erdogan, Peiró & Klehe, 2014). All of these new concerns require us to look differently at youth unemployment in order to understand the common areas and nuanced differences. The chapter begins with an introductory overview of why this is a concern to us all. I then look at three distinct global trends: first, the steady rise in youth unemployment, second, distinguishing further disadvantaged groups, most notably minorities and women. Finally, I look at the issue of education and its separation from work and labour market trends.

Why should this concern us?

What is clear from the available data is that unemployment of young people can have a profound impact, rupturing the transition to adulthood (Bjarnason & Sigurdardottir, 2003) and producing a long-term 'scarring' effect extending well beyond early adult years as a consequence of the accumulative impact of lost wages. Unemployment has long-term implications for future psychological well-being, as well as increasing the likelihood of subsequent periods of further unemployment (e.g., Gregg, 2001; Mroz & Savage, 2006). Importantly, while in the past unemployment has been treated as an individual concern, insights from recent psychological study show the failure of young people to find viable employment has consequences for the wider family and community (Peiró, Hernández & Ramos, 2015). Further, key organizations, such as the ILO (2013, 2015a, 2017) and the Organisation for Economic Cooperation and Development (OECD, 2010), are recognising youth unemployment has implications for societies as a whole. Unemployment can produce seeds of social unrest when those people with skills are forced into lower skill-level positions, or from those who are not employed. Research shows those who are able to accumulate more socio-economic, educational and motivational resources throughout their lives have higher levels of trust in institutions (Schoon & Cheng, 2011). The current rate of those unemployed who are educated to degree level threatens to undermine career expectations and trust of the most able and diligent of youth, disenfranchising them. Access into work not only shapes subsequent life trajectories of individual citizens, but has wider economic, social/political, psychological and well-being implications at national levels.

Economic and conflict-based migration are topics that are frequently in the media, yet there have been many previous waves of young people searching for work, such as following the opening up of the former Communist countries or from refugees arriving into Europe (Baranik et al., 2018; Knappert, Kornau & Figengül, 2018; Wehrle, Klehe, Kira & Zikic, 2018). Migration of any type can affect young people critically, whether it is a re-location within their own country or internationally. In 2012, Germany had one million new immigrants, mostly due to highly educated individuals from Southern and Eastern European countries seeking work there (Taberner, 2012). This country has also been an important destination for Syrian refugees (Gericke, Burmeister, Löwe, Deller & Pundt, 2018; Obschonka, Hahn & Bajwa, 2018). Thus, while recent levels of migration have been high, migration of such size is not uncommon. Indeed, re-location denotes a high level of personal adaptability, relating positively to career adaptability (Tolentino et al., 2014). However, it has been found that this positive impact can be reduced by forced migration, such as refugees (Campion, 2018). The resulting immigration, however caused, can include many challenges and complications, such as the emotional toll of separation from extended families, language difficulties, and cultural adjustment by both job seekers and employing organizations. These consequences can be particularly marked for refugees (Baranik et al., 2018; Campion, 2018; Pajic, Ulceluse, Kismihók, Mol & den Hartog, 2018). Mass migrations can create tensions in host communities (Baran, Valcea, Porter & Gallagher, 2018), with increasing competition for local resources and potentially scarce youth employment opportunities. Further, in countries where tertiary education is paid for by governments, the loss of a highly educated workforce represents a reduced return on their investment.

For example, the brain and skills drain from some developing and southern European Union (EU) countries has been considerable. Evidence from Italy shows that those who do not return by the time they are 30 years old are likely to stay away from their country of birth for the majority of their adult lives (Tolentino et al., 2014). This has consequences for those that remain, especially as they age and can become more dependent on the State to support them.

The mass movement of skilled individuals deprives nations of future talents and skills, having implications for their potential to innovate, as well as weakening their economies. It can also cause profound shortages in key skills, such as in health care with the high mobility of those with medical and nursing qualifications. Large-scale migration of young people has significant implications for both their previous country and the new society, fragmenting families and producing perplexing burdens in one context, and increasing resources and demands in another. In this way, economies are deprived of the tax and pension contributions required in order to maintain their current economic models. The loss of this income from young people places increased pressure on pension resources, welfare and social care provision demanded by ageing family members who would have previously been looked after within their own families. Conversely, young people without the support of wider family members are far more vulnerable and at risk of exploitation by others in their new country (Mason-Jones & Nicholson, 2018).

When we look at employability, it is important to consider it as a multi-dimensional concept involving relatively broad components concerned with workers' human and social capital, their work-related identity, and their personal adaptability (Fugate, Kinicki & Ashforth, 2004). As we shall see, evidence from across many countries suggests pressures are subtly different but that there are many perplexing common features, indicating that this is an endemic issue facing the young. The recent exposure to mass youth unemployment and labour market uncertainty may produce a serious generational legacy; there will be many individuals whose failure or very challenging experiences of trying to get work will leave them feeling dissatisfied, disaffected and disengaged from employing organizations and their societies. Indeed, inability to access a suitable level of work may be a contributing factor in terrorism (Gill, Horgan & Deckert, 2014). Work is an important means of integration and therefore lack of viable access, coupled with reduction in economic resources and the subsequent depletion of social security and pension provisions, can compound into the decline of psychological and physical health and well-being (Corner & Gill, 2015).

Uncertainty in the labour market requires young people to be resilient and adaptable, however national education and employment policy may be failing to promote such qualities. Reports gathering information for many different countries identify concerns about the problems facing young people (ILO, 2013, 2015a, 2015b, 2017; OECD, 2015). While there is growing recognition of this problem, there remains a pernicious and on-going decline of work opportunities at suitable levels for young people. In addition to the growing economic inactivity of young people, there are also apprehensions about the increasing levels of poverty and the precariousness of the work that they find, especially for those in the developing world. Further, the inattention towards equality of access for minorities and women is threatening to exacerbate the economic and social divisions in many countries. Given that young people have historically been catalysts for revolution and social unrest, as witnessed by the 'Arab Spring' uprisings in the Middle East, we need to pay attention to their experiences and concerns. Looking at the headline trends, however, masks three clear challenges: first, this is a growing problem as youth unemployment rates were climbing prior to its peak during the global financial crisis of 2008 but remain persistently high. Second, this is a youth issue as, regardless of the regional context examined, young people are now three times more likely than their adult counterparts to be without work (ILO, 2017). Finally, there is a critical difference emerging in the current unemployment situation compared with the past, as higher levels of education no longer offer protection. These three dimensions will now be explored in detail.

Underlying rising trend

Increases in youth employment over the last decade reveal a worrying trend, and raise fears about the effectiveness of previous and current government and organizational policy and actions aimed at younger workers. The global recession increased the necessity of governments to focus attention on older workers, with policies designed to raise, or remove, retirement age caps (Peiró, Tordera & Potocnik, 2012). Although analysts contend there is no causal link between provision for older workers and the impact on the young (George, Metcalf, Tufekci & Wilkinson, 2015), it is clear the needs of the two groups are different. Further, evidence from Spain (Peiró, Sora & Caballer, 2012) shows the growing insecurity of young workers in contrast to older workers, with the increasing use of temporary or zero hours contracts making it harder for young workers to obtain the training necessary to make their work situation less precarious. Young people are willing to forgo job security for good training opportunities and work variety (Ng, Schweitzer & Lyons, 2010), but this is done on the basis of receiving continuing opportunities for learning and development (Bradley & Devadason, 2008). Indeed, research from the Netherlands shows simple ways to use informal learning to enhance the value of temporary work (Preenen, Verbiest, Van Vianen & Van Wijk, 2015).

Perplexingly, concurrent with policy attention on provisions for older workers, research shows a declining impact of previously lauded exemplars of national youth work policies, such as Germany's apprenticeships and dual career route (Heinz, 2002). The restructuring of work to allow organizations greater flexibility, coupled with deregulation of many national school-to-work labour market transitions, has disrupted previously smooth routes into work, with consequent impoverishment of the quality and scale of skills and training, and reduction in socialisation that such training creates (Eberl, Clement & Möller, 2012). The resultant underemployment sees many young people failing to find work at the right level for their skills. Over time such mismatches reduce job satisfaction and the desire to look for more appropriate work (Béduwé & Giret, 2011). Perniciously underemployment erodes both individuals' self-confidence and their skill base.

Triple youth unemployment rates

National unemployment figures indicate that young people are more likely to be unemployed than adults. In exploring the differences across regions, it is striking that, during the recent recession, young people's work opportunities were and remain the hardest hit in developed economies and EU countries. Over the next 15 years the situation is likely to remain challenging, coupled with rising inequality between rich and poor within countries and across the globe, increased social unrest, and further high levels of migration due to conflict and economic needs. Yet, during this period, over one billion young people will be new entrants to the labour market, with real concerns as to their ability to find meaningful and on-going work (ILO, 2015a, 2017).

Examining different regions of the world reveals a clear and persistent unemployment level for young people at least twice, if not more than three times, the level of adult unemployment (ILO, 2015a). Within the EU (2007 to 2017) youth unemployment levels have improved since their 2013 peak, but remain at more than 15.6% (of the total unemployment rate) and there are persistently high rates (above 30%) in Italy, Spain and Greece. While trends outside the EU in Central and South-East Asia and the Confederation of Independent States (CIS) are showing reductions in unemployment rates for both the overall population and the young workforce, youth unemployment levels are still substantially higher than adult levels. Further, young people experience distinct problems in both gaining and retaining work. In Latin American and Caribbean contexts prospects for young people have been in decline despite the transition from informal to formal employment. Youth unemployment remains high but stable in sub-Saharan Africa, and Eastern and Southern Asia. Conflict in the Middle East has created on-going challenges with pushes for young people to migrate into other countries' labour markets. The Arab Spring has had a marked and inadvertent impact, creating some of the world's highest unemployment rates. However, there is in each context the same clear underlying trend for young people to be three times more likely than older people to be without work.

One important commodity dividing older and younger job seekers is *social capital*. This is the sum of a person's relational resources, including the size of their social network, its strength and quality. By virtue of these relationships, those seeking work find job opportunities (e.g., Kogan, Matković & Gebel, 2013) and those within the network can offer assurance as to the abilities, personal qualities and fit-for-job requirements (Fugate et al., 2004). In some countries, these personal connections are the only routes into work. Therefore, young people's reduced levels of experience and connections to organizational insiders result in more limited levels of social capital. While family and school connections are part of young people's networks, these are not usually the job decision-makers. Further, it is clear that those migrating between countries are likely to have less social capital at their disposal, making accessing work even more challenging. More dynamic research shows how initial financial difficulties and social exclusions can be important mechanisms that exhaust and deplete job seekers, while psychological capital (a personal resource) is able to ameliorate such fatigue. In this way spirals of inequality merge with job search fatigue leading to subsequent lower-quality employment, which in turn results in lower organizational commitment and greater intention to quit the new employer (Lim, Chen, Aw & Tan, 2016).

Experiences of unemployment are, of themselves, a way that social capital can be denuded. A Chinese study revealed how financial resources and the loss of face from being unemployed compounded the challenges of finding work, as interactions became confined to others in similar situations (Zeng, 2012). Therefore, a social network of other non-working individuals, while potentially offering invaluable emotional support, can significantly undermine the job search process. In addition, there are genuine fears of what happens to young people when they are idle; enhancing their exposure to risky or criminal behaviours, or becoming involved in organised violence and protest (Gough, Langevang & Owusu, 2013; World Bank, 2013).

Particularly vulnerable groups

Looking in more detail under the headline unemployment rates is an important process, revealing distinct groups that experience disproportionately more adversity in their search for work (Brown & Lent, 2016). First, those from minorities in every context have greater difficulty due to the discrimination they often face during the job search process (Wanberg, 2012) and application processes (Derous & Ryan, 2012). Studies conducted in Belgium show that female Arab candidates were rated more favourably than their male counterparts, especially when applying for jobs with client contact (Derous, Ryan & Serlie, 2015). These findings identify explicit ethnic prejudice from recruiters, which becomes more pronounced for applicants with a less clear job–qualification fit. Research using correspondence audits shows that simply obtaining an interview is problematic for those from a minority, even when the details on their applications were standardised (Derous, Ryan & Nguyen, 2012; Hiemstra, Derous, Serlie & Born, 2012). While gender has been found to have some impact on this ethnicity effect, minority groups are less successful than the dominant majority.

The on-going systematic prejudice against migrants in many countries threatens to undermine societal integration, fostering resentment within new refugee communities. While sadly there is nothing new in such experiences, the growing inequality within many societies, coupled with reductions in welfare provisions for low-income families, are likely to fuel perceptions of injustice and exacerbate further the risk of radicalisation for those who feel left out of their new society. This can be particularly marked in refugee communities (Eggenhofer-Rehart et al., 2018; Ivlevs & Veliziotis, 2018; Newman, Nielsen, Smyth, Hirst & Kennedy, 2018). Clearly migrants do not have the social capital required to access work experience and opportunities, but such discrimination is a different and more pernicious experience for those who *do* have good skills and abilities (Gericke et al., 2018).

Studies examining the impact of unemployment on different socio-economic groups reveals differences in the levels of skill and resilience of young people. Those from higher socio-economic groups have greater knowledge about available work options and, more importantly, demonstrate more ability in navigating the diverse and complex decision pathways associated with choices about education, training and employment (Yates, Harris, Sabates & Staff, 2011). In addition, those from a higher socio-economic group are more likely to remain more positive during periods of economic recession (Taylor & Rampino, 2014). In contrast, where there is misalignment of individuals' aspirations and educational expectations, coupled with uncertainty of occupational direction, this will exacerbate the likelihood of not being in employment, education or training (NEET) by age 18 (Yates et al., 2011).

Women are the second group at a worldwide-level who experience reduced opportunities and access to well-paid work (ILO, 2015a, 2017). Across the globe current figures show women make up a greater proportion of those categorised as NEET (34.4% compared with 9.8% for males). The problem is also multi-stranded. Although educational discrimination creates an on-going disadvantage in securing stable work for women in many contexts, the issue is more pernicious in developing contexts, in which four out of five NEETs are women, and in Southern Asia it is nine out of ten (ILO, 2017). Even in developed contexts where girls and young women are not denied access to education there are challenges. For example, despite often being better qualified than their male counterparts and having greater occupational aspirations (Schoon, Martin & Ross, 2007), their formal qualifications fail to translate into better-paying jobs. This issue is particularly striking for young women whose parents have fewer qualifications (Iannelli & Smyth, 2008). By contrast, in the Middle East and North Africa, boys and young men are more likely to receive education, so girls simply get left behind. Without the benefit of human capital, women continue to be at a disadvantage. Further, being in school can be an important factor in protecting children from violence and exploitation by adults (Gjermeni et al., 2008). Given these circumstances, it is hardly surprising unemployment levels are elevated for women. Yet, research from Germany has shown how direct interventions can make women more aware and skilled in two vital areas: networking and career planning (Spurk, Kauffeld, Meinecke & Ebner, 2015).

Examining job options that exist for women in developing countries reveals further differences; most work is informal, being responsible for 89% of all new work (ILO, 2015a). Lack of education and limited economic options makes girls and young women more likely to be forced into early marriages, or through exploitation in the form of slavery and trafficking (Tuwor & Sossou, 2008; Storkey, 2015). Indeed recent attention by psychologists at the United Nations (Saxena et al., 2015) reveals how informal work contexts further exacerbate women's exposure to risk, including: lower or irregular incomes, inequitable distributions of pay between the sexes, poor and often unsafe conditions for work, absence of social and medical benefits, compulsory overtime, exposure to chemical and other dangerous agents (without either protective clothing or due training), and a high risk of violence and sexual exploitation (World Bank, 2013). Therefore, it is unsurprising that high rates of ill-health and poverty follow those working in informal labour markets. Yet, without the advantage of human capital from education, insecure informal economies and self-employment routes remain the only viable options for work for many young women, particularly in sub-Saharan Africa, South Asia, the Middle East and North Africa.

In addition to the human capital challenges for women, there are many hidden cultural dimensions putting young women at further disadvantage in the labour market, with family obligations often being compounded with ethnic dimensions (Mayrhofer, Meyer, Schiffinger & Schmidt, 2008). Having children has a pronounced effect on career trajectories and early parenthood has been found to adversely impact occupational success for both sexes (Hobcraft & Kiernan, 2001). However, this has a disproportionately pernicious influence on women, particularly those from more disadvantaged backgrounds (Schoon et al., 2007). An Australian study of female Chief Executive Officers highlighted the vital importance of selecting the right partner in women's progression to the top (Fitzsimmons, Callan & Paulsen, 2014). In some communities, motherhood is pushed more quickly as an alternative career option onto young women rather than their male counterparts (Tuwor & Sossou 2008; Storkey 2015), where both may have similarly failed to find employment or quick work progression. The removal of women from the labour market into childbearing and childrearing roles effectively removes any need to attend to the underlying inequality of labour market access. Although evidence does suggest that fathers pay more attention to occupational equality when their daughters are entering the labour market, this is a generation too late for their wives (Dahl, Dezső & Ross, 2012). But the genderised structure of work does vary. For example, the labour market of East Asia shows higher unemployment rates for young men compared with young women (ILO, 2015a). This is because of the type of work being offered (e.g., assembly-line factory work), which, while offering some economic reward, has little psychological benefit.

In summary, the evidence is clear: young people do not have equal access to the labour market as their adult counterparts and the problem is growing. Youth unemployment is rising from a global average of twice the adult rate to three times that rate. In addition, there are further gender and ethnicity divides based on prejudice rather than real skill differences that need to be identified, challenged and steps taken to reduce. The next section considers in more detail the question of underemployment and over-qualification.

Reduced protection of tertiary education

Human capital is a key component of employability, and education an important means of enhancing that capital. In the past education has offered an
important buffer to young people, allowing them to side-step recessions. Over
recent years many countries have introduced policy changes effecting young
people, for example extending the provision of formal education up to 18 years
of age. Reports for OECD countries show that more than 80% of young workers now attain upper-secondary education. In addition, rates of those receiving
university-level education across the 36 OECD countries have risen by almost
10% since 2000 (OECD, 2013, 2017). Evidence from Spain confirms that early
school-leavers are now at a disadvantage compared with young job seekers with
higher levels of schooling (Vallejo & Dooly, 2013). Similarly, research from
Ireland indicates that those with a low level of academic attainment and lack
of basic fundamental literacy and numeracy, coupled with recent experiences of
unemployment, have more challenges in finding work (Kelly, McGuinness &
O'Connell, 2012).

Changes such as increasing formal education levels, however, often inad-
vertently create a greater separation of education from work. They can produce
increasing mismatches between what employers are looking for, and what vocational education is delivering (Bailey, Hughes & Moore, 2004; Billett, 2009).
Concern about the preparedness of graduates is evident in McKinsey's (2012)
report, reflecting that only 42% of recruiters believing college graduates were
adequately prepared to enter the job market. Critically, while college graduates
do have higher rates of employability, achieving a university degree does not necessarily produce a clear path to employment. Indeed, those countries with lower
youth unemployment rates have good connections between education and work,
and with educational institutions sending strong signals about job seeker skills
and abilities (Breen, 2005). Those with greater clarity about their future work
'self' can positively develop important career-enhancing behaviours, including
career awareness and planning, as well as proactive skills development (Taber &
Blankemeyer, 2015).

In looking at preparation from further education, many countries have
accompanied extensions to the length of secondary education with shifts in the
provision and delivery of careers education; with teachers now having to provide
advice especially for those from lower socio-economic groups. Critically, teachers
have a pivotal role in helping pupils to navigate subject choices and university
options, particularly for talented young people from less privileged backgrounds
(Koshy, Brown, Jones & Portman Smith, 2013). In these roles teachers support
both young people and parents, especially those from a migrant background,
who lack awareness and understanding about how best to achieve career goals
(St. Clair, Kintrea & Houston, 2013). A German study showed that teachers can
be especially effective in enhancing training prospects for young women from
lower socio-economic groups (Haase, Heckhausen & Köller, 2008). Yet, evidence
reveals a repetition of ineffective approaches to career-related competences and

aspirations failing both employers and young people. Careers support may not encourage reflectivity or support young people to identify what are meaningful actions and useful interactions (Kuijpers, Meijers & Gundy, 2011). In contrast, job search skills directly enhance employment (Wanberg, 2012). Studies from both Finland and the Netherlands show the effectiveness and value of preparing young people's transition into work (Akkermans, Nykänen & Vuori, 2015). Yet, many government policies and employment services require individuals to take up any offers of work, even when such actions may be misguided and counterproductive. Evidence suggests that those who rejected ill-suited jobs went on to have subsequent employment of a much higher quality (Zikic & Klehe, 2006).

More recently, research (Hirschi & Valero, 2015) has begun to differentiate individual employability dimensions including those associated with adaptation (such as career exploration, planning, or decision-making difficulties and occupational self-efficacy beliefs), from those related to individual adaptability (concerning core self-evaluations and proactivity). This work shows important elements are linked to perceived internal and external marketability that are significant in negating job and career insecurity (Spurk, Kauffeld, Barthauer & Heinemann, 2015). This type of research allows more effective and nuanced interventions to be developed. Considerable work being done in the Netherlands to reform practices for those with long histories of unemployment (e.g., Koen, Klehe & van Vianen, 2015; Nauta, van Vianen, van der Heijden, van Dam & Willemsen, 2009). Findings from a meta-analytic study (Liu, Huang & Wang, 2014) show that central to the effectiveness of these initiatives is their attention towards the psychological mechanisms and specific training content. This includes training on job search skills and goal setting, improvements to self-presentation and self-efficacy, and a focus on boosting proactivity and enhancing social support. Further, the strengthening of social networks is an important way young people can find out about work and be endorsed over others (Wanberg, 2012).

Other enablers

A group playing a critical role in helping young people with work decisions are parents. One longitudinal study shows the significant impact of parents' knowledge for post-16-year-olds' career decisions (Schneider & Stevenson, 2000), with parental involvement being important to reduce young people's indecision (Feldman, 2003). However, there can be clear transference from parents' own experiences of job insecurity to the level and type of career indecision of their children. It is, therefore, critical that options and reasons for their rejection are examined to ensure they are pertinent for *that* young person, and not based on inaccurate parental suppositions. Yet, how much knowledge *can* and *do* parents actually have about current career options or the different employment training programmes that are available? Such insights can be especially important for migrants who may have many untested suppositions about the labour market based on their previous home country, being unaware of critical differences. Further, parents feel acutely the pains of their children in trying and failing to find work. A recent study from Spain reveals the spill-over of mental health consequences (Peiró et al., 2015). Therefore, it is important that young people and their families have knowledge and support, along with the ability to navigate the diverse and complex array of options available to them.

Amongst the key enablers of work is work experience, which is critical to young people developing the type of professional attitude and confidence to secure and retain a job. Work experience is also a good predictor of later quality and stability of employment for young people (Ling & O'Brien, 2013). Yet, there are tensions in balancing the need for young people to acquire work experience and the pressure for them to achieve the grades necessary to access tertiary education. As a result, many young people have little work exposure or even ideas about what they want to do. A study of Greek college students showed more than half the participants had no interest in working while in education (Mihail & Karaliopoulou, 2005). Similarly, an Australian study of graduates found that, during their period of study, students had a belief that attending university and achieving good grades were critical to obtaining a good job. Sadly, they often realised too late that a degree was simply the price of admission, and insufficient alone in delivering high quality employment (McKeown & Lindorff, 2011). In contrast, young scholars obtaining internships and work-based learning tend to have more secure paths to employment (Shoenfelt, Stone & Kottke, 2013). However, there can be important and subtle differences depending on the area of study. A representative sample from a Spanish university found that academic area moderated this relationship (Yeves, Gamboa & Peiró, 2009). The authors reveal that for those studying health sciences, natural sciences and technology, work experience during their period of study had a negative impact in predicting the quality of subsequent employment (for up to five years later). Yet, those studying social sciences and education obtained better-quality jobs if they had work experience, even if this was part-time. Greater value was found if the work experience was related to their area of academic study. In a USA college a recruiters' survey endorsed these findings, with three out of four recruiters preferring job candidates to have relevant experience (Outlook, 2009).

Study of labour markets reveals disconnections between perceptions of postsecondary level education as a requirement for young workers, and the actual demands of the job. For example, statistics from the USA show that occupations with the fastest levels of growth are in health and social care, such as home health and personal care aides, occupational therapists, or installation technicians for wind and solar energies (US Department of Labor, 2014). Therefore, many of the areas of demand in the new knowledge-based economy are in fact "old economy" jobs, and do not require a degree. A further challenge for young people is foreseeing what might happen to their career options. The speed of technological change and the increasing transnational nature of organizations' economic decisions compound the difficulty in navigating and making career choices. For example, globalization has produced a shift in the viability of women's career decisions in sub-Saharan Africa, with hairdressing emerging as a better decision than becoming a seamstress (Langevang & Gough, 2012). The unanticipated export of old clothes from well-meaning countries has undermined the demand for local products, and has consequently radically altered local jobs (e.g., Mark, 2012). Further, decisions by multinationals to invest or disinvest from an area or region can have dramatic consequences for workers regardless of their age.

Despite the removal of the buffer to unemployment for those attending university, there is a clear tension with credential inflation, with former non-degree work roles becoming graduate-only positions (MacDonald, 2011). While some suggest this situation presents an opportunity for more qualified employees to craft these positions, making them more of their level (Erdogan, Bauer, Peiró & Truxillo, 2011), there remains scant evidence of organizations trying to utilise more fully the skills of overeducated workers. As a result, many jobs for young people are poor alternatives. Flemish research shows the 'entrapment' of individuals in poor-quality jobs, with the probability of them transitioning into adequate employment diminishing once they have work. The new lower-quality skills are often limited in their transferability and are an active and negative signal to other potentially more suitable employers (Baert, Cockx & Verhaest, 2013).

Successfully navigating how to get work as a young person involves support from parents but also teachers and the wider community. More awareness about the value and employability of particular degrees is required, but it is also for educators to think more critically to ensure work-based skills and experience are central to their programmes. Efforts to make employers reflect on whether they are pitching vacancies and youth employment programmes at the right level of qualifications are likely to pay dividends, especially for bright young people without the financial resources and support to go on to university. Many of these efforts will reduce the underemployment that can insidiously reduce psychological capital and well-being.

Conclusions

This chapter shows that the nature and degree of youth unemployment across the world is clearly high. This issue reveals a greater magnitude of long-term impact for young people, with the previously successful escape route of further education now having a declining effect. As a result, there are distinct threats to young people's economic and psychological well-being that are likely to create long-term consequences for families and societies. While parents in some parts of the world are taking drastic steps to try and secure better futures for their young people by sending them to other countries, such actions can actually make them more vulnerable to exploitation. Instead, evidence shows young people and their families are becoming more adept in navigating training options and career choices. However, it is often those from higher socio-economic groups who are able to leverage their social capital to the advantage of their children, and thus are simply exacerbating further socio-economic divisions within society. Two key groups are important in changing the outcomes for young people: their teachers and parents, both of whom require greater evidence-based knowledge of what is effective in helping young people to become more employable.

National policies that restrict access to education from primary to tertiary levels on gender, ethnic and economic grounds must be scrutinised, as they undermine the ability of those in clearly disadvantaged groups to reach their full potential. In addition, reforms to labour markets transforming them from informal to more formal employment options create more secure work for all, but particularly for women and minorities. Evidence shows limited equality and the artificial constraint of employment equality across most countries for key groups including those from lower-socioeconomic groups, minorities and new migrants, and women.

While young people might be perceived as more adaptable than older workers, they need support to enhance these characteristics, especially in helping them to form and then realise their future work identities. Programmes that up-skill young people regarding tangible career search (human capital) and networking (social capital) can be very effective (e.g., Klehe, Zikic, van Vianen, Koen & Buyken, 2012; Savickas et al., 2009). Interventions offering more person-centred approaches are found to be even more important in supporting the long-term unemployed get back into work (Koen et al., 2015). Critically, studies of psychologically-based interventions combining both psychological mechanisms and content can be more effective in actually transforming people's lives (Koen et al., 2015). For example, more attention paid to preparing young people for the transition from school into work has dividends in developing their career adaptability, enhancing their sense of control, as well as improving their engagement with job search and selection processes. More critically, research shows those receiving such training achieve qualitatively better jobs (Koen, Klehe & van Vianen, 2012). In addition, future programmes for young people need to promote cultural adaptation to benefit both newcomers, and those working alongside them, to improve their integration into society. This is particularly relevant as countries strive to integrate refugees and migrants into their workforces. Without more active efforts in this regard the risks of radicalisation amongst bored unemployed migrants are likely to grow. This chapter demonstrates youth employment and underemployment are global problems, with local dimensions and interventions that can be improved through the application of psychological insights.

References

Akkermans, J., Nykänen, M. & Vuori, J. (2015). Practice makes perfect? Antecedents and consequences of an adaptive school-to-work transition. In J. Vuori, R. Blonk & R. H. Price (Eds), *Sustainable working lives*, pp. 65–86. New York, NY: Springer.

Baert, S., Cockx, B. & Verhaest, D. (2013). Overeducation at the start of the career: stepping stone or trap? *Labour Economics*, 25, 123–140.

Bailey, T. R., Hughes, K. L. & Moore, D. T. (2004). *Working knowledge: work-based learning and education reform*. Abingdon, UK: Routledge.

Baran, B. E., Valcea, S., Porter, T. H., & Gallagher, V. C. (2018). Survival, expectations, and employment: An inquiry of refugees and immigrants to the United States. *Journal of Vocational Behavior*, 105, 102–115.

Baranik, L. E., Hurst, C. S. & Eby, L. T. (2018). The stigma of being a refugee: a mixed-method study of refugees' experiences of vocational stress. *Journal of Vocational Behavior*, *105*, 116–130.

Béduwé, C. & Giret, J. F. (2011). Mismatch of vocational graduates: what penalty on French labour market? *Journal of Vocational Behavior*, *78*(1), 68–79.

Billett, S. (2009). Changing work, work practice: the consequences for vocational education. In R. Maclean & D. Wilson (Eds), *International handbook of education for the changing world of work*, pp. 175–187. New York, NY: Springer.

Bjarnason, T. & Sigurdardottir, T. J. (2003). Psychological distress during unemployment and beyond: social support and material deprivation among youth in six northern European countries. *Social Science & Medicine*, *56*(5), 973–985.

Bradley, H. & Devadason, R. (2008). Fractured transitions: young adults' pathways into contemporary labour markets. *Sociology*, *42*(1), 119–136.

Breen, R. (2005). Explaining cross-national variation in youth unemployment: market and institutional factors. *European Sociological Review*, *21*(2), 125–134.

Brown, S. D. & Lent, R. W. (2016). Vocational psychology: agency, equity, and well-being. *Annual Review of Psychology*, *67*(1), 541–565.

Campion, E. D. (2018). The career adaptive refugee: exploring the structural and personal barriers to refugee resettlement. *Journal of Vocational Behavior*, *105*, 6–16.

Corner, E. & Gill, P. (2015). A false dichotomy? Mental illness and lone-actor terrorism. *Law and Human Behavior*, *39*(1), 23–34.

Dahl, M. S., Dezső, C. L. & Ross, D. G. (2012). Fatherhood and managerial style: how a male CEO's children affect the wages of his employees. *Administrative Science Quarterly*, *57*(4), 669–693.

Derous, E. & Ryan, A. M. (2012). Documenting the adverse impact of resume screening: degree of ethnic identification matters. *International Journal of Selection and Assessment*, *20*(4), 364–474.

Derous, E., Ryan, A. M. & Nguyen, H. H. D. (2012). Multiple categorization in resume screening: examining effects on hiring discrimination against Arab applicants in field and lab settings. *Journal of Organizational Behavior*, *33*(4), 544–570.

Derous, E., Ryan, A. M. & Serlie, A. W. (2015). Double jeopardy upon resumé screening: when Achmed is less employable than Aïsha. *Personnel Psychology*, *68*(3), 659–696.

Eberl, P., Clement, U. & Möller, H. (2012). Socialising employees' trust in the organisation: an exploration of apprentices' socialisation in two highly trusted companies. *Human Resource Management Journal*, *22*(4), 343–359.

Eggenhofer-Rehart, P. M., Latzke, M., Pernkopf, K., Zellhofer, D., Mayrhofer, W. & Steyrer, J. (2018). Refugees' career capital welcome? Afghan and Syrian refugee job seekers in Austria. *Journal of Vocational Behavior*, *105*, 31–45.

Erdogan, B. & Bauer, T. N. (2009). Perceived overqualification and its outcomes: the moderating role of empowerment. *Journal of Applied Psychology*, *94*(2), 557–565.

Erdogan, B., Bauer, T. N., Peiró, J. & Truxillo, D. M. (2011). Overqualified employees: making the best of a potentially bad situation for individuals and organizations. *Industrial and Organizational Psychology*, *4*(2), 215–232.

Feldman, D. C. (2003). The antecedents and consequences of early career indecision among young adults. *Human Resource Management Review*, *13*(3), 499–531.

Fitzsimmons, T. W., Callan, V. J. & Paulsen, N. (2014). Gender disparity in the C-suite: do male and female CEOs differ in how they reached the top? *The Leadership Quarterly*, *25*(2), 245–266.

Fugate, M., Kinicki, A. J. & Ashforth, B. E. (2004). Employability: a psycho-social construct, its dimensions, and applications. *Journal of Vocational Behavior*, 65(1), 14–38.

George, A., Metcalf, H., Tufekci, L. & Wilkinson, D. (2015, June). Understanding age and the labour market. Report from the Joseph Rowntree Foundation (JRF), p. 17. www.jrf.org.uk/work/labour-markets, downloaded 10/08/2014.

Gericke, D., Burmeister, A., Löwe, J., Deller, J. & Pundt, L. (2018). How do refugees use their social capital for successful labor market integration? An exploratory analysis in Germany. *Journal of Vocational Behavior*, 105, 46–61.

Gill, P., Horgan, J. & Deckert, P. (2014). Bombing alone: tracing the motivations and antecedent behaviors of lone-actor terrorists. *Journal of Forensic Sciences*, 59(2), 425–435.

Gjermeni, E., Van Hook, M. P., Gjipali, S., Xhillari, L., Lungu, F. & Hazizi, A. (2008). Trafficking of children in Albania: patterns of recruitment and reintegration. *Child Abuse & Neglect*, 32(10), 941–948.

Gough, K. V., Langevang, T. & Owusu, G. (2013). Youth employment in a globalising world. *International Development Planning Review*, 35(2), 91–102.

Gregg, P. (2001). The impact of youth unemployment on adult unemployment in the NCDS. *The Economic Journal*, 111(475), 626–653.

Haase, C. M., Heckhausen, J. & Köller, O. (2008). Goal engagement during the school–work transition: beneficial for all, particularly for girls. *Journal of Research on Adolescence*, 18(4), 671–698.

Heinz, W. R. (2002). Transition discontinuities and the biographical shaping of early work careers. *Journal of Vocational Behavior*, 60(2), 220–240.

Hiemstra, A. M. F., Derous, E., Serlie, A. W. & Born, M. P. (2012). Fairness perceptions of video resumes among ethnically diverse applicants. *International Journal of Selection and Assessment*, 20(4), 423–433.

Hirschi, A. & Valero, D. (2015). Career adaptability profiles and their relationship to adaptivity and adapting. *Journal of Vocational Behavior*, 88, 220–229.

Hobcraft, J. & Kiernan, K. (2001). Childhood poverty, early motherhood and adult social exclusion. *The British Journal of Sociology*, 52(3), 495–517.

Iannelli, C. & Smyth, E. (2008). Mapping gender and social background differences in education and youth transitions across Europe. *Journal of Youth Studies*, 11(2), 213–232.

International Labour Office (ILO) (2013). *Global employment trends for youth 2013: a generation at risk*. Geneva: International Labour Office.

International Labour Office (ILO) (2015a). *Towards solutions for youth unemployment: a 2015 baseline report*. Geneva: International Labour Office.

International Labour Office (ILO) (2015b). *World employment and social outlook*. Geneva: International Labour Office.

International Labour Office (ILO) (2017). *Global employment trends for youth*. Geneva: International Labour Office.

Ivlevs, A. & Veliziotis, M. (2018). Beyond conflict: long-term labour market integration of internally displaced persons in post-socialist countries. *Journal of Vocational Behavior*, 105, 131–146.

Kelly, E., McGuinness, S. & O'Connell, P. J. (2012). Transitions to long-term unemployment risk among young people: evidence from Ireland. *Journal of Youth Studies*, 15(6), 780–801.

Klehe, U. C., Zikic, J., van Vianen, A., Koen, J. & Buyken, M. (2012). Coping pro-actively with economic stress: career adaptability in the face of job insecurity, job loss, unemployment and underemployment. In P. L. Perrewé, J. R. B. Halbesleben & C. C. Rosen (Eds), *The role of the economic crisis on occupational stress and well being*, Vol. 10, pp. 131–176. Bingley, UK: Emerald Group Publishing Limited.

Knappert, L., Kornau, A. & Figengül, M. (2018). Refugees' exclusion at work and the intersection with gender: insights from the Turkish-Syrian border. *Journal of Vocational Behavior*, 105, 62–82.

Koen, J., Klehe, U. C. & van Vianen, A. E. M. (2012). Training career adaptability to facilitate a successful school-to-work transition. *Journal of Vocational Behavior*, 81(3), 395–408.

Koen, J., Klehe, U. C. & van Vianen, A. E. M. (2015). Employability and job search after compulsory reemployment courses: the role of choice, usefulness, and motivation. *Journal of Applied Psychology*, 64(4), 674–700.

Kogan, I., Matković, T. & Gebel, M. (2013). Helpful friends? Personal contacts and job entry among youths in transformation societies. *International Journal of Comparative Sociology*, 54(4), 277–297.

Koshy, V., Brown, J., Jones, D. & Portman Smith, C. (2013). Exploring the views of parents of high ability children living in relative poverty. *Educational Research*, 55(3), 304–320.

Kuijpers, M., Meijers, F. & Gundy, C. (2011). The relationship between learning environment and career competencies of students in vocational education. *Journal of Vocational Behavior*, 78(1), 21–30.

Langevang, T. & Gough, K. V. (2012). Diverging pathways: young female employment and entrepreneurship in sub-Saharan Africa. *The Geographical Journal*, 178(3), 242–252.

Lim, V. K. G., Chen, D., Aw, S. S. Y. & Tan, M. (2016). Unemployed and exhausted? Job-search fatigue and reemployment quality. *Journal of Vocational Behavior*, 92, 68–78.

Ling, T. J. & O'Brien, K. M. (2013). Connecting the forgotten half: the school-to-work transition of noncollege-bound youth. *Journal of Career Development*, 40(4), 347–367.

Liu, S., Huang, J. L. & Wang, M. (2014). Effectiveness of job search interventions: a meta-analytic review. *Psychological Bulletin*, 140(4), 1009–1041.

McKeown, T. & Lindorff, M. (2011). The graduate job search process—a lesson in persistence rather than good career management? *Education + Training*, 53(4), 310–320.

McKinsey (2012). *Education to employment: designing a system that works*. New York, NY: McKinsey. www.mckinsey.com/industries/social-sector/our-insights/education-to-employment-designing-a-system-that-works, downloaded 24/2/17.

MacDonald, R. (2011). Youth transitions, unemployment and underemployment: plus ça change, plus c'est la même chose? *Journal of Sociology*, 47(4), 427–444.

Mark, M. (2012). Europe's secondhand clothes brings mixed blessings to Africa. *The Guardian*, 7 May. www.theguardian.com/world/2012/may/07/europes-secondhand-clothes-africa?newsfeed=true, downloaded 24/2/17.

Mason-Jones, A. J. & Nicholson, P. (2018). Structural violence and marginalisation. The sexual and reproductive health experiences of separated young people on the move. A rapid review with relevance to the European humanitarian crisis. *Public Health*, 158, 156–162.

Mayrhofer, W., Meyer, M., Schiffinger, M. & Schmidt, A. (2008). The influence of family responsibilities, career fields and gender on career success: an empirical study. *Journal of Managerial Psychology*, 23(3), 292–323.

Mihail, D. M. & Karaliopoulou, K. (2005). Greek university students: a discouraged workforce. *Education + Training*, *47*(1), 31–39.

Mroz, T. A. & Savage, T. H. (2006). The long-term effects of youth unemployment. *Journal of Human Resources*, *XLI*(2), 259–293.

Nauta, A., van Vianen, A., van der Heijden, B., van Dam, K. & Willemsen, M. (2009). Understanding the factors that promote employability orientation: the impact of employability culture, career satisfaction, and role breadth self-efficacy. *Journal of Occupational and Organizational Psychology*, *82*(2), 233–251.

Newman, A., Nielsen, I., Smyth, R., Hirst, G. & Kennedy, S. (2018). The effects of diversity climate on the work attitudes of refugee employees: the mediating role of psychological capital and moderating role of ethnic identity. *Journal of Vocational Behavior*, *105*, 147–158.

Ng, E. S. W., Schweitzer, L. & Lyons, S. T. (2010). New generation, great expectations: a field study of the millennial generation. *Journal of Business and Psychology*, *25*(2), 281–292.

Obschonka, M., Hahn, E. & Bajwa, N. u. H. (2018). Personal agency in newly arrived refugees: the role of personality, entrepreneurial cognitions and intentions, and career adaptability. *Journal of Vocational Behavior*, *105*, 173–184.

Organisation for Economic Co-operation and Development (OECD) (2010). *Off to a good start? Youth labour market transitions in OECD countries*. Paris: OECD Publishing.

Organisation for Economic Co-operation and Development (OECD) (2013). *Education at a glance 2013: OECD indicators*. Paris: OECD Publishing.

Organisation for Economic Co-operation and Development (OECD) (2015). *The missing entrepreneurs 2015*. Paris: OECD Publishing.

Organisation for Economic Co-operation and Development (OECD) (2017). *Employment outlook 2017*. Paris: OECD Publishing, https://doi.org/10.1787/empl_outlook-2017-en.

Outlook, J. (2009). National Association of Colleges and Employers, 2008.

Pajic, S., Ulceluse, M., Kismihók, G., Mol, S. T. & den Hartog, D. N. (2018). Antecedents of job search self-efficacy of Syrian refugees in Greece and the Netherlands. *Journal of Vocational Behavior*, *105*, 159–172.

Peiró, J. M., Hernández, A. & Ramos, J. (2015). The challenge of building human capital and benefiting from it: a person-centric view of youth unemployment and underemployment. In L. M. Finelstein, D. M.

Truxillo, E. Fraccaroli, & R. Kanfer (Eds), *Facing the challenges of a multi-age workforce: a user-inspired approach*, 83–104. New York, NY: Routledge.

Peiró, J. M., Sora, B. & Caballer, A. (2012). Job insecurity in the younger Spanish workforce: causes and consequences. *Journal of Vocational Behavior*, *80*(2), 444–453.

Peiró, J. M., Tordera, N. & Potocnik, K. (2012). Retirement practices in different countries. In M. Wang (Ed.), *The Oxford handbook of retirement*, pp. 510–540. New York, NY: Oxford University Press.

Preenen, P., Verbiest, S., Van Vianen, A., Van Wijk, E. (2015). Informal learning of temporary agency workers in low-skill jobs: the role of self-profiling, career control, and job challenge. *Career Development International*, *20*(4), 339–362.

Savickas, M. L., Nota, L., Rossier, J., Dauwalder, J.-P., Duarte, M. E., Guichard, J., Soresi, S., Van Esbroeck, R. & van Vianen, A. E. M. (2009). Life designing: a paradigm for career construction in the 21st century. *Journal of Vocational Behavior*, *75*(3), 239–250.

Saxena, M., Sall, E., Scott, J. C., Rupp, D. E., Saari, L., Thompson, L. F. & Mallory, D. (2015). News from the SIOP-United Nations team: exploring work experiences of informal workers and promoting decent work for all. *The Industrial-Organizational Psychologist*, *53*(3), 172–174.

Schneider, B. L. & Stevenson, D. (2000). *The ambitious generation: America's teenagers, motivated but directionless.* New Haven, CT: Yale University Press.

Schoon, I. & Cheng, H. (2011). Determinants of political trust: a lifetime learning model. *Developmental Psychology, 47*(3), 619.

Schoon, I., Martin, P. & Ross, A. (2007). Career transitions in times of social change. His and her story. *Journal of Vocational Behavior, 70*(1), 78–96.

Searle, R. H., Erdogan, B., Peiró, J. M. & Klehe, U. C. (2014). *Youth employment,* SIOP White Paper series. Bowling Green, OH: Society for Industrial and Organisational Psychology.

Shoenfelt, E. L., Stone, N. J. & Kottke, J. L. (2013). Internships: an established mechanism for increasing employability. *Industrial and Organizational Psychology, 6*(1), 24–27.

Spurk, D., Kauffeld, S., Barthauer, L. & Heinemann, N. S. R. (2015). Fostering networking behavior, career planning and optimism, and subjective career success: an intervention study. *Journal of Vocational Behavior, 87,* 134–144.

Spurk, D., Kauffeld, S., Meinecke, A. L. & Ebner, K. (2015). Why do adaptable people feel less insecure? Indirect effects of career adaptability on job and career insecurity via two types of perceived marketability. *Journal of Career Assessment, 24*(2), 289–306.

St. Clair, R., Kintrea, K. & Houston, M. (2013). Silver bullet or red herring? New evidence on the place of aspirations in education. *Oxford Review of Education, 39*(6), 719–738.

Storkey, E. (2015). *Scars across humanity: understanding and overcoming violence against women.* London: SPCK.

Taber, B. J. & Blankemeyer, M. (2015). Future work self and career adaptability in the prediction of proactive career behaviors. *Journal of Vocational Behavior, 86,* 20–27.

Taberner, P. (2012, 2 June). *Germany's one million new immigrants.* www.neurope.eu/article/germany-s-one-million-new-migrants, downloaded 22/2/17.

Taylor, M. & Rampino, T. (2014). Educational aspirations and attitudes over the business cycle. *Economica, 81*(324), 649–673.

Tolentino, L. R., Garcia, P. R. J. M., Lu, V. N., Restubog, S. L. D., Bordia, P. & Plewa, C. (2014). Career adaptation: the relation of adaptability to goal orientation, proactive personality, and career optimism. *Journal of Vocational Behavior, 84*(1), 39–48.

Tuwor, T. & Sossou, M. A. (2008). Gender discrimination and education in West Africa: strategies for maintaining girls in school. *International Journal of Inclusive Education, 12*(4), 363–379.

US Department of Labor, Bureau of Labor Statistics (2014). *Employment projections: fastest growing occupations.* www.bls.gov/emp/ep_table_103.htm, downloaded 22/2/17.

Vallejo, C. & Dooly, M. (2013). Early school leavers and social disadvantage in Spain: from books to bricks and vice-versa. *European Journal of Education, 48*(3), 390–404.

Wanberg, C. R. (2012). The individual experience of unemployment. *Annual Review of Psychology, 63*(1), 369–396.

Wehrle, K., Klehe, U. C., Kira, M. & Zikic, J. (2018). Can I come as I am? Refugees' vocational identity threats, coping, and growth. *Journal of Vocational Behavior, 105,* 83–101.

World Bank (2013). *Jobs: World Development Report 2013.* Washington, DC: The World Bank.

Yates, S., Harris, A., Sabates, R. & Staff, J. (2011). Early occupational aspirations and fractured transitions: a study of entry into 'NEET' status in the UK. *Journal of Social Policy, 40*(3), 513–534.

Yeves, J., Gamboa, J. P. & Peiró, J. M. (2009). El papel del trabajo durante los estudios universitarios en la calidad de la inserción laboral de los titulados: ¿Existen diferencias en función del área académica? [The role of work during university studies on the quality of the placement of graduates: are there differences in academic areas?] *Psicologia dell'Educazione e della Formazione*, *11*(2), 191–222.

Zeng, Q. (2012). Youth unemployment and the risk of social relationship exclusion: a qualitative study in a Chinese context. *International Journal of Adolescence and Youth*, *17*(2–3), 85–94.

Zikic, J. & Klehe, U. C. (2006). Job loss as a blessing in disguise: the role of career exploration and career planning in predicting reemployment quality. *Journal of Vocational Behavior*, 69(3), 391–409.

3 The voice of young people
Finding the right fit

Angela J Carter and Afreen Hussain

Introduction

Many young people face being unemployed and are continually seeking work. We can presume that this is not a pleasant state, but what is it really like to be young (under 24 years), unemployed, never having had work and not expecting to get a job in the next few years? This chapter seeks to answer this question and to hear what young people have to say about their journey from education to work.

To put this question in context it is useful to look back in history to see what we can learn about youth employment. An article in the *Employment Gazette* in 1978 describes how being young and out of work is disproportionately worse for young people during a recession. This is a result of employers reducing their labour force in response to lower demand, reducing recruitment and making staff redundant to lessen their overall costs. These cutbacks in recruitment affect young people in many ways. Not only are there less jobs around, there are also less entry-level roles that allow young people to start their working lives recognising that they have little work experience. Employers are seeking experienced staff to cover several roles and there is no room for the luxury of having a training role that will develop a young person for the future.

Traditionally the UK labour market has had more young workers (under 20 years of age) than many other European countries (Eurostat, 2013), with more young people leaving education to seek work rather than continuing to further or higher education. This trend was notable in the 1960s at a time of post-war growth when many young people found employment soon after leaving education. However, along with this increase in youth employment there has also been an incremental rise in youth unemployment (Ashton, Maguire & Spilsbury, 1990) measured by the number of young people registered as unemployed. Ashton and colleagues examined the ratio of young men (under 20 years) who were unemployed and compared this with the adult male population. They found a close relationship, with young men being 1.7 times more likely to be unemployed when compared with males of all ages. Similarly, the number of young women (under 20 years) registered unemployed was related to the overall unemployment of women of all ages, but by a ratio of three times the rate of unemployed females of all ages.

These relationships suggest that while some experienced unemployed males are taking employment opportunities that may be available from young males, more female workers are taking employment opportunities that would have been open to young women. These authors, writing more than 35 years ago, call for employment measures to specifically assist young people as a disadvantaged group.

More recently, a report from the House of Lords Select Committee on Social Mobility (2016) examined the school-leaving preferences of 16 to 17 year olds, finding that 53% of young people chose to discontinue education and seek work, with 47% continuing in advanced level education. The report concludes that young people not going to university are "overlooked" (p. 13) by an education system that over-emphasises higher education over training options. This research highlights the close relationship between employment and the school leaving age.

School leavers at particular risk of unemployment are those having low skills and few or no qualifications (e.g., King, 2014). These young people are made unemployed sooner, most often, for longer and with the most serious consequences to their future lives (Hussain, 2015; Tovey, 2014). Evidence suggests that training programmes aimed at low-qualified and low-skilled young people have had little impact on their ability to gain work (Grayling, 2011). Grayling, a previous government minister for employment, describes the underperforming UK benefits system as shunting too many people from "dole queue to training room and back again".

However, not all young people who have left education and are not working register as being unemployed. These young people are classified as Not being in Employment, Education or Training (NEETs) and this category offers a broader measure of youth exclusion from the labour market. Within the NEET group are those who are unemployed along with many other subgroups of those who are not available for work due to family responsibilities or disabilities (Eurofound, 2012). While the NEET classification covers a large number of young people between the ages of 15 and 24 years in Europe, there are several common characteristics. The NEETs are more likely to have a low educational level, have a difficult family environment or immigration background, and are not accumulating human capital through formal channels of education, training or employment (Eurofound, 2014, p. 5). There is evidence that the number of young people classified as NEETs has increased to 14.6 million (EU28, 2012), representing 15.9% of the entire youth population in Europe (aged 15–29) (Eurofound, 2014). This report notes that finishing education should be an exciting time for young people setting out to embark on a career after many years of education. However, in reality this transition is fraught with insecurity; often the process of getting the first job is a lengthy process and young people are forced to be less selective about the type of job that they are prepared to accept (p. 1).

While these reports and descriptions of UK or European trends in the labour market are useful to gain an overall picture of the problems and issues young people face, they are based on aggregate data that tells you little of young people's actual experiences. Further, the majority of young people are positioned in the middle ground between those in higher education and those that are NEET. The Lords Select Committee on Social Mobility (2016) reminds us that this group are rarely considered by policy makers (p. 13).

Little is known about the attitudes and preferences of young unemployed people who have suffered rises in school leaving age, increasing costs to gain further and higher education, difficulties in gaining secure and well paid jobs, and increases in house prices, making it hard for them to achieve fulfilled independent lives within society. This chapter examines a series of studies undertaken by the authors listening to the experiences of young people in England aiming to gain a realistic account of the issues and problems they face in their transition from education to employment.

What do we know about young unemployed people?

Studies of young unemployed people are few and, even for experienced scientists, this is a hard-to-reach group often not wishing to participate in research. At the beginning of my journey (first author) to explore youth employment I had the delightful opportunity to work with a group of second-year psychology students (aged 19 to 25 years) wishing to find out about careers in work psychology. This created an opportunity to work in partnership with the Department for Work and Pensions (DWP) who were keen to see how they could support the young unemployed. We set out to examine the needs and attitudes of young unemployed people (aged 18 to 24 years) in a large northern city with a high rate of youth unemployment. Over a period of four months eight students contacted and talked to young unemployed people in their networks, using either one-to-one interviews or focus groups (small group interviews). Simple, open, non-judgemental questions were used asking: "Tell me about yourself"; "What do you do most days"; "What is your favourite/least favourite part of the day"; and "If no barriers what would you like to do?" exploring young people's activities and attitudes.

The first thing student researchers found out was that few young people wanted to talk to them about their experience of unemployment. But, with perseverance, persuasive use of friendship groups and expansion of the research locality they captured data from eight interviews (with four men and four women) and one focus group (with three males) with young unemployed people and a comparative focus group of four female students (Carter, 2013a). Interview and focus group data was transcribed and explored using template analyses (King, 2004), with the research questions being used to organise the data and allowing themes of similarity or difference to be noted.

A majority of those interviewed enjoyed seeing family and meeting friends on a daily basis, but reported being bored during the daytime with activities restricted as they had little money. At least half of the group explored opportunities for work on the internet every day, while others pursued personal interests (drawing and a playing musical instrument). Of the eight young people interviewed, only five claimed Job Seekers' Allowance, the other three believing that others misused job allowances and two feeling there was a negative stigma associated with being a claimant.

The focus groups allowed comparison between the unemployed and student groups. Daily routines of seeing friends and socialising were similar for both groups, with the student group also going to university, working and watching television. Both groups enjoyed evening activities spent with their friends. Dislikes for the student group were travelling to and from university, while the unemployed group disliked feeling bored during the day and doing jobs around the house. The most interesting comparisons were the different aspirations of the two groups. The student group considered gaining experience and increasing qualifications as their goals, while the unemployed group had clear and distinct work aspirations (in property development, studying law at university with the aim to become a lawyer, computer maintenance, and setting up a computer business).

This small study offers valuable insights into the day-to-day activities of young unemployed people. The findings showed that young people who were not working were active during their day, had strong ambition and work aspirations, were directed and focussed about seeking work, and considered values and circumstances before claiming benefits. Indeed, the unemployed young people appeared more focussed in their job seeking and work ambitions compared with the students we spoke to. These findings challenge popular viewpoints of 'lazy youth enjoying a life on benefits' and 'young people have no ambition'. Further, they demonstrate that young people have strongly held values about claiming unemployment benefits, with less than half of the participants interviewed choosing not to claim the Job Seekers' Allowance. These findings suggest likely inaccuracies of unemployment data about young people (usually based on registered job seekers) and question whether unemployment provision is appropriate for young people today. In addition, there is evidence that some young people have adapted to their experience of not having work in a similar way as described by Peter Warr and colleagues (Warr, 1987), suggesting the experience of unemployment can become tolerable over time having found other useful things to do with their time.

The student group commented that youth unemployment was "horrendous", with young people struggling to find jobs with few opportunities being available to them considering their educational qualifications. They wanted more support from the Job Centre offering them information about potential qualifications and postgraduate opportunities. Further, they felt that schools had a "massive" role to play in assisting young people to find work, stating that schools and parents should provide them with more fundamental guidance about job seeking. The students were very concerned that "people are claiming benefits when they shouldn't", suggesting there should be further investigation into the unemployment benefits that are being claimed.

Exploring young unemployed people's views of the support offered to them by JobCentrePlus suggests these young people had few positive views, feeling "too self-proud to go to the Job Centre". They recommended: a) improving advertising and marketing with a view to reducing the negative stigma attached to Job

Centers; b) to segment DWP clients by age group allowing the needs of each age cohort to be catered for more effectively; and c) to conduct motivational workshops or classes within Job Centres to help keep people striving in their search for employment.

This small study describes some of the issues young unemployed and university students found when seeking work in a northern city. It was interesting to note how active and focussed the unemployed young people were about their job search and their future careers compared with the students. Both groups had strong views about claiming unemployment benefits offering valuable advice to governmental support services suggesting young people's needs and career aspirations required more age-related support and advice. The student group felt there was insufficient help and advice given while they were at school or by their families to equip them to be able to perform effective job and educational searches.

While this study offers some interesting insight into young people's needs and attitudes, it was a small-scale study. What information would other studies bring?

Is the journey from higher education to work any different?

Many young people have their first experience of seeking full-time employment when they complete their undergraduate studies, but for many this will not be their first job. Up to 80% of students in the UK will have a part-time job or will have undertaken casual work while they were in education. Having taken a first degree, around 25% of graduates (Universities UK, 2012) will further delay their engagement with the labour market as they continue their educational journey into higher education by undertaking postgraduate degrees. This group of young people have progressed well in their academic studies having achieved good grades in undergraduate programmes and are attracted and encouraged to continue their education in order to achieve professional qualifications (such as in law, psychology, medicine and economics). But they have delayed their job seeking to 22 years of age or older. Therefore, do they have different experiences in finding work?

In 2013 I (first author) set out to explore the journey successful postgraduate students make after achieving Master's degrees in Occupational Psychology and Business Administration (Carter, 2013b). Having gained ethical permission to undertake this study, I contacted a group of 25 students coming to the end of their Master's programmes and asked if they would be involved in a study exploring their journey into employment. I planned to ask about their experiences of seeking work and their views about employers' attitudes to job seekers. Having a job was not critical to contributing to the study. After much encouragement four students (three aged between 23 and 25 years and one mature student) described their journey from education, the selection processes involved, the attitudes of hiring managers, and their current employment position. Participants emailed their responses to me and I used template analyses (King, 2004) to examine their responses. Two of the students were UK nationals and the others came from Eastern Europe and Hong Kong.

All the postgraduates initially focussed their job search in the area of their specialism: the mature student was "bidding for independent work" and secured "two interim roles as a Human Resource Professional". The other UK national explained: "After applying for a few roles, this role (a year-long internship) was secured around July (10 months after leaving university)". The Eastern European postgraduate took temporary roles: "I lectured for half a year, but it was home-based lecturing for e-learning course" and then had a "two-month work experience in HR department in a large international company". Sadly, neither of these experiences "has benefited much either to me or to my resume". The other postgraduate "worked in a retail store as an admin clerk for six months and then I resigned" leaving the UK to return to, and seek work in, Hong Kong.

Nine months after leaving their postgraduate education two were employed and one was conducting an extensive job search:

> I have applied for broadly known companies to small unknown business and now I have started applying to companies all over Europe. I have been looking for a range of jobs from psychology to general administrator or waitress jobs. I haven't passed (the) CV or application stage yet. Usually, I do not even get a response.

This young person eventually returned to their home in Eastern Europe to continue their job search.

When asked about the attitudes of hiring managers, one had received no communication about any of their job applications noting "Several times I have asked them to provide feedback on my application but I have had none". Another described several selection processes involving psychometric testing and interviews. They had received feedback:

> I thought it was helpful when feedback was given on something that I could realistically work on developing. (In one role) I was unsuccessful because I was not as strong as other applicants on the statistical questions. However some of the feedback wasn't very constructive and really knocked my confidence.

The mature postgraduate found hiring managers "all very helpful and respectful; and probably slightly nervous (about me)". Back in Hong Kong the other participant had been through an extensive selection process for a recruitment consultant role:

> I passed first two rounds of interviews; and failed the 3rd round with the General Manager. I knew the outcome as the hiring manager was very harsh in the interview processes and presented an annoyed feeling towards the end of the interview. He started to talk about his career path and belittled a graduated overseas student as a student who lacks competitiveness compared

to local (Hong Kong) university students. The manager stated that he did not see any good things from me, I am not competitive and aggressive; and my qualifications (a Master's degree) did not mean anything to them.

Summarising these findings, looking at the journey from postgraduate education to work, two things stand out (Carter, 2013b). First, few graduating students want to take part in this sort of research, as was found other studies. Second, the journeys from education to work are difficult and uncomfortable, with many hurdles being placed in the way of the young person seeking work. Selection processes vary in frequency and intensity and some are clearly prone to bias. Most selection processes do not generate any feedback for the applicants, which is very disheartening and does not help the young person develop or alter their job-seeking strategy. Hiring managers that do engage in feedback to job applicants show little sensitivity to the needs of the young person or appreciation of the efforts that they have put into the job-search process.

So, our studies have shown that graduates and postgraduate students make difficult journeys into employment after their time in education. Next we will consider if it is better to start on the employment journey earlier. However, it is often assumed that most people seeking work immediately after the completion of compulsory education are those with few or no qualifications or skills.

What is it like for the young and unemployed with few qualifications and skills?

Young people leaving school with few or no qualifications and few skills form a vulnerable group in our society that is rarely given a voice. Having a job enables people to feel financially secure, and for many young people this means taking the first steps in becoming independent from their families. Having work also helps young people to improve their self-confidence and social connectedness (Tilbury, Buys & Creed, 2009), assisting them in their quest for autonomous living. Unemployment, or those not in secure employment, is likely to lower young people's self-esteem and may influence their attitudes towards the help and support available to them (Hussain, 2015). Sadly, these disadvantages have a knock-on effect of reducing curiosity and motivation to find work, making these young people less likely to want to reach out to agencies that could help develop more effective job-seeking skills.

A recent report from the Joseph Rowntree Foundation (George, Metcalf, Tufekci & Wilkinson, 2015) highlights that the employment position of young people has worsened significantly in recent years, especially for those least qualified. Being out of education, employment and training between ages 18 and 25 years is likely to inflict longer-term damage on employment prospects. One of the main barriers young people have in their quest for employment is their lack of experience in the workplace; having little information about what to do in a workplace. Currently, gaining experience of the working environment is difficult to find when you are younger and there is a plentiful supply of experienced workers. When employers have their pick of workers they are unlikely to want to risk employing a young person with little or no work experience. This often leads to recruitment practices that sift out younger applicants in favour of those aged from 25–49 years (George et al., 2015) for permanent work roles, offering the less secure work roles (such as seasonal, causal and zero-hour contracts) to young people.

Job opportunities available for the less well skilled and educated job seekers tend to be advertised on the internet, being available only for a short time until sufficient applications are received. Such jobs are often offered to local residents with the ability to travel to work during unsocial hours (Tunstall, Lupton, Green, Watmough & Bates, 2012). These jobs are low paid and often involve working at night or during the weekend in roles such as cleaners, kitchen porters and shop assistants. Due to the low wages available young people will often have a portfolio of several jobs to achieve a living wage. Casual and infrequent work opportunities are unlikely to offer young people useful work experiences, and concerns about dismissal and lay-offs are likely to increase their feelings of insecurity and low self-esteem (Metcalf & Dhudwar, 2010). Working in temporary insecure job roles sees young people moving in and out of different forms of occupation; study, temporary employment, unemployment, training, self-employment and part-time working states (Bradley & Devadason, 2008). The uncertain and temporary nature of this type of work does nothing to increase young people's skills or knowledge, and there is often a mismatch between the (many) skills young people have compared with the (few) skills required to perform these job roles. Sadly, infrequent skill use often results in a negative cycle of skill loss coupled with reducing confidence, making it difficult for these young people to break out of this difficult cycle of continuing disrupted social relations and difficult transitions into the labour market (ILO, 2013).

It is clear from these descriptions that low-skilled and poorly educated young people do not have shared experiences of transitions into the labour market from education; each having an individual journey dependent on the availability of work in their local area and the support and resources available to them from family and friends (Goodwin & O'Connor, 2005). Little is known about these young people and their perspectives on transitions into the workplace and the pathways they use to gain access to paid employment (Russell, 2014). But there is emerging evidence that constant engagement in job seeking that usually results in failure is leading this group of young people to turn away from the job market (Hussain, 2015).

Pathways for job seeking are either formal (careers guidance or centrally designed programmes providing support to young people in unemployment (Grayling, 2011)) or informal (using personal resources or support of friendship groups and communities (Thompson, Russell & Simmons, 2014)). These routes offer access to different types of work opportunities and the choice of one route over another can disadvantage the job seeker by narrowing the range of opportunities available to them. For example, informal opportunities may arise through particular interest groups, such as volunteer organizations

(Skelcher, McCabe & Lowndes, 1996), and may not reflect the true nature of job opportunities in a particular locality. However, family, friends and relatives of young people of low socioeconomic status are more likely to be disadvantaged in terms of employment opportunities (George et al., 2015) as they lack strong networks that are engaged in employment. While there have been several studies exploring informal pathways into employment, less is known about the use and value of formal pathways (Saks & Ashforth, 1997) for low-skilled and low-educated young people who are likely to need considerable support (Tilbury et al., 2009). So what exactly are the experiences of young people in this position?

Low-skilled and low-educated young people looking for work

With little being known about this group of young job seekers (Russell, 2014), we set out to explore their experiences in a city in the Midlands (Hussain, 2015). Census data (2013) revealed a high proportion of young residents in this area with no or low-level qualifications (at Level 1), and a relatively large number of young unemployed (6.8%). Semi-structured interviews were used with a preponderance of open-ended questions to give the researcher (second author) an opportunity to probe participants' responses to increase clarity and gain a more detailed understanding of the context (Spencer, Ritchie, Lewis & Dillon, 2003) of unemployment the young people were experiencing. With this research population it was important that questions were clearly worded as they could easily be misunderstood. Interview questions explored: a) what kind of experience has the young person faced being unemployed? b) what type of work do young people want to do? and c) what do young people do to gain work experience? Probe questions were used to gain further information (such as "What does the term 'a good job' mean to you?") and to encourage participants to provide more information about their experiences and shape the research into a more balanced relationship between the researcher and the participant, making them feel confident that the information they shared was valued and treated confidentially.

This type of community research is rarely undertaken as few researchers have the skills needed to attract young participants and to encourage disadvantaged persons to share the personal nature of their unemployment. We embraced this task by reaching out to a charity dedicated to supporting local youth and reducing the number of NEETs. While engaging with the charity potentially gave access to over 750 young people (aged between 18 and 24 years), through our activities only one person came forward for interview. This was a familiar problem in this type of research so we decided to use family and friendship groups to identify our initial participants and then contact more people with snowball sampling techniques. Finally, 11 young people with varying unemployment experiences volunteered for interview; seven women (three were white British and four British Pakistani) and four men (three British Pakistani and one white British). The account below describes the themes of participants' comments, with agreement being noted by the number in brackets (e.g., 4, meaning four young people agreed with this theme).

At the time of study, a majority (nine of the 11 young people) were unemployed, commenting "you didn't feel very positive at all" about the experience of unemployment. More specifically two participants were unemployed, having never been employed, noting "I thought I just had to pass my GCSEs" and explaining that they had not prepared for the challenge of gaining employment thinking it was going to be straightforward. Four young people were seeking employment (unsuccessfully) describing "you're basically looking for a job and then nothing comes from it", and three were in and out of jobs having experienced work that was either temporary or having zero-hour contracts. Two participants were currently employed but were able to reflect on their periods of unemployment that had lasted up to three years.

What is the experience of being unemployed?

Seven out of the 11 participants described using the Job Centre. This was because: a) they felt they were required to do so, "You're going to do whatever you have to do to, even though you're not happy with it", and b) felt pressured into doing something:

> (The) Job Centre keep bringing us back to square one you know; it's a bit difficult where we are stuck and we're only stuck in this little box and we're scared to get out that box at the fact that you know, it's hard it's really hard, it really hard when you're on job seekers, I think it's a horrible mess to be in, it really is.

Or c) they felt unnoticed and wanted recognition: "I was never asked what I wanted to do, what experience you had . . .".

Participants described a competitive labour market where all the employers wanted work experience in order to be considered for the work opportunity: "Everyone wants experience and it's hard to get experience if no one is replying to ya. I would never sign on again that's one thing, even if I was brook (broke) . . .".

Another participant managed to get some work experience but did not continue: "I gid (give) up, with them like because like err I was doing all this work experience I was gaining nothing out of it so I gid up with them".

Others described cycles of work experience ending in no work opportunities, taking them back to the Job Centre again:

> Went to apply for jobs; actually go to the Job Centre. It makes you feel like useless like you can't actually do anything. You feel so overwhelmed, and more overwhelming than you should be, cuz you didn't feel like very positive at all, you're basically looking for a job, they keep sending you off like to all these places that promise you a job and then nothing comes from it, so you feel like even worse afterwards. It was quite stressful at times.

For one participant these experiences meant cycling off and on unemployment benefit:

> I was actually running backwards and forward, because I was on like err I was signing for like two three weeks then I was in a job for like one two months, then I was back on sign for one two weeks and then back into work so I was backwards and forward really. It's a struggle and I wish I did better when I was younger, a lot younger.

While the majority of the participants describe similar experiences with the Job Centre, one young person had gained their support: "I know if I lose the job I'll end up losing the house and everything else. I'd prefer to go to like a company that'll actually give you a certificate at the end of it all."

In summary, the young people were active in their job seeking but were often unsuccessful. They found that the practice of having to explain these difficult experiences to the Job Centre made them feel low and inadequate and the administrative processes required left them feeling overwhelmed and useless.

What type of work do young people want to do?

A majority of participants were seeking job roles associated with working with people (4) like customer service roles: "I always wanted to work with people, doesn't matter you know what I'm doing as long as it is with people at the end of the day".

Other participants were more specific, wanting roles as a police officer (2); a gardener; a pharmacist "My dream was to be a pharmacist that was something which I was looking forward to do"; a lawyer "Well if I had all the qualifications that I needed I would have become a lawyer that was my ambition when I was younger". Office jobs were mentioned (2), either in a non-specific context or as an administrator "I've always wanted to work in a hospital as an administrator".

When asked what the term 'a good job' meant, a range of meanings were described: good pay (7) was the prominent feature embellished with "more than the minimum wage"; financially stable (2) "pays the bills without being stressed", "a salary; not an hourly rate" and "not struggling to support myself and my family" (2); being able to support myself (outside the family) and to be able to think about a future (2), for example:

> A good job means truthfully, good wages, it's about like making people happy that you've done it . . . like how they wan it and they'll keep going for ya. A good job is something that you know don't have to keep struggling. I want to be able to cope so when I have children in the future . . . they won't have to be in this situation which I'm in today. I want to be a role model.

Other features of a good job were: security (3), for example, "Tends to be a lot of jobs that temporary, so that wouldn't be a good job cuz you know even after three months you'd be out of work and be in the same positon"; doing an interesting and enjoyable job (3); being able to progress or develop a career (3); being offered training; having decent working hours (9am to 5pm); having good people to work with and a happy work environment; having a decent job (2) where you know what you are doing; a job you look forward to going to in the morning; where you can meet people's expectations and make people happy; and where you are appreciated. "Something that pays the bills without stress. At least you know that you're earning throughout the year. Something that you know you go in you're working and you're getting appreciated for and offering good service to others".

In summary, in the challenging labour market young people are forced to accept any employment opportunity that comes their way. The motivation for working is being able to make ends meet and to get by. However, given the freedom and the opportunity they can clearly see the type of work they would like to do. Their aspirations go beyond merely earning sufficient money to live, as they wish to contribute to society and offer role models for the future.

What do young people do to gain experience?

Participants were asked whether they were able to gain work experience and who they had spoken to. All had turned to the Job Centre at some point in their job search, but many did not find this a helpful experience (5), for example: "There's the Job Centre, but that doesn't help much; they didn't have much opportunities to go into work straight away because I didn't have the relevant experience".

Some found the experience of attending the Job Centre (4) diminishes their self-esteem: "it makes you feel like useless; like you can't actually do anything . . . so when you actually feel like you can do something, they make you feel like you can do a lot worse". Further, repeated failures to gain work compounded these feelings:

> Becuz you didn't feel like very positive at all, you're basically looking for a job, they keep sending you of like to all these places that promise you a job and then nothing comes from it. So you feel like even worse afterwards, you used to like be so fed at the end.

Two participants talked about work programmes that helped to develop their job search skills but three others described that they had given up with the Job Centre entirely. Four participants described the difficulties unemployment regulations gave them in their job search, for example causing difficulties in proceeding with further education:

> Yeah if they called you in unfortunately you can't go on to a 16-hour course, because you've got to be available to sign on and filling all these work sheets. Or putting you on a work programme. I can't go on to do further education because the Job Centre keep bringing us back.

One of the main issues for participants attending the Job Centre was that few felt they were being listened to, or that there was any recognition of the type of work they wanted to do: "they're just making me work towards something that they want; they just want us to work in these shops like you know, shops".

Five participants described their own job search methods of using personal contacts, asking for work experience (2), doing voluntary work, directly asking companies for work or work experience opportunities (2) and using agencies to get temporary work: "as soon as something does become available whether its temporary contract or permanent . . . you know just a few weeks days whatever they just . . . call you in and like you know it's better to do something than nothing".

Two participants had been able to find work, with one offered advice to be true to yourself:

> you're just trying to tell them what they want to hear, but the last job that I actually got I just went to her and said I've got no experience I've just worked with my uncle and erm I just want a chance; I have been looking for six months . . . she says erm she says that we'll give you that chance I actually felt, I actually thought to myself . . . erm that it actually helped just being you.

Three participants described employers' attitudes: one was supportive (see above), but two others were less positive with employers asking for a wide range of work experience and extra requirements,

> you fill in jobs you know you apply to so many jobs where you don't even get a response back that wasn't successful, you can fill in forms, you sit there, you do lots of, you know you fill them all but you get no results. It would be nice if they just said sorry you was unsuccessful this time thank you for applying.

Facilitators of work experience were described as: taking any job, even one you don't want, for experience (3); having certificated work experience (2); keeping work experiences up to date (with few gaps of not working); and having some educational qualifications. Barriers to gaining work experience were assumptions that you will go onto college (3) and not making an effort at school: "It's a struggle and I wish I did better when I was younger, a lot younger. I mean when you left school you don't think about your GCSEs". Further, participants noted having little or no career or job-seeking advice at school (2).

Summary and recommendations

This study has shown that young people are an active population investing hard work into seeking employment and expressing a 'can do and will do' attitude if they are given a chance. They aspire to find work giving them security, stability and the ability to support themselves, as well as contributing usefully to society in ways they feel they can. However, in reality they experience frequent cycles of instability and poor work that creates complex barriers for them in seeking more stable work. These descriptions clearly underline the finding from the House of Lords Select Committee on Social Mobility report (2016, see p. 45 of this chapter) that states 53% of young people who leave school at the end of their secondary education have a difficult journey into the workplace. Cycles of poor work, unemployment and periods of being on and off benefits match other reported findings (e.g., Hooley et al., 2012; King, 2014; Russell, 2014; Scarpetta, Sonnet & Manfriedi, 2010; Tunstall et al., 2012) suggesting these are not minority experiences. However, there is little evidence of any extra support being provided from education, government agencies or employers to improve these transitions.

Despite the obvious difficulties these findings offer good evidence to combat stereotypical views that young unemployed people are lazy and failing to reach out and find help to get into work. The young people feel under pressure to gain work and describe feeling both useless and stuck in a box of how they are perceived (as having few skills and qualifications). The young people felt the support they received was inadequate, lacking individuality or recognition of their own interests when jobs were recommended. Feeling pressured to take uncertain low-status work with few components that facilitate intrinsic satisfaction leads to cycles of "struggling to getting by" rather than being able to gain their independence and make a contribution to society. These young people are therefore doubly disadvantaged in making the challenging transition from education into work.

Based on these findings the following recommendations are made to assist young people with no or low-level qualifications:

- More individualised forms of support are required, taking into account young people's interests and potential areas of development as well as their level of skills and abilities. Careful consideration of individual needs and abilities would enable training to be more appropriately tailored to this group, making a better match with recommended job vacancies. Increased recognition of personal interests and aspirations may reduce the young people's feelings of being devalued in the attention they are receiving, encouraging them to continue to work with formal sources of support rather than withdrawing.
- The energy and perseverance shown by these young people suggest they may well have more to offer the work environment than their educational achievement suggests (Cunningham, 2007). Support and development of social and communication skills would help them to describe their skills and abilities more clearly to employers, and they would be better able to express their needs for support during the tough times of unemployment.
- While these young job seekers were competent to source job information online, they had little understanding of effective job searching or the issues associated with forms of temporary employment. Help, support and training in these areas would enable more effective moves to be made towards stable employment. Further, increasing young people's understanding of the skills

and abilities they bring to the workplace will help them seek a better fit between what they can do and what the job requires (Anderson, Brownlie & Milne, 2015; Green et al., 2015). Such processes will help young people to climb out of the box labelled 'unskilled/lacking in qualifications' and encourage better engagement with work, increasing the likelihood that they will succeed and maintain employment.

Commonalities in these studies

While the young unemployed are a diverse population made up of young people from many different backgrounds, life and work experiences, they have all shown they are likely to have a difficult journey from education to work. This is a reality that needs to be acknowledged by those in education, careers and employment support services in order to adequately prepare young people for the efforts they must make to secure their working futures.

Self-knowledge of skills and abilities is an important component of job searching regardless of the level of educational attainment achieved. Traditionally, career guidance and support focusses on graduates and other individuals with the high achievements that employers demand (ILO, 2013), however it maybe that those with a lower skill set could benefit more from these forms of support. Our study of urban job seekers with low skills and few qualifications highlights the need for individual differences, experiences and aspirations to be taken into account to increase young people's chances of gaining suitable employment.

Self-knowledge alone is insufficient to appreciate the range of opportunities in local and regional job markets. Knowledge of what work roles are available and where this information can be found is no longer just the domain of the employment services, requiring local government provision to bring together young people, schools, colleges, third-sector organizations and local businesses to develop tailored responses for each area. Such responses would be hugely beneficial for inner-city populations where there are high levels of youth unemployment in the UK (Tovey, 2014).

Work psychology in action

Our studies of different groups of job seekers have demonstrated a number of issues that work psychology is able to illuminate. All of the studies mentioned below are introduced in Chapter 1.

Social Identity Theory can offer explanations of several of the positions described. For example, the identity of a job seeker is a categorization of someone who is not in work and is therefore different to those who are in employment. Job descriptions calling for experienced workers offers another categorization of those with and those without experience. Further, job seekers with low skills and few qualifications are another category of job seeker, one associated with negative meanings. Young people described how they felt boxed into this type of identity by the employment services and were channelled towards low-status work roles.

Expanding people's knowledge of how we identify various groups as being close to or distant from our values in order to simplify the complexity around us can help those who are trying to break down barriers and be more inclusive of a wide range of people within the workplace. For example, workplaces that have experience of employing young people will often have young employees engaged in the recruitment and selection processes to both attract young people to the organization and to bridge gaps between various social identities, thus questioning and reducing bias against those in minority groups.

Person–environment fit theory has been used on several occasions in this chapter to describe work where young people recognise they have the knowledge, skills and attributes to contribute to these job roles. The studies described in this chapter extend the work of Carless (2005) who focussed on graduates applying for jobs that fit their skill set and accepting (or rejecting) job offers based on fit. Greguras and Diefendorff (2009) examined person–job and person– organization fit among full-time working employees. They found that fit influenced employee attitudes towards the organization and contributed towards their overall job satisfaction. The studies described in this chapter focus on the importance of fit made between the young unemployed person and factors that are important to them when job seeking (e.g., do they already have an interest in the role?). But, while all the job seekers aspire towards work that is meaningful to them and offers development, not all job roles offer these opportunities. Descriptions of low-grade insecure work illustrate examples of poor fit, offering limited opportunities to use the young person's knowledge, skills and abilities. It is little wonder therefore that such work roles are associated with lack of work engagement, poor retention and absenteeism.

We have shown that good fit is not always possible when a person needs to find paid work and is not able to choose, or wait for, the opportunity of quality employment. Urban job seekers describe poor-quality work that is often unstable and that may only be available during unsocial hours. Work of this type is not limited to the low-skilled job seekers, with graduates and postgraduates describing taking on work with limited contact to an organization (e.g., distanced tuition undertaken online only) or temporary work (e.g., in administrative roles). Recruiting employers will often not appreciate that experience gained in other job sectors can be an advantage in terms of transferable knowledge and skills to their own work sector. Sadly, many young people who have been unsuccessful at finding work in their chosen sector will often apply to any job role in order to find employment, particularly if the role is more stable and secure. Many recruitment and selection processes pick up these type of applications and disregard them when, in fact, they are from people genuinely seeking employment. Therefore, the notion of fit needs to be further nuanced to consider the stability of work opportunity available and how this fit will be attractive to someone who has had to experience less secure work in the past. Further, if employers were more open to applicants from diverse backgrounds they would be likely to gain new recruits who were resilient and change-orientated following their (often many) previously negative work experiences.

The unheard aspirations of our urban job seekers were a cry to find work conforming to the Job Characteristics Model (JCM) and its later developments. These are job roles that provide security, variety, autonomy and valued social positions. Sadly, this type of work is aspirational to many young job seekers and points to the reality that many job roles do not conform to such an idealistic model. One aspect of the JCM that all job seekers crave is some feedback from the selection process; in terms of how they fared in the procedure and what they need to do to improve another application. It is sad that many employers do not offer a receipt of application and a generic form of feedback to unsuccessful job candidates. Organizations who find they are in competition for young applicants find these processes an important part of their branding as a youth-friendly organization and, if not maintained, their number of young applicants will decrease.

Concluding remarks

This chapter has offered several studies examining the difficult transitions young people are having to make between education and employment. Having good educational qualifications is no longer the pathway to good, stable employment. There are many traps and hurdles on the way to achieving individual work goals, particularly if the young person lacks the support from others or has to provide support to others.

Work psychology offers a lens through which to examine various types of work and highlights a number of job roles that are not valued, are repetitive, offer low engagement and little feedback (Lloyd, Mason & Mayhew, 2008). Sadly, many of these roles are taken by young people in their journey from education to employment. The lack of security in many of these roles causes young people to dip in and out of joblessness, damaging their self-efficacy and self-esteem. It is hoped that closer co-operation between business, education and employment support could help to balance these inequities and develop more appropriate pathways into a range of work opportunities.

References

Anderson, S., Brownlie, J. & Milne, E.-J. (2015). *Between kith and kin and formal services: everyday help and support in the 'middle layer'*. York: JRF.

Ashton, D., Maguire, M. & Spilsbury, M. (1990). *Restructuring the labour market: the implications for youth*. Basingstoke, UK: The MacMillan Press Ltd.

Bradley, H. & Devadason, R. (2008). Fractured transitions: young adults' pathways into contemporary labour markets. *Sociology, 42*(1), 119–136.

Carless, S. A. (2005). Person–job fit versus person–organization fit as predictors of organizational attraction and job acceptance intentions: a longitudinal study. *Journal of Occupational and Organizational Psychology, 78*(3), 411–429.

Carter, A. J. (2013a). *The voice of young people and the issues they face*. Part of a symposium "Supporting Young Society" (Chair, A. J. Carter). DOP Conference, January 9–11, Chester, UK.

Carter, A. J. (2013b, July). *Supporting young society: what can psychologists do to help youth employment?* Paper given to the BPS South West Branch 'Psychology in the Pub', Exeter, UK.

Census (2013, May). *Key statistics for Walsall: borough summary.* cms.walsall.gov.uk/walsall_census_2011_summary_report_v1.0.pdf, downloaded 20/01/2013.

Cunningham, I. (2007). Disentangling false assumptions about talent management: the need to recognize difference. *Development and Learning in Organizations: An International Journal, 21*(4), 4–5.

Employment Gazette (1978, August). The young and out of work. *Department of Employment Gazette,* 908–916.

Eurofound (2012). *NEETs – young people not in employment, education or training: characteristics, costs and policy responses in Europe.* Luxembourg: Publications Office of the European Union.

Eurofound (2014). *Mapping youth transitions across Europe.* Luxembourg: Publications Office of the European Union.

European Foundation for the Improvement of Living and Working Conditions (EU28) (2012). *NEETs Young people not in employment, education or training: characteristics, costs and policy responses in Europe.* Luxembourg: Publications Office of the European Union.

Eurostat; European Commission for Employment, Social Affairs and Inclusion (2013). *Youth employment.* http://europa.eu/social/main.jsp?catId=1036, downloaded 20/01/2013.

George, A., Metcalf, H., Tufekci, L. & Wilkinson, D. (2015, June). *Understanding age and the labour market.* Report from the Joseph Rowntree Foundation (JRF), p. 17. www.jrf.org.uk/work/labour-markets, downloaded 10/08/2014.

Goodwin, J. & O'Connor, H. (2005). Exploring complex transitions: looking back at the 'Golden Age' of from school to work. *Sociology, 39*(2), 201–220.

Grayling, C. (2011). *How to tackle unemployment.* www.gov.uk/government/speeches/how-to-tackle-unemployment, downloaded 20/04/2015.

Green, A., Sissons, P., Broughton, K., De Hoyos, M., Warhurst, C. & Barnes, S. A. (2015). *How cities can connect people in poverty with jobs.* www.jrf.org.uk/sites/files/jrf/cities-poverty-jobs-full.pdf, downloaded 10/08/2014.

Greguras, G. J. & Diefendorff, J. M. (2009). Different fits satisfy different needs: linking person–environment fit to employee commitment and performance using self-determination theory. *Journal of Applied Psychology, 94*(2), 465.

Hooley, T., Devins, D., Watts, A. G., Hutchinson, J., Marriott, J. & Walton, F. (2012). *Tackling unemployment, supporting business and developing careers.* London: UK Commission for Employment and Skills (UKCES).

House of Lords Select Committee on Social Mobility (2016). *Overlooked and left behind: improving the transition from school to work for the majority of young people.* London: The Stationery Office Ltd.

Hussain, A. (2015). What is it like to be young and unemployed? Unpublished dissertation submitted in part requirement for the Degree of MSc Occupational Psychology of the University of Sheffield, Sheffield, UK.

International Labour Office (ILO) (2013). *Global employment trends for youth: a generation at risk.* www.ilo.org/wcmsp5/groups/public/---.../wcms_212423.pdf, downloaded 09/05/2015.

King, E. (2014). *Tackling unemployment: towards a participation plan for Victorians.* http://vcoss.org.au/documents/2014/11/Tackling-unemployment.pdf, downloaded 20/05/2015.

King, N. (2004). Using templates in the thematic analysis of text. In C. Cassell & G. Symon (Eds), *Essential guide to qualitative methods in organizational research*, pp. 256–270. London: Sage Publications Ltd.

Lloyd, C. L., Mason, G. & Mayhew, K. (2008). *Low-wage work in the United Kingdom*. New York, NY: Russell Sage Foundation.

Metcalf, H. & Dhudwar, A. (2010). *Employers' role in the low-pay/no-pay cycle*. York: Joseph Rowntree Foundation.

Russell, L. (2014). Formerly NEET young people's pathways to work: a case-study approach. *Power and Education*, 6(2), 182–196.

Saks, A. M. & Ashforth, B. E. (1997). A longitudinal investigation of the relationships between job information sources, applicant perceptions of fit, and work outcomes. *Personnel Psychology*, 50(2), 395–426.

Scarpetta, S., Sonnet, A. & Manfriedi, T. (2010). *Rising youth unemployment during the crisis: how to prevent negative long-term consequences on a generation?* OECD Social, Employment and Migration Working Papers, No. 106. Paris: OECD Publishing. www.oecd-ilibrary.org/docserver/download/5kmh79zb2mmv-en.pdf?expires=1488721812&id=id&accname=guest&checksum=996F088615C8D3BD12FD89C6383AFB7D, downloaded 20/05/2015.

Skelcher, C., McCabe, A. & Lowndes, V. (1996). *Community networks in urban regeneration*. Bristol, UK: Policy Press.

Spencer, L., Ritchie, J., Lewis, J. & Dillon, L. (2003). *Quality in qualitative evaluation: a framework for assessing research evidence*. London: Cabinet Office, Strategy Unit.

Thompson, R., Russell, L. & Simmons, R. (2014). Space, place and social exclusion: an ethnographic study of young people outside education and employment. *Journal of Youth Studies*, 17(1), 63–78.

Tilbury, C., Buys, N. & Creed, P. (2009). Perspectives of young people in care about their school-to-work transition. *Australian Social Work*, 62(4), 476–490.

Tovey, A. (2014). Attempts to tackle youth unemployment have failed, claims think-tank. The *Telegraph*, 8 April. www.telegraph.co.uk/finance/jobs/10752255/Attempts-to-tackle-youth-unemployment-have-failed-claims-think-tank.html, downloaded 20/05/2015.

Tunstall, R., Lupton, R., Green, A., Watmough, S. & Bates, K. (2012). *Disadvantaged young people looking for work: a job in itself?* York: Joseph Rowntree Foundation. http://eprints.lse.ac.uk/47212, downloaded 01/06/2015.

Universities UK (2012). *Patterns and trends in UK higher education*. www.universitiesuk.ac.uk/facts-and-stats/Pages/facts-and-stats.aspx, downloaded 23/5/2015.

Warr, P. W. (1987). *Work, unemployment and mental health*. Oxford: Clarendon Press.

4 Unemployment at a young age

A work psychological analysis of its nature, consequences and possible remedies

Eva Selenko

Introduction

Youth unemployment is a serious and widespread issue in most European countries nowadays. Despite seeing some decline recently, at the time of writing over 3.5 million young people between the ages of 15–24 years are unemployed in the European Union; an unemployment rate that still remains consistently higher than the adult unemployment rate and reflects the difficulties of young people in finding a job (Eurostat, 2018).

Unemployment at a young age is different to experiencing unemployment as an adult. It is likely to have devastating effects on economies, societies and individuals and their future lives. While there are quite a number of economic studies and policy reports available on the macro-level effects of youth unemployment, there is scarce data on the individual experience of unemployment by young people themselves. More seriously lacking are systematic investigations into how individual experiences of unemployment at a young age can be alleviated, how people can be assisted and how longer-term scaring can be reduced to a minimum.

Work psychology can offer a breadth of empirical insights, thanks to over 100 years of research on the effect of unemployment on individuals, the challenges of reemployment and career development in general (see, e.g., Paul & Moser, 2009; Wang & Wanberg, 2017). Building on this theoretical knowledge could allow for a more structured and informed approach towards understanding the situation of young people out of work. A better understanding of the issues facing young unemployed adolescents will also allow for the development of empirically and theoretically robust intervention strategies for getting young people into jobs, education or apprenticeships.

Despite the theoretical developments, young unemployed people still constitute an elusive cohort in academic research that somehow fall between the cracks. Unemployment researchers tend to disregard young unemployed adolescents as they often are not on unemployment benefits and have not yet been in formal employment for a sufficiently long time to be counted with other unemployed people. Similarly, educational researchers regard unemployment only as an outcome of dropping out of school, but little attention is paid to those who have already left education and are trying to get into the workplace.

This chapter will illustrate how work psychology can offer new ways of understanding the issue of youth unemployment. First, I will explore the nature of youth unemployment from a psychological point of view. I will bring forward several arguments and empirical support to suggest that being unemployed at a young age is experienced differently than at an adult age. Adolescents who are not in employment, education or training face a particular and highly complex set of demands warranting special attention. Next, I will illustrate how the psychological consequences of unemployment at a young age might affect future career outcomes. This chapter closes with a cautious evaluation of a recent initiative of the European Union to keep young people in education and training (the Youth Guarantee) in light of the psychological literature.

The focus of this chapter will be on adolescents who are not in education, employment or training but have completed the minimum amount of schooling (in most European countries up to an age of 15 years). The chapter will concentrate on the experience of being in unemployment, outside education and training, with particular focus on the social context young people are in and the psychological consequences of this situation. While the reasons for becoming unemployed and falling out of education and training can be manifold, this chapter suggests that the situation of being unemployed at a young age has particular consequences in itself, warranting attention on its own. To understand the risk factors that lead young people to become unemployed, the reader might want to refer to other literature (such as Eurofound, 2012).

Unemployment at a young age is different

Unemployment as an adolescent can be the result of two situations; either a person has lost employment or they have not found a job. Research shows that these two situations do not differ in their impact on the well-being of adolescents, rather they seem to be similarly detrimental (Winefield & Tiggemann, 1989). Unemployment is a pervasively negative experience at any age. In that sense, it is no surprise that unemployment will have negative effects on the lives of young people as well. However, there is evidence that shows that younger adults may be particularly affected by unemployment, more so than middle-aged people.

The pervasive negative effects of unemployment on people's lives, well-being, private and social relations have been widely documented ever since the classic Marienthal studies by Lazarsfeld, Zeisel and Jahoda in the early 1930s (Jahoda, Lazarsfeld & Zeisel, 1971/2017). What empirical research on unemployed people also showed is that while almost everyone suffers from unemployment, not everyone suffers equally. One of the decisive factors for the effect of unemployment is a person's age. Young people are differently and disproportionally more affected by unemployment than middle-aged people. In a meta-analysis on the negative effects and moderators of unemployment that scrutinised the empirical evidence of over 300 (cross-sectional and longitudinal) studies surveying nearly half a million people, Paul and Moser (2009) found an unexpected u-shaped relationship between age and health deficits during unemployment. Younger (and older) people it seemed, suffered disproportionally more from unemployment than middle-aged people. Also other meta-analyses (McKee-Ryan, Song, Wanberg & Kinicki, 2005) found that the experience of unemployment leads to worse mental health among school leavers than among adults. Do these findings indicate that younger people are worse off than middle-aged unemployed people, or do they show that middle-aged people are better off than the younger ones (as Paul and Moser (2009) argue)? The reality might be more complex. Young people might apprehend and cope with unemployment in different ways than middle-aged people, simply due to being at different stages in their lives.

First, young people might not have had the chance to build up the positive resources provided by employment. Being out of work deprives people of essential human experiences, which are central for well-being and happiness (Jahoda, 1982). Employment, for example, offers the chance to contribute something meaningful to society, and to achieve more than a person would be able to achieve on their own. Employed people meet other people through work and at work, which not only widens their social circle beyond family relations and friends, but also offers new sources of status recognition and feedback. Furthermore, employment structures one's time into on-the-job time and leisure time, and work automatically activates people into action. Unemployed people can have these experiences as well, but they are more difficult to sustain outside work. These five so called 'latent' (because not immediately obvious) benefits of work have been related to well-being in numerous studies (e.g., see Muller & Waters, 2012, for a review). Jahoda is not alone in suggesting that having work is essential for well-being. In a similar analogy, Peter Warr suggests the existence of job-related characteristics that have a vitamin-like effect on well-being (e.g., Warr, 1987, 2013). Some scholars (e.g., Ryff, 1989) even go so far as to propose that work *is* well-being, in that doing something meaningful can be understood as a form of eudaimonic well-being (as opposed to the hedonic 'feeling happy' type of well-being). However, due to a short or non-existing employment experience, unemployed adolescents would have had fewer of these beneficial well-being-enhancing experiences.

Second, having a negative experience at the career-entry stage might taint and cast a shadow over future aspirations and the development of professional self-efficacy. Young people might simply not have had enough positive professional learning experiences to develop enough knowledge and confidence in their skills to cope with unemployment (e.g., Bandura, 1982). In this sense, young people might be less well equipped to deal with set-backs and blows to their career and professional sense of self.

There are even biological reasons as to why unemployment during adolescence might be experienced more severely than in a later stage of life. Adolescents are in a particularly turbulent period in their lives, undergoing substantial hormonal and social changes in their transitioning from childhood to adulthood. According to Life Span Theory (e.g., Heckhausen & Tomasik, 2002; Heckhausen, Wrosch & Schulz, 2010) people under the age of 20 years face several challenging life goals that are accompanied with varying waxing and waning windows of opportunity in which to achieve them. For example, the life goal of finishing an education and commencing a first job falls within the period between mid-teens to mid-twenties. Also important are other life goals that start to become relevant in this period (e.g., finding a partner, beginning a family, becoming financially independent). In this sense, adolescence can be considered an extra stressful period that asks young people to suddenly negotiate a number of life demands at once. Adolescents who are not in employment, education or training are confronted with an obstacle in achieving the important life goal of landing a first job. In addition, since they do not continue into higher education, unemployed adolescents are also low achievers on another life goal: finishing an education. These two situations are likely to induce stress, followed by a variety of coping behaviours.

To summarise, there are plenty of theoretical and empirical reasons to expect that younger people will be more affected by unemployment than middle-aged people. Data from meta-analytic studies confirms that unemployment at a young age has more pervasive effects on well-being than at middle age. Theoretically there are several ways to explain this different effect: adolescents might have had fewer opportunities to benefit from the well-being-enhancing experiences of employment (simply due to having had less work experience), and adolescents might have fewer alternative activity sources to compensate for unemployment (e.g., by caring and family duties, volunteer work). In addition, adolescents have to deal with hormonal and developmental challenges along with the stress of achieving central life goals, which might create additional strain to which middle-aged people might not be exposed in that form.

This implies that in order to support young adolescents who are not in employment, education or training it may not be enough to solely look at the factors that lead them into this situation, but also to regard the negative aspects specific to the experience itself.

Psychological consequences of unemployment at a young age

The long-term consequences of youth unemployment are well established, as unemployment seems to predict future unemployment. People who have been unemployed in their lives have a higher risk of becoming unemployed in the future. Longitudinal studies show that adolescents who experienced longer spells of unemployment experience a wage penalty in the form of lower life-time earnings than those who spend the same period in education or training (Mroz & Savage, 2006). The period of being not in employment, education or training hence leads to a 'scarring' effect on a young person's career that is visible over a longer period of time (OECD, 2010). Furthermore, adolescent unemployment is presumed to be a risk factor for future social exclusion (Kieselbach, 2003; Sen, 2000). How can these longitudinal effects be explained? On a psychological level, unemployment, not being in education or failing a life goal will have a variety of effects. These effects are likely to impact on an adolescent's choices, behaviours and future chances to succeed. The present chapter particularly focusses on well-being, regulatory abilities, individual human capital and identity development.

Effects on adolescents' well-being and regulatory abilities

Unemployment is bad news for the well-being of any unemployed person. Unemployment has pervasive effects on mental health, life satisfaction and physical well-being. It enhances the chance for developing depression and is associated with an increased risk for suicide (McKee-Ryan et al., 2005; Paul & Moser, 2009). Lowered well-being and light spells of depression are often accompanied by a loss of interest, low aspirations, a low sense of competence, difficulties concentrating and an overall pessimistic goal outlook. These symptoms will stand in the way of presenting oneself well in upcoming job interviews, or performing well in future educational programmes, training or work. In order to successfully master a job, an education or a training, adolescents need to have sufficient regulatory abilities. They need to be able to set realistic goals for themselves, select effective strategies and invest the right level of energy and persistence to achieve those goals. If things go wrong in an educational setting, at work or in a short training course, people need to be able to adapt their strategies on their own and regulate their effort in the right way. This requires a persistent investment of extra energy that is going to be more challenging for people suffering from low well-being. Subsequently, the inability to invest enough energy to regulate their efforts might lead to future setbacks and experiences of underachievement. In other words, the negative well-being consequences of unemployment at a young age are likely to put adolescents in a worse starting position for their future career.

In addition, compared with older people, younger people will have a less well-developed repertoire of behavioural strategies and, by being in the depriving situation of unemployment at a young age, they are likely to find it more difficult to build adaptive coping abilities. As different from employed young people or those in formal training and education, unemployed adolescents are likely to have fewer opportunities to succeed in work-related tasks that enable them to develop their skills and confidence in a work context. The belief that they can master these challenges is essential in the development of adaptive self-efficacy (Bandura, 1982).

Further, the experience of failure offers a potentially maladaptive opportunity for learning about one's own knowledge, skills and ability. Rather than learning what they *can* do, adolescents who are not in employment, education or training may get feedback about what they *cannot* do (e.g., succeed in landing a place on a training programme, finish an education, get a first job). According to social cognitive learning theory (Bandura, 1982), new potentially anxiety-evoking situations are presumed to be more influential learning contexts for the development of knowledge, skills and abilities than situations that have been encountered (personally or as a witness) before. In this sense, first-time experiences (such as being unemployed or applying for a job) are going to have greater impact on a person's knowledge of their regulatory abilities than experiences that have been encountered before. Consequently, the experience of failure at a young age might have a more pervasive effect than at an older age.

Therefore, repeated experiences of individual failure are likely to undermine a person's self-efficacy creating negative affect, frustration and irritability.

These negative experiences and feelings can have long-lasting effects on socio-psychological development. Longitudinal studies have shown that lower self-esteem in adolescence can be related to lower mental health, worse economic prospects and higher levels of criminal behaviour during adulthood (Trzesniewski et al., 2006). Lower self-esteem and reduced self-efficacy will also impact a person's goal-setting. Without the belief in their own ability to achieve something, and without knowledge of what they can do, i.e., their competencies, young people are less likely to set themselves ambitious and realistic goals for their future career.

Effects on development of psychological skills and abilities

Not succeeding in getting a job or an apprenticeship is also going to have pervasive effect on an individual's human capital and self-development. As Sen (2000) notes: "People not only 'learn by doing', they also 'unlearn' by 'not doing'" (p. 19). Therefore, adolescents who are unemployed are doubly affected; not only do they not practise (and hence possibly unlearn) the skills they already possess, they also do not learn essential novel skills, abilities and knowledge since they no longer participate in work or further education.

According to classic human capital perspectives (Becker, 2002), prolonged periods of being unemployed, not in education or training are going to affect the individual's capital that they need to proliferate in later careers. Whereas unemployment as an adult deprives people of the opportunity to practise already existing skills, knowledge and abilities, unemployment as an adolescent implies that people are not developing those skills in the first place. In other words, people who spent their teens unemployed are likely to possess a lower level of education than their peers remaining in education and lower levels of work experience than their colleagues gaining valuable work experience. At least from a human capital point of view, this will make them less competitive in the job market later on in comparison with other candidates who spend this time in further education or in employment. In this regard, young unemployed people face the double deprivation of employment and education.

In addition, not practising existing knowledge, skills and abilities, and not learning additional and novel things through education, means that unemployed adolescents are also at risk of learning maladaptive coping strategies. Coping strategies can vary in light of potential goal failure, with some enhancing their efforts or changing their strategies to achieve their goals. Or, they may re-evaluate their goals and their relative importance, or even withdraw from attempts of goal achievement altogether. In other words, adolescents experiencing longer spells of unemployment may reconsider the benefits of being employed all together and, feeling hopeless in their attempts to gain employment, they may withdraw from job seeking or self-improvement activities all together. Diary studies of unemployed people reapplying for jobs show that the individual's ability to detach from unsuccessful experiences is very important. The more people were able to disengage from negative experiences, the less these experiences will have an effect on their self-efficacy, affect and subsequent job-seeking behaviours (Wanberg, Zhu & Van Hooft, 2010).

Effects on identity development and belonging

Unemployment at a young age is believed to be a disenfranchising experience, leading to an estrangement from politics, state and civic duties (Banks & Ullah, 1987). How these longer-term effects come to be are less well understood. Young unemployed people may not yet have found their place in society professionally speaking. McKee-Ryan and colleagues (McKee-Ryan et al., 2005) argue that the additional burden of developing an occupational identity might also explain why young people's well-being is more affected by unemployment. Not having access to the labour market, not being in training or education, may undermine the development of an understanding of who one is, occupationally and professionally. Indeed, in a study among high-school leavers, Gurney (1980) suggested that not being able to get work was associated with a confused sense of self.

According to Social Identity Theory (Tajfel, 1982), people define themselves in terms of social categories (or group memberships). In industrialised societies, what one does for a living, the occupational self-categorisation, is a common form of description. In informal conversations, when being introduced to new people, one of the first things asked is often "What do you do for a living?" In this sense, when defining oneself, people often refer to their occupation or the work that they do. Unsurprisingly, who one is and what one does are very closely related categories. Stating what one does for a living not only tells a lot about a person's background, it also allows a person to locate themselves in relation to others. In this sense, it tells them 'who they are' (see also Selenko et al., 2018).

An unemployed young person with only fleeting membership in an occupational setting would have difficulties establishing a positive self-categorisation as a member of a certain occupation. Someone who has only worked for a short time in a profession is unlikely to define themselves in terms of that profession. Having fewer chances to try out one's potential is also likely to limit that individual's identity development, given that 'who one is' very often depends on what one does or is able to do. Unemployed adolescents who are not in training are deprived of the opportunity to learn social and technical skills in a variety of areas that will enable them to enlarge their behavioural repertoire. They are missing opportunities to develop a stable sense of self and an occupational identity (Côté, 1996). This will make it more difficult for adolescents to know who they are and what they can do, which in turn is likely to affect future career behaviours. Without a clear understanding of the self, a sense of the range and limits of one's abilities, future career-goal planning and adaptive coping will be a much more difficult task (Inceoglu, Selenko, McDowall & Schlachter, 2018). Whereas an adult unemployed professional with an established sense of occupational identity is more likely to direct their re-employment efforts towards getting a job in that occupation again, the re-employment strategies of a person without an occupational identity will be much less focussed. Being able to gain any job may alleviate the negative situation of unemployment; however, not every job might be suitable or satisfactory for that person.

The disrupted development of a stable occupational identity is also likely to affect adolescents' feeling of belonging to general society. In a recent study comparing British employed and unemployed adults it could be shown that people who are unemployed feel less included, less part of the general working society, which then explained part of their reduced levels of well-being (Stadler, Selenko & Patterson, 2016). Whereas middle-aged and older adults might have alternative resources allowing them to participate in society (such as financial reserves, a wider social network, varied family and social obligations), younger adolescents might not yet have been able to develop these resources.

What can be done? Analysing the benefits of Youth Guarantee Programmes from a psychological perspective

Youth unemployment has been recognised as a main target by policy makers and politicians throughout Europe and the industrialised world. To tackle this issue, in 2014 all member states of the European Union ratified the Youth Guarantee scheme. By adhering to this programme, EU member states are committed to offer employment, apprenticeships, or continued education to people under the age of 25 years, within four months of them leaving school or losing a job (European Commission, 2014). The precise nature and shape of the implementation of Youth Guarantee Programmes varies between the EU member states but the underlying logic is the same: to ensure that no young person is inactive for longer than four months. The Youth Guarantee aims to enable young people to gain suitable employment, education and training in order to enhance their chances to find a way 'back in' to the labour market.

The presumed benefits of Youth Guarantee Programmes are large; adolescents would no longer be unemployed and at the same time would be able to gain more skills, knowledge and abilities (depending on the programme). Little is known yet about the success of these programmes, but anecdotal evidence from countries where the Youth Guarantee programmes have been in place for several years (e.g., Austria, Finland, Sweden), suggests a two-fold response (Eurofound, 2012). These Youth Guarantee Programmes are successful at getting young people into suitable employment, but dropout rates can be high. Without going into detail about the structural and delivery aspects of these programmes, I will consider those of the psychological factors discussed previously that may be affecting the success of the Youth Guarantee schemes.

From a psychological point of view, having been through a spell of unemployment, or not being in education and training, is likely to have after-effects, at least in the short term. Adolescents entering a Youth Guarantee Programme may suffer from a 'survivor' syndrome; they have just been through a period of adversity that has affected their skills development, well-being and identity. The lowered levels of well-being they experience due to unemployment and unsuccessful job search are likely to affect their ability to cope with the demands of a Youth Guarantee Programme in the short term. This reduced sense of self-efficacy may make it difficult to achieve the realistic but challenging goals encouraged by a Youth Guarantee Programme that will provide a good learning experience. A young person with a confused sense of self is likely to find it difficult to see what they can achieve with the training, employment or education offered by the Youth Guarantee Programme. Therefore, it is crucial to know an individual's background, their levels of well-being, self-efficacy and stage of occupational identity development in order to plan a successful journey through such a programme.

Further, the young person's future prospects in a programme are likely to vary according to their individual circumstances. Neither overcoming adversity nor participating in a Youth Guarantee Programme takes place in a vacuum. Socio-economic background, age, migration experience and available social support have all been found to moderate the negative effect of unemployment. Similarly, these factors may also play a role in the experience of unemployment among adolescents. Parents and parental support is of primary importance during the transition between childhood and adulthood. Adolescents tend to recover better from adversity if they have a positive relationship with a supportive adult during the time of adversity (Masten, Best & Garmezy, 1990). Indeed, in a recent study exploring the factors responsible for the success rate of a Youth Guarantee Programme, Selenko and Pils (2016) found support for this assumption. Adolescents who reported having a more positive relationship with their parents at the onset of the programme were more likely to continue their education after one year, or to have found employment, or been offered an apprenticeship outside the programme after one year. Having a good relationship with parents helps not only when coping with unemployment and unsuccessful job search, but will also be of importance during the demanding times of the Youth Guarantee Programme.

The nature and forms of the services offered under the Youth Guarantee vary substantially, but one defining unifying characteristic is their swiftness. Youth Guarantee schemes target all adolescents within a four-month period of being unemployed, or not in education or training. From a psychological viewpoint the short duration of the deprivation experience is likely to be a crucial element in the success of these programmes. Not only would the negative effect of spells of inactivity be limited but, if this period can be quickly and successfully mastered, this is likely to contribute substantially to the young person developing resilience.

Resilience describes a person's ability to overcome adverse situations, recover from negative events quickly and avoid risks. It is a mix of a variety of psychological ingredients, such as self-efficacy, competence and coping skills (Olsson, Bond, Burns, Vella-Brodrick & Sawyer, 2003). Resilience is a highly beneficial personality trait; not only helpful with coping with future adversity, but also providing confidence for more proactive career behaviours (such as ambitious goal-setting or undertaking entrepreneurial activities). Resilience can develop in the face of adversity; through successfully coping with risk situations important strategies for handling emotions and problems are learned. Managing adversity successfully at a young age can contribute to the development of resilience (Fergus & Zimmerman, 2005). Therefore, if Youth Guarantee Programmes could assist young people in becoming more resilient, the experience of unemployment might be transformed into something positive. In such an ideal world, having been unemployed, unable to find a job and outside education could then be nothing more than a bad dream from which a young person awoke better equipped and with fresh perspectives to deal with novel challenges of their own careers.

References

Bandura, A. (1982). Self-efficacy mechanism in human agency. *American Psychologist*, 37(2), 122–147.

Banks, M. H. & Ullah, P. (1987). Political attitudes and voting among unemployed and employed youth. *Journal of Adolescence*, 10(2), 201–216.

Becker, G. S. (2002). *The age of human capital* (pp. 71–89). Retrieved from: media.hoover.org.

Côté, J. E. (1996). Sociological perspectives on identity formation: the culture–identity link and identity capital. *Journal of Adolescence*, 19(5), 417–428.

Eurofound (2012). NEETs – *young people not in employment, education or training: characteristics, costs and policy responses in Europe*. Luxembourg: Publications Office of the European Union.

European Commission (2014). Memo: the EU Youth Guarantee. Retrieved from the European Commission Press Release Database: http://europa.eu/rapid/press-release_MEMO-14-571_en.htm.

Eurostat (2018). *Unemployment statistics*. Retrieved from: http://ec.europa.eu/eurostat/statistics-explained/index.php/Unemployment_statistics.

Fergus, S. & Zimmerman, M. A. (2005). Adolescent resilience: a framework for understanding healthy development in the face of risk. *Annual Review of Public Health*, 26, 399–419.

Gurney, R. M. (1980). The effects of unemployment on the psycho-social development of school-leavers. *Journal of Occupational Psychology*, 53(3), 205–213.

Heckhausen, J. & Tomasik, M. J. (2002). Get an apprenticeship before school is out: how German adolescents adjust vocational aspirations when getting close to a developmental deadline. *Journal of Vocational Behavior*, 60(2), 199–219.

Heckhausen, J., Wrosch, C. & Schulz, R. (2010). A motivational theory of life-span development. *Psychological Review*, 117(1), 32–60.

Inceoglu, I., Selenko, E., McDowall, A. & Schlachter, S. (2018). (How) do work placements work? Scrutinizing the quantitative evidence for a theory-driven future research agenda. *Journal of Vocational Behavior*, 110(B), 317–337.

Jahoda, M. (1982). *Employment and unemployment: a social-psychological analysis*. Cambridge: Cambridge University Press.

Jahoda, M., Lazarsfeld, P. F. & Zeisel, H. (1971/2017). Marienthal: the sociography of an unemployed community. Abingdon, UK: Routledge.

Kieselbach, T. (2003). Long-term unemployment among young people: the risk of social exclusion. *American Journal of Community Psychology*, 32(1–2), 69–76.

Masten, A. S., Best, K. M. & Garmezy, N. (1990). Resilience and development: contributions from the study of children who overcome adversity. *Development and Psychopathology*, 2(04), 425–444.

McKee-Ryan, F., Song, Z., Wanberg, C. R. & Kinicki, A. J. (2005). Psychological and physical well-being during unemployment: a meta-analytic study. *Journal of Applied Psychology*, 90(1), 53–76.

Mroz, T. A. & Savage, T. H. (2006). The long-term effects of youth unemployment. *Journal of Human Resources*, *41*(2), 259–293.

Muller, J. & Waters, L. (2012). A review of the latent and manifest benefits (LAMB) scale. *Australian Journal of Career Development*, *21*(1), 31–37.

Olsson, C. A., Bond, L., Burns, J. M., Vella-Brodrick, D. A. & Sawyer, S. M. (2003). Adolescent resilience: a concept analysis. *Journal of Adolescence*, *26*(1), 1–11.

Organisation for Economic Co-operation and Development (OECD) (2010). *Off to a good start? Jobs for youth*, position paper. Retrieved from: www.oecd.org/els/emp/46717876.pdf.

Paul, K. I. & Moser, K. (2009). Unemployment impairs mental health: meta-analyses. *Journal of Vocational Behavior*, *74*(3), 264–282.

Portes, A. & Haller, W. (2010). The informal economy. In N. Smelser & R. Swedberg (Ed.), *The handbook of economic sociology*. Princeton, NJ: Princeton University Press. Retrieved from: Google Books.com.

Ryff, C. D. (1989). Happiness is everything, or is it? Explorations on the meaning of psychological well-being. *Journal of Personality and Social Psychology*, *57*(6), 1069–1081.

Selenko, E., Berkers, H., Carter, A. J., Woods, S. A., Otto, K., Urbach, T. & De Witte, H. (2018). On the dynamics of work identity in atypical employment: setting out a research agenda. *European Journal of Work and Organizational Psychology*, *27*(3), 324–334.

Selenko, E. & Pils, K. (2016). The after-effects of youth unemployment: more vulnerable persons are less likely to succeed in Youth Guarantee programmes. *Economic & Industrial Democracy*, https://doi.org/0143831X16653186.

Sen, A. (2000). *Social exclusion: concept, application, and scrutiny*. Social Development Papers No. 1. Manila: Office of Environment and Social Development, Asian Development Bank.

Stadler, T., Selenko, E. & Patterson, M. (2016). Bedeutet Arbeitslosigkeit gleich sozialen Ausschluss? Der Einfluss des Anstellungsgrads auf Belongingness und Gesundheit [Does unemployment equal social exclusion? The impact of employment status on belongingness and health], German Congress of Psychology, Leipzig, September.

Tajfel, H. (1982). Social psychology of intergroup relations. *Annual Review of Psychology*, *33*(1), 1–39.

Trzesniewski, K. H., Donnellan, M. B., Moffitt, T. E., Robins, R. W., Poulton, R. & Caspi, A. (2006). Low self-esteem during adolescence predicts poor health, criminal behavior, and limited economic prospects during adulthood. *Developmental Psychology*, *42*(2), 381–390.

Wanberg, C. R., Zhu, J. & Van Hooft, E. A. (2010). The job search grind: perceived progress, self-reactions, and self-regulation of search effort. *Academy of Management Journal*, *53*(4), 788–807.

Wang, M. & Wanberg, C. R. (2017). 100 years of applied psychology research on individual careers: from career management to retirement. *Journal of Applied Psychology*, *102*(3), 546–563.

Warr, P. B. (1987). *Work, unemployment, and mental health*. Oxford: Oxford University Press.

Warr, P. B. (2013). Jobs and job-holders: two sources of happiness and unhappiness. In S. A. David, I. Boniwell & A. Conley Ayers (Eds), *The Oxford handbook of happiness* (pp. 733–750), Oxford library of psychology. New York, NY: Oxford University Press.

Winefield, A. H. & Tiggemann, M. (1989). Unemployment duration and affective well-being in the young. *Journal of Occupational Psychology*, *62*(4), 327–336.

5   It's a hard knock life

Youth unemployment in London

Yeşim Guner

Introduction to youth services

Young people under the age of 25 years have the greatest disadvantage in the UK labour market (George, Metcalf, Tufekci & Wilkinson, 2015) and thus local authorities have set up Early Intervention and Prevention Services focussing on providing 'hard-to-reach' young people with suitable tools to succeed in life. These young people include those who may be from more deprived socio-economic backgrounds, with poor or no role models to whom to aspire, they may have undiagnosed mental health issues and/or learning difficulties, they may be involved with gangs, drugs and, at times, may have regular police contact. The other end of the spectrum are those young people who are highly academic and the pressure they place on themselves to be 'perfect' has, on countless occasions, resulted in self-harm.

The key to identifying the needs and issues facing young people is utilising adequate assessment tools. The Department of Education and Skills (2004) Green Paper *Every Child Matters* proposed the introduction of a Common Assessment Framework (CAF) as a central element of the strategy for helping children, young people and their families. The CAF gathers and records information about a child or young person for whom a practitioner has multiple concerns in a standardised format that can be shared with the other professionals involved. In doing this, the needs of the child or young person are identified and unnecessary duplication amongst teams of practitioners or professionals prevented. These teams include: Youth and Family Services, Sure Start Children's Centres, GP practices, schools, multi-agency faith groups, Safer Families Projects and social care including Leaving Care. The use of CAF plays a key part in delivering front-line services in an integrated and consistent format.

Support for young people is provided by a range of different agencies working across universal, targeted and statutory services. London boroughs employ full-time Targeted Youth Workers (TYWs); for example, I and nine other TYWs each have caseloads of up to 25 'targeted' young people at any one time. Targeted Youth Support (TYS) aims to provide timely, effective and co-ordinated support for vulnerable or 'at risk' young people aged 9 to 19 years (and up to 25 years for those with learning difficulties and disabilities). Targeted Youth Workers receive referrals from a range of services such as: schools, social care, Child and Adolescent Mental Health services (CAMHs), Family Focus Teams, General Practitioners, the police, young people's Drug and Alcohol Services, parents and sometimes self-referrals. These referrals may be for a specific piece of work such as youth conditional cautions, attendance work, youth work (e.g., self-esteem, anger management, Keeping Safe workshops), positive activities, counselling, child sexual exploitation cases, or for more general support such as careers advice, housing and financial support.

Youth work is underpinned by statutory requirements (set out in Section 507B of the Education and Inspections Act, 2006) to provide targeted social education opportunities for young people (via youth work and positive activities) and is delivered in a variety of settings. Service locations include Youth and Community Centre-based work, mobile provision, residential and project work. Detached youth work is also undertaken (sometimes called outreach work) with the aim of identifying and providing support to vulnerable young people in their own 'territory' such as streets, cafés and parks. This work is aimed particularly at reducing youth-related anti-social behaviour and has been recognised as being successful in encouraging healthy lifestyles, sound decision-making and supporting transitions to adulthood (Jeffs & Smith, 2010). In order for TYW to be successful, multi-agency working in collaboration and partnership with schools, social services, Leaving Care teams, family focus teams, police and other local partner organisations (such as Mencap, Mind, Drug & Alcohol Services and Solace, which supports young people in relation to domestic violence) is essential.

Austerity cuts in youth services

Local authorities are experiencing spending cuts that are being made as part of austerity measures in England. Currently youth and family services are delivered by either commissioned or council services and the budget for TYW (2015–2017) has been reduced by £1.7 million. The National Youth Agency (2014) published a paper exploring the impact of these spending cuts, concluding that the funding situation would continue to worsen over the next 18 months. One London local authority predicted they would be: "staring at a financial black hole of around £19 billion by 2020 unless things changed".

Financial cuts are making youth work increasingly difficult and influencing the number of vulnerable young people TYWs are able to support. In addition, youth workers are no longer able to provide continuity in their support for young people, with many services being commissioned as three-month specific pieces of work in areas such as anger management, attendance improvement and positive activities. The London borough where I work has now become a commissioned service, which means that TYWs are now required to turn around young people's negative patterns of behaviour (or situations such as first-time entrance into the criminal justice system, gang activity, or entry into secure mental health institutions) in a three-month period. After this time, if little or no progression is being made with the young person, a written report is completed by the allocated TYW and a managerial decision is made as to whether this work is extended or withdrawn. This timeframe was put in place to avoid long waiting lists (e.g., CAMHs have waiting lists of up to six months at present as a result of last year's £50m budget cuts (Buchanan, 2015)) as there are far more referrals than the number of TYWs.

The impact of these cuts has seen a number of Youth and Community Centres closing. This leaves fewer places for young people to 'hang out' and groups gathering in local parks or on street corners has resulted in some young people entering the criminal justice system. Locally, there are increased numbers of young people possessing and frequently smoking cannabis. In some instances, softer drug use can be one of the early indicators of gang involvement; for example, cannabis is being used as the 'hook' to influence young people to join a gang (Williams, 2018).

In summary, youth work is complex multi-agency work that is subject to financial governance. In order to more fully understand the nature of this work some case studies will be explored.

Real-life stories

As many young people have multiple and numerous issues affecting their welfare I will describe two real-life case studies showing the detail and complexities of this work. In order to protect the identity of these young people their real names have not been used.

Case study one – Lucy

Lucy is aged 16 years and has recently moved to North London from another London borough where she previously lived with her father. I received a referral from CAMHs and from the school admission team to provide Lucy with weekly one-to-one support to aid her transition into a suitable place of education. In order to introduce myself to Lucy and explain the purpose of the referral and the proposed sessions on offer I initially made telephone contact with her to identify how we could work together effectively. This is ordinary practice in youth work to gauge whether or not the client is willing to engage with the service. It became apparent through telephone conversations with Lucy and her mother that she was not present enough to engage in education or training. I came to this conclusion as Lucy repeatedly told me that she "was unable to leave her house as she would be sick". Her mother informed me that Lucy's behaviour had become repetitive and cleanliness had become her obsession. I had challenged Lucy on a number of occasions over the telephone by asking if she had ever actually been sick, to which she would say "no, but the feeling of being sick is so intense". As Lucy was on the waiting list for CAMHs in her new location I agreed to carry out one-to-one sessions with Lucy on a weekly basis for at least three months.

I initially arranged a home visit to meet Lucy face to face, as she expressed deep anxiety at the thought of meeting me anywhere else. I carried out the home visit together with a colleague, following a thorough risk assessment that involves completion of a risk matrix devised and developed by management and frontline staff (with reference to Kemshall & Pritchard, 1997) to ensure the safety and well-being of the TYW as well as the client (e.g., is there risk of being attacked, falling, or being hurt?). The severity of the risks identified in these domains inform the two key dimensions of impact and likelihood (Kemshall, 2007), which determine whether we offer a home visit as an option. Our policy for home visits is that we telephone a colleague at the office to inform them that we are about to enter the home and the approximate time we are due to leave. It is known practice within our service that if we were to call the office at any point during the home visit and incorporate the words "blue folder" into a sentence, the other person would be notified that we felt somewhat uneasy and uncomfortable with the current situation and would like to be checked up on again shortly. However, if the words "red folder" were to be incorporated into a sentence, the team member designated as the risk assessment "phone buddy" would know that their colleague(s) was/were in "serious danger" or "at risk of a dangerous situation" and thus would immediately notify the police, followed by senior management, before driving to the home address with another colleague.

During the home visit Lucy explained that her father showed no sympathy towards her current fear of becoming sick: "he just doesn't believe me and thinks I'm making it all up for attention but I'm not!" I used the ABC model to analyse behaviour (Skinner, 1953) during our initial meeting in order to explore the details of what happened to Lucy before ('Antecedents'), during ('Behaviour' patterns) and after (the young person's perception of 'Consequences') the development of severe anxiety and signs of agoraphobia. I suggested she request Cognitive Behaviour Therapy (CBT) sessions with CAMHs as this has a proven track record of being successful in improving negative thought patterns and situations (Fuggle, Dunsmuir & Curry, 2012). Lucy was able to arrange an initial appointment with CAMHs the following week and her allocated therapist would set her small challenges (following our telephone conversations and e-mail exchanges) such as attending one-to-one sessions with me at the youth centre. I had arranged a session with Lucy and her mother for the following week and, because she did not attend, I telephoned her and offered to meet a few days later, in the hope that she would feel more ready. Lucy did attend this time together with her mother.

Our weekly one-to-one sessions consisted of home visits, telephone conversations or meetings at our main youth centre. I used solution-focussed (setting realistic and achievable goals at the end of each session) and self-reflective approaches (asking Lucy how she felt about what was being discussed during sessions). I also incorporated mindfulness into our sessions. Mindfulness-based interventions have been shown to improve stress, anxiety, depressive symptoms and quality of life in adolescents (Kallapiran, Koo, Kirubakaran & Hancock, 2015; Rogers, 2010). I would set Lucy short-term goals that were specific, measurable, achievable, realistic and time-bound (SMART). For example, in the first instance I highlighted the importance of Lucy attending her CAMHs sessions weekly in order for her to feel more ready to engage with others. My aim with Lucy was to carry out our sessions together at one of two youth centres located at either end of the borough and thus this was a specific goal (S) for our next session. In order to be able to achieve this goal, we set a manageable time-frame (M) of two weeks (T), and thus Lucy was able to take smaller steps throughout the two weeks (e.g., spend time outside on the balcony at the family home, go for a walk round the block or go to the shops with her mother) in order to achieve the overall goal. We made this goal realistic and achievable (R, A) by agreeing that her mother would accompany her for our first few sessions at the youth centre.

I incorporated assertiveness training and relaxation techniques in a couple of our one-to-one sessions with the aim of helping Lucy to change her negative behaviour patterns. Two months later she started CBT and hypnotherapy sessions at a private clinic funded by her father to provide her with adequate support to overcome her phobias. The techniques I was using with Lucy worked hand in hand with her CAMHs sessions and Lucy responded well to these techniques.

By our seventh session, Lucy was coming up to her 17th birthday and she was not in employment, education or training (and therefore classified as NEET). The Education Welfare Officer, her mother and I were keen to support Lucy in identifying a suitable place of training or education. Lucy expressed a strong interest in becoming a make-up artist, and her mother explained that this was something she had always had an interest in and she was regularly trying out her skills on family and friends. The option that Lucy favoured the most, out of those presented to her, was attending the London College of Beauty Therapy to study for a Level 2 National Vocational Qualification (NVQ) in Beauty Therapy. It was important that the education programme Lucy chose matched her personality, as evidence suggests that this is most likely to lead to her success and satisfaction (Holland, 1997). However, this was a privately funded college meaning that Lucy would need to cover the annual fees herself. As her father used to provide her with an allowance she was relying on him to support her entry onto the course, as her mother was not in a position to be able to do so. In this instance Lucy's father stated that he was not going to be able to financially support her on this programme and thus I looked into alternative funding opportunities.

While researching funders I came across The Prince's Trust Development Awards and I discussed this opportunity with Lucy. The criteria for the funding was that the applicant had to be a UK resident, 14–17 years old, with no General Certificate of Secondary Education (GCSE) grades A–C (or not expecting to achieve these grades) or 17–25 years of age and currently NEET. Funding could be used for tools or equipment directly related to the training programme or job, such as hairdressing or beauty kits, interview clothes, transport to the job until their first pay was received, or to go towards the completion of Level 1 and Level 2 NVQ courses. I completed all the relevant paperwork on behalf of Lucy and initially succeeded in getting her the one-year grant to study on the Level 1 NVQ in Beauty Therapy. Lucy did so well on this programme that she went on to successfully apply to the Princes Trust for further funding of Year 2 of the NVQ.

However, The Prince's Trust grant would not cover Level 3 qualifications and so her father agreed to pay for Lucy's final year of education. Eighteen months later I was informed by Lucy's mother that she had completed the Level 3 in Beauty Therapy and was working part-time in a local beauty therapy salon; a job she had secured with the support of her college tutors. We held a celebration event during National Youth Work Week (www.nya.org.uk/supporting-youth-work/youth-work-week) at which a number of young people received certificates of achievement for continuous perseverance and determination to succeed despite many challenges on their journey. Lucy came to the event with her mother, grandmother, sister and boyfriend and, though she was too shy to go up on stage to receive her certificate, she expressed feeling happy and her mother stressed how proud all the family were of Lucy's fantastic achievement.

Evaluation

At the end of youth-work sessions with young people we ask them (and/or their parents/guardians) to provide us with feedback by completing a standardised survey exploring what went well or what could have been improved in order to shape our future practices. Below is the testimonial that I received from Lucy's mother:

> Yeşim has been my daughter's Targeted Youth Support worker for 18 months, during this time my daughter had major mental health issues. Yeşim often visited my daughter at home as she was unable to leave the house. My daughter suffered a severe break down after witnessing her school friend being stabbed to death. Lucy suffered from Agoraphobia, Emetophobia (linked to fear of vomiting), a number of obsessive compulsive disorders and panic attacks. Without Yeşim's help convincing and talking to Lucy I don't think my daughter would be where she is today. Yeşim changed my daughter's life for the better as she would not have achieved all these hurdles in her life without Yeşim's help.

Lucy's story describes a young person with good motivation and vocational ability once the right match for her interests was found. She had a number of mental-health problems that were holding her back and, once they had been alleviated, she was able to move on in her transition to work. However, other young people may have more special needs as the next case study will describe.

Case study two – Jay

A number of young people we work with suffer from mild to moderate or, in some cases, severe Special Educational Needs and Disabilities (SEND). When these disabilities are coupled with mental-health issues, they will significantly impact on the potential employment opportunities available for the young person, particularly if these young adults are left to their own devices after completing their statutory schooling. At the time of writing, UK law specifies that compulsory schooling ends after the completion of GCSE examinations, even though many young people remain in some form of education or training until they reach 18 years of age. However, individuals with SEND who are 'statemented' (requiring specific support to assist their education) while at school will all too often end up doing menial jobs in the school itself while their classmates are sent out for work experience to local employers. Not every child with special needs is statemented, particularly if the school is able to meet a child's needs during their education. Those young people who are not statemented whilst in school can be put forward to an education panel of local authority professionals who decide if the young person is eligible to receive an education health care plan. Such a plan entitles young people with special needs to receive one-to-one support and equipment required for their education or training until they reach 25 years of age.

The Head of Employer Engagement at Mencap (Mark Capper, November 2015) stated: "People with a learning disability have the lowest employment rate amongst disabled people. Just 7% of people with a learning disability have a paid job, yet around 80% can work". A press release by the Department for Education and Member of Parliament Edward Timpson (UK Government Press Release, 2015, 12 March) highlighted that people with the most severe forms of SEND can find it difficult to enter the world of work, with their employment rate being as low as 7%. However, a government trial of supported internships resulted in 36% of participants with SEND gaining paid employment.

I am the link practitioner from the local authority to a Pupil Referral Unit (PRU) for young people who suffer from severe mental health issues. This PRU is based in a separate building beside the local hospital to ensure that young people who are assessed by CAMHs and deemed unfit for mainstream schooling can continue to receive an education. I work with a number of young people with severe to moderate mental health issues and/or learning difficulties. The following case study is an example of a young person to whom I provided support over an eight-month period and describes the impact youth work incorporating IAG (Information, Advice and Guidance) has on self-confidence, motivation and progression.

I was allocated to support Jay, a 15-year-old male, with the aim to improve his school attendance and to find a suitable place of education to enable him to move away from the PRU. This facility only offers short-term provision during a period of transition. For example, if a young person has attempted suicide and is sectioned in hospital, once they are deemed well enough by senior clinical staff they must return to part-time education. This London-based PRU offers small-group tutorial sessions helping participants not to miss out on their education. However, this was not the case with Jay who ended up at this hospital PRU due to becoming "lost in the system" as there were no records of him under any London authority between the ages of 13–15 years. This meant that Jay had not received any form of education for two years prior to starting at this specialist school.

Further, he had poor numeracy and literacy skills meaning he would not be able to cope in a mainstream school. Both of Jay's parents also suffer from moderate to severe learning difficulties. Apart from issues with educational attendance, Jay had social inclusion needs; he often struggled to engage with other students at the PRU and would regularly isolate himself during break times, avoiding contact with others. I would often refer to the *Guide for practitioners in communicating with vulnerable children* (Jones, 2003) for extra guidance in supporting Jay.

During my initial assessment with Jay I used the STAR assessment tool to gather information that may not have been included on the referral form (for an example of the STAR assessment tool see Figure 5.1). This type of assessment is a way of monitoring outcomes and client progress, offering a way to record client outcomes. The use of such a tool enables services to collate, analyse and aggregate outcome data to enable learning across a service. The STAR is used by many Mental Health Trusts as a tool for optimising individual recovery and gaining information to create a recovery-focussed care plan. The STAR chart is a flexible tool that can be amended to meet the needs of different young people. It is co-developed by the service user and the staff member in partnership, it covers ten life domains and it can be adapted to meet the needs of different young people.

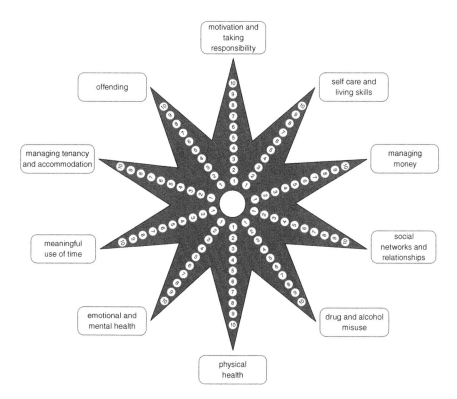

Figure 5.1 An example of the STAR assessment tool.

When using the assessment, I began with 'motivation and taking respon-sibility' and with an open-ended question to Jay: "What are your interests or what do you particularly enjoy doing?" Taking Jay's interests as a starting point is likely to increase the chances of him opening up to me, as devel-oping a young person's trust in their allocated TYW is key in determining whether or not future sessions will be successful. Jay told me he loved films and would like to pursue a course involving film in the future. As he was socially isolated at present, it was agreed by the school, Jay's parents, Jay and I that he would benefit from having twelve 45-minute mentoring sessions with me on each visit to the PRU.

During our sessions we would work on building Jay's self-esteem, motivation, goal-setting and future planning. I would ensure our sessions did not clash with his small-group tuition classes by liaising with the PRU administrator as Jay was to be entered for GCSE Foundation Level in Mathematics, English, Science, Religious Education and Information and Communications Technology (ICT) in the summer. Further, I utilised basic exercises with Jay such as the Getting to Know Me questionnaire and a goals progress chart so we could monitor the pro-gress he made over future sessions. Examples of some of the questions I asked Jay and the answers he gave are listed in Figure 5.2 below.

I worked on supporting Jay to identify his strengths and weaknesses and set him challenges to develop these areas (using the Support vs Challenge model, see Figure 5.3, from LaVigna & Willis, 2005). It was evident from our initial meetings that Jay felt he had a low level of support from home as his parents

GETTING TO KNOW ME:

	Often	Sometimes	Never
I am shy	✓		
I get angry easily		✓	
I worry about the future	✓		

GOALS PROGRESS CHART:

DATE	GOALS	ACHIEVED
06/01	To join other PRU students during break and lunch-time rather than sitting on your own.	Yes
13/01	To complete homework for English test next week.	Partly
21/01	To ask the teacher for help during class if not sure about the topic being covered.	Yes

Figure 5.2 Example questionnaire items and responses.

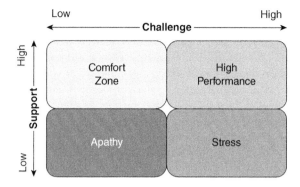

Figure 5.3 Support vs Challenge framework of LaVigna & Willis, 2005, based on the work of Sanford, 1967.

suffered from learning difficulties, which consequently meant that he was not being challenged for long periods of time. As I set him tasks and challenges like the ones above (Figure 5.2), he started to show interest in doing better by being more forthcoming to accept the tasks and challenges being set for him.

Evaluation

Jay's transition review meeting (eight weeks after our initial session) was going to decide if this London-based hospital PRU was best suited for his development and progression or whether alternative mainstream education was to be sought for him. The meeting was attended by Jay, his parents, his PRU tutor, a senior educational psychologist, a Special Educational Needs coordinator and myself. It was felt overall that Jay was growing in confidence and his numeracy and literacy skills had improved. However, his attendance was still poor and needed much greater improvement.

Jay engaged well at the review meeting and said that he would like to go to college after completing his GCSEs at the PRU. He expressed an interest in studying Information Technology, poetry, web design or media. However, as Jay still lacked the social skills for a mainstream college course, he was referred to and started on a programme called 'Bridging the Gap', a special provision to support those over 16 years towards positive transitions from school, either into Level 2 college courses, apprenticeships or work.

Young people like Jay have a range of needs requiring the support of a number of different agencies before he is able to achieve any level of independence. Jay was able to explain what he wanted and liked to do, however there are many young people with SEND living in London who are less able.

Now I would like to change focus to examine what it is like to be a job seeker in a city.

The nature of job seeking in a city

Job seeking in cities has changed since the 1990s. At that time young people with low or no qualifications were able to leave school education and gain a place on an apprenticeship scheme or go into employment. Now, it is often university graduates who are taking on these roles. With greater numbers of young people entering further or higher education and paying student fees it is hard for these young people to find work after they leave education. High student debt and a very competitive job market is pushing young people to take on work that may not require a higher level of educational qualification. Sadly, this type of work leaves graduates underemployed, but it also removes work opportunities for those who are less well educated.

Competition for jobs between the least qualified and the well qualified is unlikely to change in the medium term. Bolton (2016) wrote a paper for the House of Commons on student loans and stated that the government's projected outstanding cash value of publicly owned student debt in England will increase to around £100 billion in 2016–2017, £500 billion in the mid-2030s and £1,000 billion (£1 trillion) in the late 2040s. This is highly concerning, particularly for young people who may not get into the jobs they had originally set out to achieve after their education, or gain the financial income they had hoped to receive. Now, more than ever, is a critical time to educate young people about the future job market and how to best equip themselves for success in the competitive marketplace. It is crucial that young people take every opportunity for work experience, apprenticeships, work placements or volunteering opportunities that give them greater knowledge of the workplace to act as a springboard into paid employment in the more competitive fields.

Summary

As highlighted at the start of this chapter, young people under the age of 25 years have the greatest disadvantage in the UK labour market (George et al., 2015) and thus local authority Early Intervention and Prevention Services such as Targeted Youth Workers and Family Practitioners have been working hard to provide hard-to-reach young people with suitable tools to succeed in life. Currently youth and family services are delivered by either commissioned or local authority services, with the budget for Targeted Youth Work being reduced by £1.7 million (2015–2017). Therefore, vulnerable young people like Lucy and Jay who have multiple issues affecting their welfare may be receiving less support in the future.

References

Bolton, P. (2016). *House of Commons student loans statistics.* Downloaded on 1/05/2015 from: www.parliament.uk/commons-library.

Buchanan, M. (2015). Children's Mental Health Services 'cut by £50m'. *BBC News,* 9 January. Downloaded on 30/04/2015 from: www.bbc.co.uk/news/education-30735370.

Department for Education and Skills (2004). *Every child matters*. Downloaded on 21/4/2016 from: www.education.gov.uk/consultations/downloadableDocs/ACFA006.pdf.

Education and Inspections Act (2006). London: The National Archives. Downloaded on 18/04/2016 from: www.legislation.gov.uk/ukpga/2006/40.

Fuggle, P., Dunsmuir, S. & Curry, V. (2012). *CBT with children, young people and families*. Thousand Oaks, CA: Sage.

George, A., Metcalf, H., Tufekci. L. & Wilkinson, D. (2015, June). *Understanding age and the labour market*, report from the Joseph Rowntree Foundation. Downloaded on 10/08/2014 from: www.jrf.org.uk/work/labour-markets.

Holland, J. L. (1997). *Making vocational choices: a theory of vocational personalities and work environment* (3rd Ed.). Odessa, FL: Psychological Assessment Resources.

Jeffs, T. & Smith, M. K. (Eds) (2010). *Youth work practice*. Basingstoke, UK: Palgrave Macmillan.

Jones, D. P. H. (2003). *Communicating with vulnerable children*. London: Gaskell

Kallapiran, K., Koo, S., Kirubakaran, R. & Hancock, K. (2015). Effectiveness of mindfulness in improving mental health symptoms of children and adolescents: a meta-analysis. *Child & Adolescent Mental Health*, 20(4), 182–194.

Kemshall, H. (2007). Risk assessment and risk management: the right approach? In M. Blyth, E. Solomon & K. Baker (Eds), *Young people and 'risk'*. Bristol, UK: The Policy Press.

Kemshall, H. & Pritchard, J. (Eds) (1997). *Good practice in risk assessment and risk management 2: protection, rights and responsibilities*. London: Jessica Kingsley Publishers.

LaVigna, G. W. & Willis, T. J. (2005). A positive behavioural support model for breaking the barriers to social and community inclusion. *Tizard Learning Disability Review*, 10(2), 16–23.

National Youth Agency (2014). *Youth services in England: changes and trends in the provision of services*. Downloaded 19/04/2016 from: www.nya.org.uk/wp-content/uploads/2015/01/Youth-services-in-England-changes-and-trends.pdf.

Princes Trust Development Awards (n.d.). Downloaded on 19/04/2016 from: www.princes-trust.org.uk/help-for-young-people/get-funding-train-learn.

Rogers, V. (2010). *Working with young women: activities for exploring personal, social and emotional issues* (2nd Ed.). London: Jessica Kingsley Publishers.

Sanford, N. (1967). *Where colleges fail: a study of the student as a person*. San Francisco, CA: Jossey-Bass.

Skinner, B. F. (1953). Some contributions of an experimental analysis of behavior as a whole. *American Psychologist*, 8(2), 69–78.

Star Assessment Tool (n.d.). Willerby: Humber Teaching NHS Foundation Trust. Downloaded on 20/04/2016 from: www.humber.nhs.uk/about-our-trust/recovery-star.htm.

UK Government Press Release (2015, 12 March). *Young people with SEND to benefit from £5 million work scheme*. Downloaded on 19/04/2016 from: www.gov.uk/government/news/young-people-with-send-to-benefit-from-5-million-work-scheme.

Williams, P. (2018). *Being matrixed: the (over) policing of gang suspects in London*. London: StopWatch, www.stop-watch.org?uploads/documents/Being_Matrixed.pdf, downloaded 13/02/2018.

6 Building individual futures

Education to prepare people for work

Dawn Gosden and Rebecca Levi

Introduction

The world of work is ever evolving, with the effects of digitalisation and globalisation demanding new skills. In parallel, the abolition of the default retirement age in the UK has led to the prediction that four generations of workers will be in the workplace by 2030. The impact of these changes will be seen as early as 2020, when 50% of the workers are predicted to be Generation Y (young people born between 1979 and 1991), whilst the number of economically active people aged 65 or over is predicted to have risen by a third (George, Metcalf, Tufekci & Wilkinson, 2015; Inkson, Dries & Arnold, 2015; UKCES, 2014).

Against this backdrop of labour market and workplace changes, individuals will be required to demonstrate a flexible and fluid approach to career development and planning, seeking jobs that provide them with a wide range of skills and experience, with a focus on enhancing employability across a diverse number of employers, rather than gathering the skills needed to pursue a traditional career path in a single organization (Inkson et al., 2015). With promotions harder to achieve and life-long service in one organization an aspiration of the past, individuals' expectations of promotion and hierarchy (Levinson, 1976; Super, 1957, 1980) are expected to be replaced by more frequent lateral moves in and out of organizations to gain relevant experience (Inkson et al., 2015). An individual's ability to cope with frequent job changes will require an understanding of essential skills for future success, outlined by the UKCES (2014) as: motivation, career decision-making, flexibility, adaptability and resilience. In turn, there will be increasing need for individuals to take full responsibility for their careers and ensure their skills are kept continuously up to date in order to guarantee life-long employability.

For over a decade now, young people have been experiencing difficult transitions between education and work, with reasons being poor links between schools and businesses (IPPR, 2014), poor achievement at post-secondary education, and a failure to equip young people with occupation-ready skills (Symonds, Schwartz & Ferguson, 2011). The UK Commission for Employment and Skills (UKCES, 2011) call upon employers to work with education to build young people's experiences of working and to provide feedback on training requirements at both local and national levels (p. 12). These thoughts were echoed in the Economic and Social Research Council's Centre on Skills, Knowledge and Organisational Performance report a year later (SKOPE, 2012). Additionally, England is the only country in which the Organisation for Economic Co-operation and Development (OECD) found young people's literacy and numeracy skills to be worse than those of their grandparents (Ramesh, 2013). The OECD indicate that the implications of these findings for England and Northern Ireland "is that the stock of skills available to them is bound to decline over the next decade, until significant action is taken to improve skills proficiency among young people" (Ramesh, 2013).

Bridging the gap between the skills employers demand and the skills the education systems develop is affected by industrial trends; with some industries growing (e.g., technology sector) and others shrinking (e.g., manufacturing). Hence the skills demanded by employers are changing over time and these changes are difficult to plan for. The ongoing need to predict future job trends and skills requirements is illustrated in the UKCES *The Future of Work* report (2016), where modelling and projections of expected occupational changes by sector for the period 2014 to 2024 reveals an anticipated strong growth in higher-level occupations; mostly professional occupations and many associate professional and technical roles as well as caring, leisure and other service occupations. In contrast, the report reveals that net job losses are anticipated for the same period in administration and secretarial occupations, skilled trade occupations and plant and machine operatives.

This chapter examines a secondary school's focus on developing their students' career competencies and work-ready skills by working with employers and external business professionals to help their students make the transition from education to employment shorter, easier and more focussed. The school equips its young people for the world of work, encouraging the development of strong work identities by enabling access to working people who are willing to describe their work and coach the students whilst they make decisions about their future career paths (Levi & Gosden, 2014).

Research on transition from education to work

Work psychologists are beginning to examine issues of youth employment and are concerned that employers believe young people are not motivated to work and are not ready for the discipline of the working environment (Carter et al., 2013; Carter et al., 2014). Research has focussed on the need to prepare students for the world of work, whereas an equal focus on how employers can work with students to help them prepare has been less apparent. In order to bridge this gap, recent research has concentrated on how employers and education can work together to help young people overcome the obstacles and difficulties they face as they start out in their early careers (Carter, 2015a; Carter et al., 2015).

Careers research

Schools have been failing to provide students with key competencies needed in the workplace, leaving this responsibility to universities (Paton, 2010). Moreover, key competencies are seen as being developed within university, with the workplace facilitating consolidation (Watson & Grant, 2012). As a result, employers are now placing more emphasis on employees acquiring skills and competency rather than pure education, with reports highlighting employers' complaints about the standards of those leaving education (e.g., Pring, Hayward & Hodgson, 2012, p. 3). This dialogue highlights the critical role employers play in youth employment. Whilst young people have a strong desire to gain employment, available work can all too often be low skilled, low paid and lacking in stability (being either part-time and/or having zero-hour contracts). Young people who are not offered the opportunity to use their skills to the full can become disillusioned with the world of work, leading to a perception by their employers that they are demonstrating the wrong attitude and are less motivated to do a good job (Stern, Stone, Hopkins & McMillion, 1990).

To maximise their chances of obtaining a job making the best use of their skills, it is important for young people to understand their unique strengths, skills and abilities, which make them stand out from the crowd and differentiate them from other candidates (Triener, Wilson & Rebow, 2011). A research study examining how career advisers could best support graduates to compete in the job market revealed that the key ways are by: understanding their strengths, weaknesses and the qualities that differentiate them from other graduates; making the right career choices; choosing the right options to pursue based upon realistic self-awareness and presenting themselves confidently to recruiters (Triener et al., 2011, p. 11). These strengths are not unique to graduates, being generalisable to all young people, and they should inform any planning and development undertaken in preparation for the working world.

In their preparation for work, young people also need to be aware of changes in the labour market that have led to the requirement to take responsibility for their own careers (Francis-Smythe, Haase, Thomas & Steele, 2013). This change of emphasis to career self-management has led to the development of a framework of career competencies to help people plan their own careers. Seven career competencies have been identified within this framework, as follows (Francis-Smythe et al., 2013):

- goal setting and career planning;
- self-knowledge;
- job-related performance effectiveness;
- career-related skills;
- knowledge of office politics;
- networking and mentoring; and
- feedback-seeking and self-presentation.

These career competencies were used to develop the Career Competency Indicator (CCI) (Francis-Smythe et al., 2013) to help individuals to understand their career strengths and areas where they might need to develop further. A research study using the CCI with a small group of police officers enabled improvement of self-awareness and highlighted the importance of taking personal responsibility for careers. This study concluded that developing career competencies involves both reflection and planning (Haase, Thomas & Francis-Smythe, 2013). Therefore, if it takes reflection and planning for adults to develop career competencies, this infers that young people also require these skills, but it may take longer for young people to develop them. From this work we deduce that the career-planning requirements of young people may require a different approach.

Inspecting the CCI's career competencies we find that some are too sophisticated and business focussed for young people to understand (e.g., job-related performance effectiveness and knowledge of office politics). Additionally, these competencies are not widely adopted in the UK's national educational curriculum and are likely to be new concepts for both young people and their teachers to assimilate. A simpler, less sophisticated set of competencies needs to be developed to which both young people and their teachers can relate. Such a career competency framework, tailored specifically for young people, will help them to identify their strengths and enable them to plan their early careers. Such a framework will also appeal to employers, helping them to design assessment methods in their recruitment and assessment processes that are capable of spotting the potential young people may bring to their organization.

With the ever-changing demands of the future career, it is vitally important for young people to learn to develop their career competencies. Self-managing their careers in this way will equip them with essential coping strategies and help them develop the skills necessary to sustain employability (UKCES, 2014). These studies suggest that career competency frameworks and interventions should be introduced as early as possible in secondary schools' educational curricula.

Positive Psychology strengths-based research

In parallel with evolving research about careers, a growing importance and emphasis has been placed on the use of Positive Psychology strengths-based approaches in education (van Nieuwerburgh & Passmore, 2012a). Positive Psychology focusses on the optimistic aspects of life such as happiness and life satisfaction. Young people who are happy and possess improved well-being are better able to face challenges and problems in life, to cope with stress and, importantly, to make better decisions about their future career. Developments in Positive Psychology have encouraged a different perspective in stress and well-being research, which has often been criticised for focussing on negative aspects of well-being, possibly implying that there is something wrong with an individual that needs to be fixed. Positive Psychology takes the opposite view, examining what is intrinsically good about an individual and how their strengths can be further enhanced. A central tenet of the Positive Psychology movement is that if individuals identify and use their strengths, whilst at the same time pursuing the things they are passionate about, they will feel more engaged in the process and success is more likely to follow (Peterson, 2006). These concepts are central to the development of career competencies.

Competency frameworks are designed with the expectation that people will be able to develop equally in all competency areas. In reality, some competencies will not naturally resonate with a person's strengths and, as a result, they find them more difficult to develop and build capability. Positive Psychology research has identified 24 strengths that people could possibly identify as their assets (Peterson & Seligman, 2004). However, it is likely that most people will have five main strengths they use on a frequent basis (Peterson & Seligman, 2004). These five top strengths are linked to the person's sense of identity and, when used to the full, people feel more able to achieve the goals they have set for themselves (Linley, Harrington & Garcea, 2009; Peterson & Seligman, 2004). Therefore, using these top strengths regularly is likely to have an effect on an individual's happiness and well-being (Seligman, Steen, Park & Peterson, 2005) and thus it can be concluded that, in order to survive in the competitive world of the future, young people should strive to identify and continuously use and build upon their top strengths (Proctor & Fox Eades, 2009, quoted in Proctor et al., 2011).

Evidence suggests that students who have identified their strengths are likely to be more motivated and perform at a higher level (Seligman, Ernst, Gillham, Reivich & Linkins, 2009). There is a strong argument to encourage young people to identify and build upon their strengths, given that all young people have unique and different strengths (Peterson, 2006; Proctor & Fox Eades, 2009, quoted in Proctor et al., 2011). By building an understanding of their strengths, young people start to learn from an early age what makes them stand out and differentiates them from others (Proctor & Fox Eades, 2009, quoted in Proctor et al., 2011).

Coaching psychology research

Coaching complements Positive Psychology interventions (Biswas-Diner, 2010) and is playing a growing and increasingly important role in secondary education. Coaching in schools is seen to have an influence on students' social skills and abilities, encouraging them to take greater personal responsibility. Further, coaching also helps to develop students' self-confidence and self-awareness (van Nieuwerburgh, Zacharia, Luckham, Prebble & Browne, 2012).

Many young people, especially those from poorer backgrounds, lack hope, face inequality gaps in their lives and have significant barriers to achieving their full potential in life (UNICEF, 2010; WHO, 2008). Hopeful people are motivated, have belief and confidence in their abilities and have clear plans as to how they will achieve their goals (Snyder, Rand & Sigmon, 2002). Whilst self-awareness, self-confidence and well-being are important to achieving their full potential, young people also need to have hope in order to be able to plan for their future and identify the steps they need to take in order to achieve progress (Synder et al., 2002).

The ability to be flexible, adaptable and resilient is becoming increasingly important in the workplace (Luthans, Vogelgesang & Lester, 2006). Resilience is seen as a competency that can be developed, with studies providing evidence that both adults and children can be taught skills to increase their resilience (Adams, 2016; Clough & Strycharczyk, 2012; Seligman et al., 2009; Timson, 2015). Coaching can help young people to become more resilient, encouraging them to develop flexibility, adaptability and resilience, and the need for these skills is likely to grow in importance as young people prepare for the workplace of tomorrow (Clough & Strycharczyk, 2012). In particular, developmental coaching has been identified as valuable in supporting young people as they face the adolescent life transition (Palmer & Panchel, 2011). Adolescence is the fifth of Erikson's eight stages of adult development, described as a time of identity versus role confusion (Erikson, 1950, 1995, quoted in Palmer & Panchel, 2011, p. 4 and 6). It is during this time that young people start to develop a sense of their own identity quite separate to that of their family and peers and, whilst this transition can be difficult, it can also present opportunities for development and learning (Palmer & Panchel, 2011; Erikson, 1950, 1995, quoted in Palmer & Panchel, 2011, p. 4 and 6). Providing developmental coaching to young people at this important transitional life stage supports them whilst they build a strong sense of identity and start to focus on their future careers (Palmer & Panchel, 2011).

In addition to developing resilience, an important requirement for job-search activities, undertaking coaching can also increase young people's hope through supporting and encouraging them to consider a number of possible career options that match their aspirations for future employment. Coaching at this time will also help students to develop confidence in their ability to obtain the goals they set for themselves (Synder et al., 2002).

The ASPIRE coaching programme developed at the Axe Valley Community College (AVCC) provides a practical example of the integration of Positive Psychology and a coaching intervention in the educational context (Green, Oades & Robinson, 2012). One of the strengths of the ASPIRE coaching programme is that it takes its students on a journey of self-discovery, supporting the development of competencies from a young age and enabling students to start to take responsibility for their own life and career choices as early as possible within their secondary-school education. In the next section we will describe the development and the evaluation of the ASPIRE programme.

Case study: the ASPIRE programme

Based in the heart of rural East Devon, AVCC is positioned between two successful and highly academic schools where competition to attract top students is high. Axe Valley Community College needed to differentiate itself, wanting to find a niche in the local educational market. The school recognised a need to develop students and prepare them for a more competitive and complex future as part of the ever-changing and fast-moving world of work. Some key issues that they were aware of were:

- a career for life is almost non-existent;
- by the time students are in their mid-20s they will have had numerous jobs rather than one specific career;
- internet and digital age will take over many jobs that exist today; and
- the work that students may undertake in future does not currently exist.

Further, while there was recognition that the education system is focussed on developing academic results, there was less emphasis on preparing students for their lives beyond education. How could the school support their students and develop them for the world they will be working in? How could they help students achieve their potential and develop a confident and strong workforce for the benefit of the UK economy? Inspiring students and developing their aspirations could really differentiate the school from others around them and provide their students with a competitive advantage. The school chose to design a programme that would help students feel motivated to achieve their potential, provide them with opportunities to learn about themselves, as well as to develop their interpersonal and employability skills (e.g., self-confidence, self-awareness and self-esteem) while discovering their strengths. All the activities in the programme would be designed to increase the students' possibility of success.

The ASPIRE programme was launched in 2011, initially supporting the top 10% of students in each year cohort and focussing on three key areas: a) providing insight into the world of work from early secondary schooling years; b) introducing work-related competencies and developing employability skills from their early secondary schooling to when they leave school; and c) providing one-to-one coaching from outside school as they transitioned through choosing their General Certificate of Secondary Education (GCSE) subject options to their post-16-year specialist education.

Gaining an insight into the working world

Inspiring the next generations and building their aspirations is an important part of the ASPIRE programme and bridging the gap between the working world and the education system is key to achieving these aims. This included opening the classroom walls, taking students out to see what the world of work looks like and inviting the working world into school. Blending these two worlds and connecting academic *learning* with *working* is crucial to motivating and inspiring students to want to work and allows them to understand what work roles exist and which they might want to undertake after their education.

Making contacts with local and national organizations was essential to support ASPIRE. Professionals were persuaded to come into school, talk about what they did and work with the students on practical career-based projects (e.g., about careers in law or science). The school introduced a series of events, activities and workshops enabling the students to appreciate what people did at work. As well as providing them with a unique insight, the students took part in hands-on activities teaching them what professionals really did in their daily jobs and enabling links to be explored between what they were learning at school and what they could be doing at work. Two different examples below show the breadth of these experiences.

- The school proactively developed a relationship with the Met Office at a time when Met Office Science Camps were being piloted for students. The school sent a group of students along to learn about the concept of meteorology, to absorb for themselves what the inside of a large local business looked like and to meet some working professionals who might inspire and motivate their future aspirations. The Science Camps take place on a Friday evening, include dinner and an overnight stay in conference rooms in tents, and conclude late Saturday morning after breakfast. Many volunteers from across the Met Office departments support the Science Camps, which are designed to inspire and motivate school students towards further engagement with STEM (Science, Technology, Engineering and Mathematics) subjects.
- In collaboration with Devon County Council, the school invited the Chief Bridge Engineer to teach the students about engineering and, in particular, bridge-building. This was arranged as an after-school workshop taking place each week over six weeks. Students visited local bridges, learnt the art of bridge-building, designed their own bridges, built bridges from basic materials and competed for the coveted prize of abseiling from a large viaduct in the area.

One unique aspect of the ASPIRE programme was involving primary-school children from local schools in the final two years of their primary education. The opportunity provided young students with challenging learning opportunities alongside older students, as well as starting to open their minds to higher education and work. The younger students were enthusiastic, motivated and keen to learn and take on the challenges set. They enjoyed working with the older secondary-age students and relished the chance to see for themselves where their learning could take them when they were older. Engaging young students from the age of 10 years in the working world seems a natural way of preventing them developing into the NEETs (those Not in Education, Employment or Training) of tomorrow.

Workshops of skills and competency development

A primary aim of the ASPIRE programme is to encourage students to start to take personal responsibility and become autonomous learners in their life and career planning. However, as they are accustomed to being taught in their everyday school activities, the project team appreciated that embarking on a journey to a more student-led approach to learning would take time and adjustment. Additionally, surrounded by a changing world where some future jobs were not yet created, it was agreed that the school needed to help the students to develop the skills and competencies that could prepare them for the working world. As a result, it was appreciated that plans to introduce the notion of competency would be another new concept for the students, which would require a hands-on activity-based learning approach.

In partnership with a range of professionals from outside the school (Occupational Psychologists, trainers, career counsellors and people development consultants), a series of workshops was designed to help students understand and develop their employability skills. Important *Skills for Success* were identified, based on one aim: that these were skills students would need to develop in order to achieve their potential and succeed as they grow into adulthood. Being resilient, adaptable, flexible, positive and proactive were all identified as vital employability skills required for any future workforce. Thus the AVCC strengths-based *Skills for Success* framework comprises of six competencies:

- Emotional Intelligence (e.g., Self-Awareness, Self-Confidence);
- Teamworking;
- Leadership (taking initiative);
- Creativity and Innovation;
- Communication and Presentation Skills; and
- Problem-Solving and Decision-Making.

The *Skills for Success* framework underpinned the workshops designed to help students to analyse and understand themselves, and to recognise their strengths, abilities and development needs. They were also planned to provide stepping-stones to the world of work, to harness great examples of their positive behaviours and work readiness at an early age. From Year 7 (ages 11 to 12 years) to Year 11 (ages 15 to 16 years), after the school day had finished, ASPIRE students undertook workshops that were developed to include practical activities, worksheets and discussions to develop their learning. Workshops explored: a) teamworking; b) communication and presentation skills; c) creativity and problem-solving skills; and d) emotional intelligence. Two examples of these workshops are described below.

Teamworking

This workshop tested teamworking skills by dividing the students into small teams and asking them to design and run a restaurant. This was a fun activity allowing the students to demonstrate to each other listening skills, planning and organising their work against time deadlines, encouraging others to participate and using the important strengths and skills within their team. Working with the students following the exercise on what made each team successful or even chaotic, the students quickly grasped and understood the concepts and essential positive behaviours. They were then given the opportunity to undertake the task again, thus learning from their mistakes and immediately implementing and consolidating their learning.

Emotional Intelligence

The students were introduced to the concept of emotional intelligence (Goleman, 1996) and awareness was developed that this was a competency they could continually build and develop. The students were given the opportunity to create an awareness of themselves and how they communicate and interact with others. This was done by asking the students to develop a collage depicting themselves and their lives. Students worked through this task and, although their verbal responses to workshop facilitators were minimal, the work they produced proved they understood the concepts of the relationship between themselves and others, having been introduced to the importance of differing and diverse skills and strengths in successful teams. Often students at this stage in life believe being the same as their peers is important, allowing them to feel safe and secure in "group alikeness", but, having explained the importance of diversity and strength in teams of unique individuals, they were able to show their true and unique personalities, skills and passions in their collages.

The notion of the students attending an after-school workshop was a whole new concept for many and required strong engagement with the students, parents and school staff to describe the benefits and rewards of developing future employability skills alongside achieving their academic results.

Once in the 6th Form, ASPIRE students were invited to attend a one-day Development Centre outside school. Taking students out of the school environment and undertaking ASPIRE events at professional business offices was paramount to inspiring students and widening their horizons. The Development Centre is an event assessing the skills and competencies of individuals and providing an individual development plan to help them focus on key personal development needs. The Development Centre included a number of individual and group exercises and a mock interview that focussed on gaining evidence of the *Skills for Success* competencies.

Interviewers and assessors of the Development Centre exercises were external coaching professionals from the working world. With the design emphasis on students benchmarking their strengths against the competencies, the coaches provided feedback and reflective coaching after each exercise. For example, students were given the opportunity to make a formal presentation to a panel of coaches of their key strengths and skills. They were provided with feedback by the coaches on how well they had performed and how confidently they presented, focussing particularly on the competency of Communication and Presentation Skills. After the Development Centre each student was provided with an individual development plan and the opportunity to gain some career advice and guidance at an important time in their lives, as they moved towards higher education or the world of work.

ASPIRE coaching

The third area of the ASPIRE programme is coaching. Students are provided with a supportive one-to-one coach from when they are in Year 9 (aged 13 to 14 years) and choosing their GCSE options through to Year 13 (aged 17 to 18 years) whilst undertaking their post-16-year qualifications. The coaching programme focusses on continuing to build the students' emotional intelligence and employability skills, and helping them to develop an understanding of their differentiating strengths and unique characteristics to prepare them for the strong competition they will encounter during recruitment and selection processes when applying for jobs.

The school worked hard to develop a pool of 20 local professionals willing to commit their time and wanting to share their expertise, knowledge and investment in inspiring the next generation, and equally seeking a personal development opportunity to support these capable students (van Nieuwerburgh & Passmore, 2012b). In exchange for coaching students, coaches gained valuable experience of working with younger children, sharing their knowledge and experience and acting as strong role models. This personal development for the coaches took them out of their day jobs, allowed them to share their experiences, prepared them for supervising other staff or parenthood and ultimately inspired the next generation into the world of work. Having worked in a variety of organizations, many of these volunteers had never coached young people before and each one was given the opportunity to undergo training in effective coaching techniques. They attended a briefing on the current education system and the type of issues young students might be facing. Coaches were equipped and prepared to undertake one-hour coaching sessions with the same students each half-term.

The ASPIRE programme is a new concept in education. It was a way of introducing students to employability skills, providing them with one-to-one role-modelling mentors and presenting opportunities for them to learn from doing, while also weaving in guidance and exploration of various career opportunities. Many lessons were inevitable along the way and the school had to experience a change of culture to enable the programme to become business as usual within the school.

Work psychology meets education: reflections and lessons learned

Bridging a gap between the working world and education, and developing students to prepare and indeed motivate them for the world of work, were the original aims of the ASPIRE programme. These aims were not easy to achieve and many reflections have developed.

- Influencing teenagers to spend time after school to focus on soft skills, speaking on a one-to-one basis with adults and just presenting the concept as a great personal advantage to them was never going to be easy. It was clear that we needed to persuade and influence not only the students but also their friends to ensure students would attend.

- Key to maintaining the students' interest and enthusiasm was having activities that were interactive, fun and engaging, enabling them to gain feedback that would benefit their learning.
- Parents will often refer to their own education in developing their expectations of what the education system should be like today. The ASPIRE concept is new and, for some parents, difficult to understand. Encouraging some students to participate and take part in ASPIRE activities was challenging and influencing parents to support and guide their children to attend and understand the value of the programme was a greater challenge.
- Influencing the *whole* school was critical; all teachers, assistants, governors and support staff needed to be aware of the programme and what it wanted to achieve. The importance of this broad understanding of the programme purpose cannot be underestimated. A range of stakeholders from the school helped to market and represent the programme in the community, and this good will was vital when relying on the volunteering of so many individuals and organizations.
- The ASPIRE programme is built on the vision and ambition of one school with a supportive and ambitious leader and, without this support, the programme would never succeed. The education system is focussed on academic achievements and finding the time and resource to focus on a programme like ASPIRE could be seen as frivolous and unnecessary. However, as schools move towards needing to report on the destinations of all their students *after* education, they may decide to look carefully at the employability skills of their students and how they are developing their students for the world of work.

Introducing career competencies

Facilitating the competency workshops whilst working with an audience of teenagers provided many tumbleweed moments where it appeared that the students were bored or not listening. Their apparent disinterest was first noticed in a workshop designed to introduce ASPIRE students to the concept of emotional intelligence (Goleman, 1996). However, the subsequent production of compelling collages during their table work proved that the students had taken on board the content of the workshop and understood the concepts. Workshop facilitators quickly learnt not to assume that students had not grasped the concepts that were under consideration. As in adult development, the school teachers and leaders learnt that participation in development programmes and the hunger to develop relies on the student's maturity and self-awareness. The students needed to be encouraged to be motivated and to want to achieve their goals. It was clear that some were already demonstrating these skills and competencies while others needed more input and feedback.

Teamworking and Communication were probably easier competencies to introduce as these are a regular feature in mainstream education. Emotional Intelligence and Leadership were harder to grasp. Students often naturally believe leadership means taking charge, directing people and dictating decisions on behalf of a group, rather than influencing and guiding a group through role modelling and engagement. For Emotional Intelligence, talking to students about self-esteem, self-confidence and empathy towards others were 'deeper delves' into their core as human beings and required them to soul search and really think about how they interact with others, and this posed a challenge for many teenagers. However, having taken part in the competency workshops and the coaching sessions, the students reported that they learnt a great deal about the Skills for Success, which they recognised were useful in all aspects of their lives.

Attempting to transfer adult career competencies into the educational environment has created challenges due to the business-focussed language of the adult career competencies. Key employability skills that were identified to help the students achieve their potential and become more work ready (the Skills for Success) proved both helpful and useful to both developers and students.

Introducing coaching

While the aspiration is always for coaching to be a voluntary rather than a mandatory activity, coaching was a new adult-oriented practice introduced to the ASPIRE students. Coaching became the hardest part of ASPIRE to sell to the students, yet one of the most powerful activities once it was taken up. Until the coaching relationships were formed, there were a number of no shows by students for their coaching appointments. Additionally, the ASPIRE students did not immediately appreciate the value of coaching and needed to be encouraged to attend their sessions. In a rural East Devon community students were not used to communicating confidently with adults they had never met before and needed to be persuaded about the benefits of undertaking coaching with a professional from the business world. For many, their mind-set was that their education came to a conclusion at mid-afternoon each day. Convincing students to stay and spend time talking to an unknown adult took hard selling by the school staff. Strong role models in the lives of many of these capable young people were few and far between but some parents attended the first coaching sessions to learn more about what was involved and who this one-to-one mentor might be. After one or two sessions many students began to realise the true benefits of developing these relationships and what these experienced business professionals could offer them in external advice and personal guidance. The programme team also learnt that both parents and students involved in ASPIRE needed equal engagement and encouragement to buy in to the coaching programme.

Many of the coaching sessions ran as directive mentoring interventions rather than facilitative student-led coaching interventions. The differences between mentoring and coaching can be explained as follows:

Coaches act as facilitators while Mentors give advice and expert recommendations. Coaches listen, ask questions and enable coachees to discover for themselves what is right for them. Mentors talk about their own personal experience, assuming this is relevant to the mentees.

(Roskinski, 2004, p. 5)

As the coaching programme continues to embed, students become more comfortable within the coaching relationships they have built and share these benefits with their peers. We anticipate that, over time, the balance between mentoring and coaching will change, with students becoming more engaged and participating in coaching rather than needing mentoring relationships.

Additionally, while the students enjoyed working with older people from industry, they also related well to younger role models, but the key factor for success in the coaching sessions was providing them with inspiring and enthusiastic people. Enthusiasm was critical to effectively influencing young people, not age. Many of us recall enthusiastic teachers in our schooling days, no matter what age they are, inspiring us to take a certain direction or path in our careers. The same is true for the ASPIRE coaches.

Evaluation of the ASPIRE programme

Evaluation has indicated that coaching students to increase their self-confidence, self-awareness, general employability and career decision-making skills has been a successful intervention.

A two-part external evaluation study was conducted at the request of AVCC, which included:

- A Masters in Occupational Psychology study (*the MSc study*); a small-scale research project that surveyed 26 ASPIRE students, examining their proactivity, self-efficacy and well-being in relation to their career decision making (Wang, 2014).
- A qualitative study of seven ASPIRE stakeholders (*the stakeholder study*) considered a broader view of the programme and examined its strengths, areas for development and future opportunities. The stakeholders who took part in this study were companies and organizations associated with the programme, ASPIRE coaches, ASPIRE teaching staff, and a school governor (Carter, 2015b).

Successful decision-making is pivotal to career planning and a smooth transition from education to employment. Moreover, young adults who are more confident with their academic achievement and social interaction and have the ability to cope with stress are more likely to make better career decisions (Wang, 2014, p. 11). The MSc study revealed that, when associated with the ASPIRE programme, students were likely to report higher self-esteem and were more likely to solve problems and make decisions when faced with challenges. This study also revealed that ASPIRE students increased their strength of belief in their own ability to plan goals and achieve them over the time (Wang, 2014).

The stakeholder study provided evidence that students' motivation, confidence and self-esteem were boosted by the ASPIRE programme, while at the same time they were achieving at and above their educational targets. Students demonstrated an increased ability to challenge accepted practice and engage with greater risks when taking on diverse work-experience placements and educational opportunities (for example, taking up work experience opportunities further from home, in one case in India, or working in a local MP's office). Evidence suggests that the students showed an increased ability to manage their own time and anxieties more effectively and that they were more critically appraising of potential job roles.

The stakeholder study revealed that ASPIRE is seen as a successful programme at several levels (Carter, 2015b):

- Students were maturing into young people by their increased competence to make decisions about their future.
- Students have pride in the programme and are applying to universities outside of Devon (and top-quality universities such as those in the Russell Group).
- AVCC is now attracting high-quality staff who are well qualified and proactive.
- People want to be involved in ASPIRE. Parents are asking for their children to be on the programme, other schools want to be involved with ASPIRE and primary-school children want to know about the programme.
- Companies want to be associated with ASPIRE as the programme is being offered by a forward-looking school.
- Organizations want to hear what ASPIRE students have to say (e.g., Devon County Council requested students' opinions on cycle paths).
- AVCC now gets media exposure (e.g., in newspapers and on television).

The ASPIRE programme continues to be shaped and focussed by building on the wider recommendations of the evaluation. For example, AVCC will continue to monitor the progress of the programme, reflect upon the need for change and, whilst recognising the value of the coaching process, conduct a review of the coaching model used, explore the students' views of the coaching process and explore offering supervision for coaches as part of their role. The next section will look at some of these developments in more depth.

Next steps for the ASPIRE programme

Coaching interventions

The evaluation of ASPIRE has outlined a number of improvements that can be brought to the programme. Whilst AVCC adopted the GROW model of coaching (Whitmore, 2002) when the programme was first designed, future improvements should include a coaching model capable of providing a resilience coaching element and should also include a supervision offer, not only to provide support to the coaches but also to provide quality assurance of the standard of coaching delivered.

Reflections on the effectiveness of ASPIRE, as previously outlined, have revealed that students valued their relationships with their coaches but also highlighted that they identified with role models closer to their own age. This suggests that the introduction of a peer-coaching approach has the potential to further enhance the coaching experience of all ASPIRE students. Peer-coaching skills can be useful life skills to acquire as they develop young people's emotional intelligence, enhance their study skills and attitudes to learning, and improve their communication and wider problem-solving skills, all of which lead to enhanced employability (van Nieuwerburgh et al., 2012; van Nieuwerburgh & Tong, 2013). Developing peer-coaching skills would also be invaluable to young people's future careers, given the expanding and growing trend within the business environment for reverse coaching and mentoring initiatives, where more senior employees are benefiting from the skills and knowledge that younger people have to offer (van Nieuwerburgh & Passmore, 2012b; Greenes & Pitkialis, 2008, cited in Wagner, 2008).

The present AVCC model invites volunteer business coaches to become involved in the ASPIRE programme, providing the students with exposure to working people who are willing to coach and support them whilst they make their educational and career choices (van Nieuwerburgh & Passmore, 2012b). The potential disadvantage of this model is that voluntary coaches may find it difficult to sustain their input into the programme over a longer period of time due to changes in their work commitments or, if they are self-employed, a change in circumstances to a continuous flow of paid work (van Nieuwerburgh & Passmore, 2012b). Improvements could be made to ASPIRE by introducing a peer-coaching approach alongside the existing business coaching model. The combination of business coaches and peer coaching has the advantage of providing the younger students with role models they can relate to in the older student coaches, whilst maintaining the validity of the business context. This approach also caters for the peaks and troughs of supply in the external business coach model, whilst at the same time guaranteeing consistency of membership of the peer-coaching pool over time.

Career competency interventions

Advances in career research since the ASPIRE programme was launched has led to the emerging concept of Career Adapt-abilities and the design of the Career Adapt-abilities scales (Savickas, 2013). Career Adapt-ability is about helping individuals to take responsibility for their own careers, manage career transitions and developmental issues and the challenges that continuous changes in the workplace and labour market pose. Career Adapt-ability is seen as "an adaptation

to a series of transitions from school to work, from job to job and from occupation to occupation" (Savickas & Porfeli, 2012). The aim of this work is to help
individuals to adopt career planning and reflection behaviours.

The Career Adapt-ability scales consist of four scales known as the 4Cs
(Savickas & Porfeli, 2012):

- Concern: developing hope and optimism for the future;
- Control: applying personal focus to one's future;
- Curiosity: seeking to understand oneself and exploring potential options and
  possibilities; and
- Confidence: developing self-belief and confidence in achieving personal
  goals.

A self-report instrument adopting a strengths-based approach, the Career Adaptability scales invite individuals to rate how strongly they have developed their
Career Adapt-abilities (using a scale of 1 to 5 with 5 being Strongest and 1 Not
Strong). Some examples of the items are: "Becoming aware of the education and
career choices that I must make", "Thinking about what my future will be like"
and "Looking for opportunities to grow as a person" (Savickas & Porfeli, 2012).

Young people need support in learning how to continuously adapt their
competencies and skills to navigate the changing workplace and labour market
that they are likely to experience throughout their lifetime. They also need
to be encouraged to build their flexibility and resilience by developing career-
adaptability behaviours from an early age. The Career Adapt-abilities scales
have been used successfully in higher education (Bimrose, Barnes, Brown &
Hughes, 2011). However, introducing the Career Adapt-ability scales earlier
in the educational system, and into the ASPIRE programme in particular,
would enhance the coaching process, providing a consistent career-planning
instrument that coaches can use to support the students in developing specific adaptability behaviours, encouraging them to reflect upon and plan their
careers on a regular basis.

An additional area of research since the ASPIRE programme was designed
has focussed on plugging the skills gaps for young people and highlighting the
key competencies they need to develop in their first year of employment (CIPD,
2015). This study surveyed Human Resource and Learning and Development
Professionals, highlighting general skills, building confidence, communication
skills and commercial capability as the essential but also the most challenging
competencies to build. Communication skills and confidence were seen as the
most important competencies along with the capability of resilience, which young
people should concentrate on building (CIPD, 2015). From this we can deduce
that the introduction of interventions, such as ASPIRE, that help to prepare young
people for their careers early in their educational journey will gain in importance
as vital support to young people as they transition from education to employment.

Through the ASPIRE programme, AVCC has placed a strong focus on preparing their students by obtaining work-ready skills, supporting the development

of all these important skills and providing a strong foundation for its students to develop the essential career competencies needed in their first year of employment. In addition to building their general skills, confidence and communication skills, AVCC has innovatively provided exposure for their ASPIRE students to the world of work by inviting business people into the school and taking the students into industry to enable them to learn more about the modern workplace. In this way, ASPIRE students have been given opportunities to start to understand the requirements of the commercial world through their involvement in practical careers-based projects with professionals from industry (e.g., the Met Office Science Camps and the engineering bridge-building project). Continuing to provide opportunities such as these will enable ASPIRE students to start to gain a valuable understanding of the commercial world, experiencing the demands of work through not only working alongside industry professionals but also having involvement in projects that have a focus on designing and delivering services to clients.

Positive Psychology strengths-based interventions

The original ambition of the ASPIRE programme was to encourage students to identify their strengths by benchmarking themselves against the Skills for Success competency framework. All these activities were undertaken outside of formal school activities, when the students had completed a full school day and were likely to be tired. Future developments of the programme would benefit from the introduction of a positive strengths-based intervention that is fully integrated into the educational curriculum, benefiting not only those students on the ASPIRE programme but all students attending AVCC.

An example of a practical Positive Psychology strengths-based intervention in education is the Strengths Gym programme, helping young people to identify and develop their top five strengths through storytelling (Proctor et al., 2011). The Strengths Gym provides students with the opportunity to self-identify their top five strengths by undertaking strengths-based classroom exercises and applying what they have learnt in all aspects of their lives. This aims to encourage individuals to "build their strengths, learn new strengths and recognise strengths in others" (Proctor et al., 2011, p. 382). The course has three levels of implementation in the educational curriculum at Years 7, 8 and 9 and is age specific (Proctor et al., 2011, p. 382). Booklets for the course have the title 'Spotting your Strengths' and students are asked to pick their five top strengths from a list of 24 (Proctor & Fox Eades, 2009, quoted in Proctor et al., 2011).

The course consists of Strength Builder and Strength Challenge exercises. An example of a Strength Builder exercise (Year 8) involves strengths in action, asking students to think of a time when someone showed love or beauty and then write, or draw, a story about it (Proctor & Fox Eades, 2009, p. 5, quoted in Proctor et al., 2011). A corresponding Strength Challenge exercise invites students to "look for beauty on the way to school and tell a friend or family member what you notice" (Proctor & Fox Eades, 2009, p. 5, quoted in Proctor et al., 2011).

Introducing a strengths-based approach, such as the Strengths Gym, would benefit ASPIRE as the programme could be delivered as an integral part of the school day and to the benefit of all AVCC students, not just those who have been identified to receive the programme. The exercises are designed to be flexible, are linked to and can be used in AVCC's Personal Well-Being Curriculum lessons, or can be included in other lessons as appropriate. The approach would enhance and compliment the Skills for Success workshops, as the Strengths Gym invites students to identify, understand and use their top five strengths in their school activities and everyday life. At the same time, they would be offered the ability to benchmark their identified top strengths against the Skills for Success competency framework. As the students are liable to be faced with strengths-based and competency-based recruitment methods in their applications for future jobs, they would be provided with a solid understanding of their strengths and how these relate to the Skills for Success competency framework, enabling them to understand what makes them stand out and differentiates them from others whilst competing for jobs where recruiters use both approaches. An additional benefit to ASPIRE is that this approach does not require AVCC staff to undergo in-depth training or accreditation. The materials have been designed for ease of understanding and administration. Schools in this research study were provided with the materials together with background on the programme, the character strengths and the aims of the strengths builder and challenge booklets. No further training was required once all the materials had been supplied (Proctor et al., 2011).

Recommendations and conclusions

Over the last five years the ASPIRE programme has successfully integrated an education to employment transition intervention, which includes inviting employers into the classroom and introducing the students to working people willing to describe their work identities and the journey they took from education to employment. In parallel, ASPIRE introduced a strengths-based approach, coaching and a competency framework to students from an early age in the secondary school's curriculum. Discussions in this chapter have outlined future developments that could be implemented to further enhance the programme.

However, in looking to the future development of education to employment transition interventions, work psychologists, employers and schools really need to work together to develop interventions that are impactful and benefit young people as they prepare themselves for the world of work.

The evidence and arguments presented throughout this chapter lend support to developing and implementing education to work transition interventions, providing young people with support in the following areas:

- identification and development of their career competencies and top five strengths;
- provision of coaching and encouragement to develop and practise peer-coaching skills;

- development of career planning and decision-making skills along with tools and techniques to help develop flexibility, adaptability and resilience; and
- connecting students in education with the world of work as early as possible to drive motivation to work hard and develop greater understanding of what the world of work looks and feels like.

In order to survive in the competitive world of the future, young people need to strive to identify and continuously build an understanding of their strengths, together with what makes them stand out and differentiates them from others. It is also vitally important for young people to develop their career competencies. Alongside the implementation of career competency frameworks as early as possible in the educational curriculum, secondary schools should also consider introducing strengths-based interventions that help young people identify and develop their top five strengths.

Young people can also prepare themselves for their future careers by undertaking coaching and acquiring peer-coaching skills. Coaching can help young people to become resilient, flexible and adaptable and can provide useful interventions in the development of these abilities. Additionally, developing peer-coaching skills will be invaluable to young people's future careers, given the growing trend in the workplace for reverse mentoring and coaching initiatives. All young people should not only be encouraged to undertake coaching to develop their flexibility, adaptability and resilience, but also to develop and practise peer-coaching skills.

To conclude, interventions that seek to support and develop young people should include the identification and development of their career competencies and top strengths, the development of career planning and decision-making skills, along with tools and techniques to help develop flexibility, adaptability and resilience. Of equal importance to an effective intervention is the provision of coaching and encouragement to develop and practise peer-coaching skills. These requirements should be designed into any future transition model aimed at young people.

Chapter summary

The world of work is ever evolving with the effects of digitalisation and globalisation demanding new skills. Individuals will be required to look for jobs that provide them with a wide range of skills and experience. In turn, there will be an increased need for people to take full responsibility for their careers to keep their skills continuously up to date and to ensure life-long employability. In parallel to these dramatic changes in the workplace, young people have been experiencing difficult transitions between education and employment for over a decade now, with reasons given as poor links between schools and businesses (IPPR, 2014), poor achievement at post-secondary education and failure to equip young people with occupation-ready skills (Symonds et al., 2011).

This chapter has described a secondary school's focus on working with employers and external business professionals to help their students make the transition from education to employment shorter, easier and more focussed. The ASPIRE coaching programme, developed at the Axe Valley Community College, provides a practical example of the integration of a Positive Psychology and coaching intervention in the educational context. One of the strengths of the ASPIRE programme is that it takes its students on a journey of self-discovery, supporting the development of competencies from a young age and enabling the students to take responsibility for their own life and career choices as early as possible within their secondary-school education. Along the way, we have described the benefits of the programme for the students, outlined the lessons learned during implementation and made recommendations for improvements. We conclude the chapter with the suggestion that work psychologists, employers and schools should work together to develop education to employment interventions that provide students with support in developing their top five strengths, career competencies and flexibility, adaptability and resilience, through undertaking coaching and acquiring peer-coaching skills. Additionally, extending current research by adopting and analysing the usefulness of the Career Adapt-ability scales (Savickas & Porfeli, 2012) with young people earlier in the educational system (Bimrose et al., 2011), together with the adoption of fully integrated positive strengths-based interventions such as the Strengths Gym (Proctor & Fox Eades, 2009, quoted in Proctor et al., 2011), would be useful next steps for secondary schools to consider.

References

Adams, M. (2016). Developing resilience. In M. Adams (Ed.) *Coaching psychology in schools: enhancing performance development and wellbeing.* Abingdon, UK: Routledge.

Bimrose, J., Barnes, A. A., Brown, A. & Hughes, D. (2011). *The role of career adaptability in skills supply.* Wath-upon-Dearne: UK Commission for Employment and Skills.

Biswas-Diner, R. (2010). *Practising positive psychology coaching: assessment, diagnosis and intervention.* Hoboken, NJ: John Wiley.

Carter, A. J. (Chair), Richmond, P., Walker, A., Guner, Y., Gould, S., Lewis, H. & Matta, H. (2013). Supporting young society. Symposium given at the BPS Division of Occupational Psychology Conference, 9–11 January, Chester.

Carter, A. J. (Chair), Levi, R., Gosden, D., Matta, H., Palermo, G., Bourne, A., Gould, S. & Carew, D. (2014). Sustaining communities of good work. Symposium given at DOP conference, 8–10 January, Brighton.

Carter, A. J. (2015a). Youth employment – the missing facts. *The Psychologist, 28*(6), 462–465.

Carter, A. J. (2015b). *Evaluation of the ASPIRE programme.* Feedback report to the Axe Valley Community College, Institute of Work Psychology, Sheffield University Management School.

Carter, A. J. (Chair), et al. (2015). We need to tackle youth employment in other ways. Symposium given at the EAWOP Congress, 20–23 May, Oslo, Norway.

Chartered Institute of Personnel Development (CIPD) (2015). *Developing the next generation: today's young people, tomorrow's workforce.* A Learning to Work Research Report. London: Chartered Institute of Personnel Development. Downloaded on 13/03/2016 from: www.cipd.co.uk/knowledge/work/youth/next-gen-report.

Clough, P. & Strycharczyk, D. (2012). Mental toughness and its role in the development of young people. In C. van Nieuwerburgh (Ed.), *Coaching in education: getting better results for students, educators and parents*, 75–91. London: Karnac.

Erikson, E. (1950). *Childhood and society*. New York, NY: Norton.

Erikson, E. (1995). *Childhood and society*. London: Vintage.

Francis-Smythe, J., Haase, S., Thomas, E. & Steele, C. (2013) Development and validation of the Career Competency Indicator (CCI). *Journal of Career Assessment, 21*(2), 227–248.

George, A., Metcalf, H., Tufekci, L. & Wilkinson, D. (2015, June). *Understanding age and the labour market*. Report from the Joseph Rowntree Foundation (JRF), p. 17. Downloaded on 10/08/2014 from: www.jrf.org.uk/work/labour-markets.

Goleman, D. (1996). *Emotional intelligence: why it can matter more than IQ*. London: Bloomsbury.

Green, L. S., Oades, L. G. & Robinson, P. L. (2012). Positive education programmes: integrating coaching and positive psychology in schools. In C. van Nieuwerburgh (Ed.), *Coaching in education: getting better results for students, educators and parents*, pp. 115–132. London: Karnac.

Haase, S., Thomas, E. & Francis-Smythe J. (2013). Applying career competencies in career management. *Assessment and Development Matters, 5*(1), 2.

Inkson, K., Dries, N. & Arnold, J. (2015). Understanding careers (2nd Ed.). London: Sage.

Institute of Public Policy and Research (IPPR) (2014). *States of uncertainty: youth unemployment in Europe*. London: Institute of Public Policy and Research. Downloaded on 16/04/15 from: tinyurl.com/npr765h.

Levi, R. & Gosden, D. (2014). Vision of an outward facing school. In A. J. Carter (Chair) Sustaining communities of good work. Symposium held at the Division of Occupational Psychology Conference, 8–10 January, Brighton.

Levinson, H. (1976). *Psychological man*. Cambridge, MA: Levinson Institute.

Linley, P. A., Harrington, S. & Garcea, N. (Eds) (2009). *Handbook of positive psychology and work*. New York, NY: Oxford University Press.

Luthans, F., Vogelgesang, G. R. & Lester, P. B. (2006). Developing the psychological capital of resiliency. *Human Resources Development Review, 5*(1), 25–44.

Palmer, S. & Panchel, S. (Eds) (2011). *Developmental coaching, life transitions and generational perspectives*. Abingdon, UK: Routledge, pp. 1–28.

Paton, G. (2010). Schools being turned into exam factories. The *Telegraph*, 19 March. Retrieved on 04/01/16 from: www.telegraph.co.uk/education/educationnews/7472757/schools-being-turned-into-exam-factories.html.

Peterson, C. (2006). *A primer in positive psychology*. New York, NY: Oxford University Press.

Peterson, C. & Seligman M. E. P. (2004). *Character strengths and virtues: a classification and handbook*. Washington, DC: American Psychological Association.

Pring, R., Hayward, G., Hodgson, A., et al. (2012). *Education for all: the future of education and training for 14–19 years olds*. Abingdon, UK: Routledge, p. 3.

Proctor, C. & Fox Eades, J. (2009). *Strengths Gym, Year 8*. St Peter Port, Guernsey: Positive Psychology Research Centre.

Proctor, C., Tsukayana, E., Wood, A., Maltby, J., Fox Eades, J. & Linley, A. P. (2011). Strengths Gym, the impact of a character strengths-based intervention on the life satisfaction and well-being of adolescents. *The Journal of Positive Psychology, 6*(5), 377–388.

Ramesh, R. (2013). England's young people near bottom of global league table for basic skills. *The Guardian*, 8 October. Retrieved on 31/05/18 from: www.theguardian.com/education/2013/oct/08/england-young-people-league-table-basic-skills-oecd.

Roskinski, P. (2004). *Coaching across cultures*. London: Nicholas Brealey.

Savickas, M. L. (2013). Career construction theory and practice. In S. D. Brown and R. W. Lent (Eds) *Career development and counselling: putting theory and research to work* (2nd Ed.), pp. 147–183. Hoboken: NJ: John Wiley and Sons.

Savickas, M. L. & Porfeli, E. J. (2012). Career adapt-abilities scale: construction, reliability and measurement equivalence across 13 countries. *Journal of Vocational Behaviour*, 80(3), 661–673.

Seligman, M. E. P., Ernst, R. M., Gillham, J., Reivich, K. & Linkins, M. (2009). Positive psychology, positive education and classroom interventions. *Oxford Review of Education*, 35(3), 293–311.

Seligman, M. E. P., Steen, T. A., Park, N. & Peterson, C. (2005). Positive psychology progress: empirical validation of interventions. *American Psychologist*, 60(5), 410–421.

SKOPE: ESRC Centre on Skills, Knowledge and Organisational Performance (2012, May). *Youth transitions, the labour market and entry into employment: some reflections and questions*. Research Paper No. 108. Oxford: Department of Education, University of Oxford.

Snyder, C. R., Rand, K. L. & Sigmon, D. R. (2002). Hope theory: a member of the Positive Psychology family. In C. R. Snyder & S. J. Lopez (Eds), *Handbook of Positive Psychology*, pp. 257–276. Oxford: Oxford University Press.

Stern, D., Stone, J. R., Hopkins, C. & McMillion, M. (1990). Quality of students' work experience and orientation toward work. *Youth & Society*, 22(2), 263–282.

Super, D. W. (1957). *The psychology of careers*. New York, NY: Harper Collins.

Super, D. W. (1980). A life-span, life-space approach to career development. *Journal of Vocational Behaviour*, 16(3), 282–298.

Symonds, W. C., Schwartz, R. B. & Ferguson, R. (2011). *Pathways to prosperity*. Pathways to Prosperity Project presented at Harvard Graduate School of Education, Industry Trade Federation Conference 28 July, Auckland, New Zealand.

Timson, S. (2015). Exploring what clients find helpful in a brief resilience coaching programme: a qualitative study. *The Coaching Psychologist*, 11(2), 81–88.

Triener, E., Wilson, A. & Rebow, J. (2011). Standing out from the crowd: using strengths in career development. *Assessment and Development Matters*, 3(1), 11.

UK Commission for Employment and Skills (UKCES) (2011). *The youth enquiry: employers' perspective on tackling youth unemployment*. Wath-upon-Dearne: UK Commission for Employment and Skills.

UK Commission for Employment and Skills (UKCES) (2014). *The future of work: jobs and skills in 2030*. Wath-upon-Dearne: UK Commission for Employment and Skills.

UK Commission for Employment and Skills (UKCES) (2016). *The future of work: working futures labour market projections for the period 2014 to 2024*. Wath-upon-Dearne: UK Commission for Employment and Skills.

UNICEF (2010). *The children left behind*. Report Card 9. New York, NY: UNICEF. Downloaded on 10/12/2016 from: http://unicef_irc.org/publications/pdf/rc_9_eng.pdf.

van Nieuwerburgh, C. & Passmore, J. (2012a). Coaching in secondary or high schools. In C. van Nieuwerburgh (Ed.), *Coaching in education: getting better results for students, educators and parents*, pp. 63–74. London: Karnac.

van Nieuwerburgh, C. & Passmore, J. (2012b). Creating coaching cultures for learning. In C. van Nieuwerburgh (Ed.), *Coaching in education: getting better results for students, educators and parents*, pp. 153–172. London: Karnac.

van Nieuwerburgh, C. & Tong,C. (2013). Exploring the benefits of being a student coach in educational settings: a mixed-method study. *Coaching: An International Journal of Theory, Research and Practice*, 6(1), 5–24.

van Nieuwerburgh, C., Zacharia, C., Luckham, E., Prebble, G. & Browne, L. (2012). Coaching students in secondary school. In C. van Nieuwerburgh (Ed.), *Coaching in education: getting better results for students, educators and parents*, pp. 191–198. London: Karnac.

Wagner, C. G. (2008). When mentors and mentees switch roles. *The Futurist*, January/February, 6–7.

Wang, J. (2014). *Evaluation of the ASPIRE programme*, report to the Axe Valley Community College, Institute of Work Psychology, Sheffield University Management School.

Watson, C. & Grant, C. (2012). Employability: the development and validation of a scale to measure work-related competencies. *Assessment and Development Matters*, 4(3), 13.

Whitmore, J. (2002). *Coaching for performance: growing people, performance and purpose* (3rd Ed.). London: Nicholas Brealey.

WHO (2008). *Inequalities in young people's health*. Downloaded on 4/01/2009 from: www.euro.who.int/Informationsources/Publications/Catalogue/20080616_1.

7 Increasing youth employment benefits a community

Hannah Matta

Why focus on youth employment?

The detrimental impact of the 2008 economic downturn prevailed across London as it did across the rest of the world. For one particular London borough (the focus of this case study) unemployment for young people of 16–19 years of age was among the highest of the London boroughs at 7.7% (Trust for London, 2015). This figure translates to 687 young people not in education, employment or training (NEET). Youth unemployment has a significant adverse impact on society and remains a hot topic for all Local Authorities in the UK. With the cost of every young person who is NEET estimated at around £100,000, local services have a vested interest, now more than ever, to work together to prevent and tackle its causes (Coles, Godfrey, Keung, Parrot & Bradshaw, 2010). Other evidence (Smeaton, Hudson, Radu & Vowden, 2010) shows that by the age of 21 years a young male who has been NEET for six months is three times more likely than other young men of his age to have mental health problems, five times more likely to have a criminal record and six times less likely to have any qualifications (p. 9).

The Local Authority (LA) featured in this case study was under significant financial pressure to reduce spending, resulting in downsizing of jobs and redundancies. Transformational change programmes were initiated across the LA aiming to increase efficiency and productivity, and at the same time to mitigate low staff morale that was being measured by organizational health checks and engagement surveys. Along with this large change agenda the LA had become aware that they were employing an ageing workforce. The average employee age was 44 years, indicating that 22% of staff (around 800 people) could retire in the decade 2010–2020. But at the time there were few younger people in the organization with less than 12% of the workforce being aged 30 years or less. Therefore, failing to plan for the risk of potential retirement would result in the loss of crucial skills and knowledge from the organization. Diversifying the age profile of the LA was therefore essential, coupled with the LA's commitment to Corporate Social Responsibility, so actions to get local young people into work became a top priority.

In 2009 the UK government set up the Backing Young Britain campaign to address the nation's rising youth unemployment statistics. All 33 London LA

Chief Executive Officers were asked to pledge to take on 2,000 apprenticeships collectively by the end of 2012. Thereafter, all the London LAs were committed to sustaining 2% of their workforce as apprentices, resulting in a local target of 87 apprentice starts within this timeframe. This was the antecedent for the establishment of the LA's first ever apprenticeship scheme.

The LA is a complex organization accountable for a broad range of important public services including: benefits and council tax, business and investment, health and social care, planning and regeneration, education and learning, environmental services, leisure, culture and housing. As with many LAs in the UK at this time, "local government is often characterised as bureaucratic and inefficient" (Capsley, Pallot & Levy, 2002, p. 5) and this LA was no exception. An organization-wide apprenticeship scheme would introduce a new approach into the workplace, hopefully adding fresh perspectives that would also support the on-going agenda driving organizational culture change. However, successfully introducing young people into the workplace via an apprenticeship scheme would ultimately depend on fostering a new organizational culture.

What is an apprenticeship?

Apprenticeships combine the development of theoretical knowledge about a particular occupation or range of occupations with practical experience gained from doing the job. Apprenticeship training should lay the foundation for occupational competence and the capacity to add to this as required throughout working life (Macleod & Hughes, 2006). Apprenticeships in Britain date back to the Middle Ages and the medieval craft guilds. For two centuries apprenticeships expanded and evolved, with legislation improving working conditions over time. By the mid-1960s 33% of male school leavers aged 15–17 years entered an apprenticeship programme. However, soon after the 1960s, the popularity of apprenticeships declined dramatically across various industry sectors, with the number of apprenticeships dropping from 171,000 in 1968 to 34,500 in 1990. Apprenticeships were criticised for numerous reasons; they were considered to compromise on training quality, had not kept pace with accelerating industrial, technological and scientific advances, and were male dominated (Rudd, Henderson, Usher & Hawtin, 2008). These criticisms led many employers to conclude that apprenticeships were ineffective.

There was a revival of apprenticeships in the 1990s with successive UK governments investing heavily to improve apprenticeship outcomes, introducing reforms to training activities and expanding apprenticeships to cover over 80 occupational areas. Training quality and curricula improved, evidenced by increasing numbers of organizations taking on apprentices. Between 1997 and 2009 the number of organizations taking on apprentices doubled from approximately 75,000 to around 180,000, and by December 2010 numbers exceeded 450,000 (Mirza-Davies, 2015). However, there were still issues about skills development during apprenticeships. The Dearing Report (1997) describes employers' concerns about the lack of essential skills possessed by young work recruits. This report led to the Department for Children, Schools and Families in England and the Department for Children, Education, Life-long Learning and Skills (2000) in Wales to introduce the concept of Key Skills. Key Skills are a range of essential skills underpinning success in education, employment, life-long learning and personal development. Subsequently, Key Skills qualifications have developed as an important component of 14–19 year olds' education in England, Northern Ireland and Wales. Such qualifications in Mathematics, English Language and Information and Communications Technology are now described as Functional Skills.

Apprenticeships today are integrated programmes of learning developed by the Sector Skills Council and the National Apprenticeship Service (NAS) in collaboration with organizations operating in a given field. An apprenticeship has four elements (see Figure 7.1 below): a) a Competency Qualification (previously the National Vocational Qualification, NVQ, and now a nationally recognised qualification); b) verbal and numerical skills known as Functional Skills; c) On-the-job training; and d) a Technical Certificate, a qualification that assesses the underpinning knowledge. For example, for the Business Administration Apprenticeship the Technical Certificate would assess the principles of business and administration.

The level of apprenticeship depends on the individual's capability and the learning opportunities available in the organizational role. There are different levels of apprenticeships starting at a Level 2, which is equivalent to five General Certificates of Secondary Education (GCSEs), moving on to an Advanced Apprenticeship Qualification at Level 3 equivalent to two Advanced (A) levels. More recently there has been development of Higher

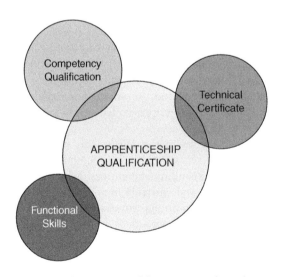

Figure 7.1 Components of the apprenticeship scheme.

Apprenticeship Qualifications allowing individuals to progress to a Level 7 qualification equivalent to the Chartered Status in many industries.

Organizational challenges

We discovered that there were a number of real challenges introducing young people and apprenticeships into the LA. First we had to let young people know that there were job opportunities available.

Employer brand

The LA conducted numerous engagement events with young people across the borough to raise the profile of the LA as an employer of choice. Early events focussed on gaining insight into young people's needs to show how the apprenticeship scheme would benefit young people, while later events focussed on promoting apprenticeship opportunities. For example, a *Question Time* event was hosted by the LA in collaboration with the local Youth Council, inviting young people living in the area to attend and ask questions of a panel of local politicians and senior LA leaders. The young people did not hold back in demanding answers to some pertinent questions and concerns about their futures. Many questions focussed on the lack of employment opportunities for young people providing a perfect opportunity to introduce the new apprenticeship scheme. Additionally, recruitment fairs hosted by Job Centre Plus (JCP) and Connexions offered opportunities for the LA to host a stand and advertise places on the apprenticeship scheme to local young people seeking work.

During these events it transpired that attracting young people to work for the LA would prove to be a challenge, one that was not initially anticipated. Responses to questions posed to young people showed that a surprising number of them had very little knowledge of what working for the LA would involve and they had misconceptions and stereotypes about the work. For example, when asked what roles LA employees might fulfil, one young person replied "They drive buses" and another said "Doesn't everyone from the LA wear grey?" When asked the question "What kind of career are you seeking?" an overwhelming number of young people did not know the answer or were very vague in their responses, for example: "Something to do with IT". These conversations highlighted that there was significant work to do to improve the employer brand and reputation, and to ensure the apprenticeship scheme was appropriately marketed to young people. The subsequent marketing campaign took every effort to do just that. The youngest (and most boldly dressed) LA employees became ambassadors for the apprenticeship scheme, working closely with schools and youth groups to promote the exciting, broad and varied career paths available in local government through the apprenticeship scheme.

In parallel to the external campaign with young people, there was an internal battle to fight. Why was there an ageing workforce? Was it simply a case that young people were not attracted to LA roles or were there other variables at play?

The ageing workforce and a diversity bias

Discussions were held within the Authority's Human Resource (HR) Department to explore why the average employee age was 44 years, with less than 12% of employees being under the age of 30 years. Demographic reports for the different departments were scrutinised and the HR Business Partners posed several different views. One line of reasoning was that the skills needed in many departments were specialised, requiring many years of experience (e.g., the role of a Social Worker). Another viewpoint was that hiring managers in the LA were reluctant to take on young people for various reasons, with some thinking young people were unreliable or not motivated to work, while others were afraid of the unknown preferring to employ people with several years' work experience. Also, there were managers who felt that they did not have time to 'handhold' entry-level employees as they felt it would be too demanding of their time. These views were consistent with anecdotal evidence shared from the local JCP and Connexions (Annual Report 2001 to 2002) based around their conversations with other local employers.

Regardless of the cause of the ageing workforce within the LA, it was clear that diversifying the age profile would add value to the organization. The ageing workforce and stereotypes inherent among some of the current workforce had implications for the organizational culture. Attitudes and values were further influenced by the current context within the organization of budget cuts and financial pressure. To realise this value, the organization needed to embrace culture change and adopt new ways of working so that the different generations of workers could work effectively together, and this would involve a shift in mindset. To move forward a comprehensive communications and engagement strategy was essential to seek buy-in and support from the LA employees as to the benefits of age diversity in the workplace.

Lack of resources

Statements like 'Doing more for less', 'firefighting' and 'walking through treacle' will sound familiar to people who have worked in public sector organizations at this time. The third prominent challenge the LA faced at the prospect of introducing an apprenticeship scheme was a strong view from the workforce that they did not have adequate resources (time, people, money or materials) to do their jobs well. How could already stretched managers be expected to take on additional responsibilities in the form of supervising a young person with little to no work experience? This was a prospect that some managers could not fathom. To offer some context to this challenge, Employee Satisfaction Surveys and Organizational Health Reports undertaken by the LA between the years of 2010–2011 highlighted these themes. Qualitative feedback from these engagement tools echoed the phrases above.

There were two sides to this dilemma; on the one hand the organization needs to introduce apprentices to support employees with their workload, while on the other hand these new apprentices will need adequate support and guidance from their manager. Similarly, introducing apprentices into a team with a manager who feels overly stretched by their current workload could cause further unnecessary burden and stress. It was clear that to succeed with this challenge careful consideration needed to be given as to where apprentices would be placed and what support structure would be available to assist both apprentices and managers alike. To ensure the apprenticeship scheme benefitted all those involved, a strategic approach was established to maximise the opportunities and realise the benefits associated with the scheme while taking measures to mitigate against some of the aforementioned challenges.

Getting started

With young people at the heart of the strategy, ensuring they were set up for success was paramount. Hence starting off with a relatively small cohort meant each young person would get the personal attention and support that they needed. This approach would also allow lessons to be learnt as the apprenticeship scheme progressed, gathering momentum along the way and allowing for larger cohorts in Years Two and Three. Thus targets were established to have in Year One 20 apprenticeship starts (2010), rising to 67 apprentice starts by the end of Year Two and finally 100 apprentices by the end of Year Three (2012).

Apprenticeships to do what?

The LA is a large and complex organization with many different roles and specialisms and, as we found at the engagement events, young people were largely unaware of the nature of LA work. Deciding what type of apprenticeships would best meet the needs of the LA was a primary consideration. Where would apprenticeships add most value to the organization? What type of apprenticeships would be most attractive to young people? Members of the HR team set out as ambassadors for the scheme to explore these questions.

First we explored the organizational metrics. Some departments operated effectively through the placement of permanent hires and continuing professional development pathways for employees (e.g., the Planning department and Customer Service teams), whereas others were considered as areas having skills shortages, characterised by an over-reliance on temporary staff to perform roles, high turnover and vacant positions that proved hard to fill. Health and Social Care was an example of a skills shortage area and offered an excellent opportunity to introduce apprentices to the workforce. Apprenticeships in these areas would offer the LA an opportunity to *grow your own* skills for the future, saving temporary staff costs while developing in-house expertise. A Health and Social Care apprenticeship could offer a career path with progression into rewarding associate social work roles for those young people with a passion to work in this field.

Second, we had to find out what type of apprenticeships would be the most attractive to young people. By exploring conversations had during the engagement events we realised few young people had any clarity about what they wanted from a future career, but there were some interests in the areas of IT, business and the caring professions. One conclusion we drew from this was that the provision of more *generic* apprenticeships, those offering a skill set transferable to most businesses or departments such as Information Technology (IT), Business Administration (BA) and Customer Service (CS), would be valuable. Provision of transferable skills through these generic apprenticeships would be especially useful for those young people lacking in clarity about their own career path and we could offer a solid foundation in skills allowing them to move into a wide range of different job roles. Therefore, the strategic decision to offer both generic apprenticeships and those in Health and Social Care (HSC) was taken. The advantages of generic apprenticeships had value to the LA; skills learned in an IT, BA or CS apprenticeship would be applicable across the breadth of LA departments. This would mean that the young person's career progression need not be limited to the department where their apprenticeship was carried out. Also, it was likely that longer-term retention would be increased and apprentices could work in different departments as and when the organization and/or the individual required, offering flexibility on both sides.

Before we went on to design the bespoke placements it was essential to draw on experiences and important lessons from other organizations, particularly other LAs who had already engaged with apprenticeship schemes.

Lessons from other boroughs

A think-tank and lobbying organization called the London Councils was responsible for reporting on LA activity towards the pledges for the Backing Young Britain campaign with networks being set up across the London LAs. Conferences, workshops and networking events were convened by this group enabling learning to be shared across the various schemes. With schemes having differing levels of maturity and experience this was a welcome development for those organizations new to employing young people, as we were.

Crucial information was gathered during these meetings, shaping our approach. For example, the importance of ensuring that apprentices receive a variety of support through dedicated mentor/buddy schemes, selecting an excellent apprenticeship training provider with low case-loads of apprentices per assessor and establishing internal apprentice networks in the organization. Other boroughs with established schemes also highlighted the importance of paying above the Apprentice National Minimum Wage to increase retention of the young people throughout the scheme.

The approach

Based on the background research carried out with other organizations as well as conducted internally, the LA apprenticeship scheme particulars were agreed and finalised in preparation for an organization-wide launch event.

Apprenticeship domains

The endorsed LA apprenticeship scheme would give preference to young people residing in the borough aged between 16–24 years and the apprenticeships offered to departments were the generic apprenticeships (e.g., ICT, BA and CS). The apprenticeship scheme aimed to: a) diversify the ageing workforce; b) provide support to over-stretched departments suffering from reduced resources; and c) make a positive contribution to reduce local youth unemployment by meeting supply with demand (Carter, 2015). This approach was based on evidence that young people would be attracted to such frameworks as they would equip them with transferable skills that they could build upon in any future career. Specific apprenticeships (e.g., HSC) would also be made available for those teams with recognised skills gaps to enable the LA to grow skills internally and offer opportunities to young people who are passionate about a career in a more specialised field.

Apprenticeship duration

The NAS stipulate that apprentices are required to work for a minimum of 30 hours per week (this changed to 16 hours per week in 2012) to include either day-release to college to study for the apprentice qualification or, if working five days per week, to be supported on the job by monthly visits from a qualified trainer and NVQ assessor and up to five off-site training courses per year. An apprenticeship qualification is delivered by an Apprenticeship Training Provider (ATP) drawing down funding directly from the government to cover the cost of training. The minimum time taken to complete an apprenticeship is 12 months but, depending on the individual learner, it could be completed in six months (Delebarre, 2016).

Apprenticeship contracts

Apprentices can be employed as permanent members of staff or they can be hired on a training contract. It is important that apprentices are hired for their *potential* to do a job, in that through on-the-job training and achieving training qualifications they will become equipped to work more autonomously. This approach is in contrast to hiring people with the skills to do a job, which would be the LA's normal practice for permanent hires. Through the promotion and marketing of the apprenticeship scheme the LA would be encouraging new practice; apprenticeship training opportunities for young people with a 12-month training contract endorsed for the scheme. Should they complete the qualification early, they would continue on in their work until their contract had been concluded. For those managers who had sufficient budget and were satisfied with the apprentice's performance the apprenticeship could be extended for a second year, allowing the young person to complete a further advanced qualification and gain additional experience.

Apprentice wage

The National Minimum Wage (NMW) for an apprentice as stipulated by NAS in 2010 was £90 per week (increased to £95 per week in 2012). The LA scheme offered apprentices a significantly higher wage than that stipulated by the minimum wage for ethical and retention reasons. A six-month increment was also built into the approach to recognise good performance and attainment of the training requirements of the apprenticeship. This meant that those apprentices who were meeting and exceeding expectations would be financially rewarded at a half-way point through their qualification.

Apprentice support

A clear message came through from communications with other boroughs, apprentices need support from a range of stakeholders to successfully complete their training and move into working more autonomously. This message was attended to and reflected in the LA approach. It was particularly important given that one driver for the apprenticeship scheme was to support already over-stretched managers, so it was essential that the scheme made provision for a range of support options for apprentices. Support included each apprentice being assigned a mentor (other than their manager) for monthly meetings, monthly visits from their NVQ assessor allocated by the ATP and monthly Apprentice Forums hosted by the LA enabling peer support among apprentices.

Apprentice forums offered an opportunity for apprentices to meet others on the scheme from different departments, to share experiences, have some fun, learn about the different challenges facing the LA and also hear from various speakers (e.g., staff, unions, LA directors, and a money advisory service). In addition, the apprentice forums were an opportunity for apprentices to provide feedback on their experience allowing changes to be made to the scheme along the way. One example of a change made as a result of the forum feedback was that not every apprentice valued having to have a mentor all the way through their employment; many felt the first three to six months was sufficient to help them settle. Hence the mentors were assigned for a minimum of three months thereafter. This early evaluation of the scheme (at reaction level) (Kirkpatrick, 1959) complemented the more thorough evaluation of the scheme that was to take place after 12 months.

Raising awareness: internal and external communication campaigns

Early research with both young people and LA managers highlighted the need to market the scheme appropriately to overcome issues of perception on both sides. Young people needed to understand what it was or was not like to work for the LA, and for the managers it was important to explore and explode some of the myths about working with young people. Hence the apprenticeship scheme communications plan was developed including both internal and externally focussed campaigns to raise awareness of the benefits of apprenticeships to apprentices and hiring managers alike.

Internally this campaign involved a high profile launch event, departmental awareness sessions with senior leadership teams, articles in the LA monthly magazine, drop-in discussion sessions in the lunch area and prominent notices on the LA intranet. Throughout the internal campaign it was important to demonstrate the added value apprentices had elsewhere. Apprentices from other organizations and their managers came along to these sessions to tell their stories. These events had a profound impact on people's views and an overwhelming number of managers pledged their support for the scheme following these awareness sessions.

Before embarking on an external campaign it was prudent to first generate some internal apprentice vacancies. This was achieved shortly after the apprenticeship scheme launch event, albeit with a fairly small number of apprentice opportunities. The external campaign commenced supported by close collaboration with local schools and partnerships with JCP and Connexions. Attendance at recruitment fairs and local youth events allowed the LA to raise the profile of the organization with young people and promote the varied and rewarding career paths available in local government. As the apprenticeship scheme recruited the first apprentices, local press campaigns promoted and reinforced the message that apprenticeship schemes have positive outcomes for all involved. The next section will describe how the impact of the apprenticeship scheme was measured and how this information was used to enhance the scheme in subsequent years.

Evaluating the impact

The internal and external marketing campaigns maintained the momentum of the apprenticeship scheme and apprentice numbers grew; by the end of the first year the LA employed over 20 apprentices directly and a further 100 through providers. The evaluation of the scheme was on-going through regular two-way feedback between apprentices, managers and the LA employees managing the scheme. But it was time for a more scientific approach to evaluation. This section will explore the evaluation method and highlight findings, including qualitative comments from the apprentices and managers who were surveyed.

TOTADO: a multi-level approach to evaluation

Drawing on the Taxonomy of Training and Development Outcomes (TOTADO) evaluation model (Birdi, 2006), an evaluation of the apprenticeship scheme was undertaken after a 12-month duration to assess the impact of the scheme and identify areas for development. The TOTADO model of evaluation goes beyond Kirkpatrick's four-level model offering a comprehensive framework that is both integrative and multi-level in its approach (Birdi, 2010). The TOTADO model allows exploration of the scheme through examination of work behaviours and the feelings of those involved. Outputs are described at four levels – individual, team, organization and society – examining the impact the apprenticeship scheme has within and outside the LA. By considering the LA as the organization and the borough as the society, this model offered the broader level of evaluation that the apprenticeship scheme needed, and this was particularly important given that one of the drivers for the scheme was to have a positive impact on young society in the borough. Moreover, the organizational benefits had multiple levels to consider: at the individual level it was about the apprentices, managers and teams involved gaining value from the scheme; at the organizational level it was about the long-term sustainability of a skilled and agile workforce. The TOTADO model offered an excellent framework through which to evaluate the impact at these multiple levels.

Evaluation data gathered from focus groups and surveys were disseminated to key stakeholders involved in the scheme, primarily the apprentices and their managers. Questions were aligned with the TOTADO framework and levels. Response rates were high (100% for apprentices and 98% for managers) with 21 and 20 respondents respectively in these groupings. This level of response was important as initially the number of apprentices was relatively small with the scheme still in its infancy, just one year in duration. Quantitative and qualitative findings were analysed using comparative methods; thematic (Braun & Clarke, 2006) and template analysis (King, 2004).

Findings from the evaluation were broadly categorised as *Highlights*, features of the scheme found to be going well, and *Lowlights*, features requiring attention. Highlights are described first along with a discussion of best practice, followed by *Lowlights* and discussion of areas for improvement.

Highlights of the evaluation

A number of highlights were found at the various levels of analysis.

INDIVIDUAL-LEVEL OUTCOMES

Apprentice experience and employer brand: the vast majority of apprentices were enjoying their work, which offered the opportunity to experience work while developing key skills, gaining qualifications and earning money. Ninety-five per cent of apprentices would describe their overall satisfaction with the scheme as 'very satisfied' or 'satisfied' and 90% of apprentices said the scheme had lived up to their expectations. For example: "I am highly satisfied with the apprenticeship programme, as it gave me a brilliant step into a real working environment, I gained so much valuable experience and transferable skills that can be used across a variety of roles". Further, 100% of apprentices would recommend working at the LA to their friends and felt the wide range of work offered by the LA would interest other young people. For example: "It's a pretty fair job; work hard and you can be rewarded. Ultimately we are serving the public so providing a service for the average man or woman on the street and in my Borough is a nice feeling".

Excellent support: for the majority, the positive experience of being an apprentice and working for the council was attributed to the support they had been given by their teams, managers, mentors and HR. Ninety-five per cent said the support received from their manager was 'good' or 'excellent'.

Apprentices show willingness to learn: findings suggest apprentices have a strong desire to learn and develop themselves. Eighty-six per cent of apprentices said they were developing skills that will help them in their future career. "I wanted to get somewhere in life and provide a better future for my two children and partner."

Managers were encouraged by apprentices' learning: despite experiencing some performance issues early on, through close supervision and feedback apprentices demonstrated the ability to take feedback on board, learn through experience and modify behaviour. For example: "I have been very satisfied with both the apprentices' approach to workload and wanting to learn anything and everything. When asked 'which of the following describes your apprentice' the top three responses were: 85% 'willing to learn', 80% 'enthusiastic' and 60% 'confident'.

TEAM-LEVEL OUTCOMES

Apprentices add value to their teams and managers: managers report championing the scheme to their peers because of the value apprentices have added to their teams. Ninety-five per cent would recommend the scheme to other managers.

Managers would take on another apprentice: when asked if they would take on another apprentice themselves 95% said 'yes'.

Apprentices bring fresh perspective to work: apprentices bring something new to the teams and departments they work in, and the 'youthful influx' of apprentices re-energises the office. Seventy per cent of managers said their apprentice brought a different dynamic to the team: "fresh ideas from a young person's perspective, move away from how it's always been".

Managing apprentices offered development opportunities for the wider team: overall, managers reported that their teams were enthusiastic and excited prior to the apprentice's start, especially where resources were stretched as many teams welcomed some extra support. Furthermore, where some managers usually managed more senior members of staff, they welcomed the development opportunity and experience of managing younger staff members: "I'm used to managing more experienced people so this is a development opportunity for me". However, it is worth noting one manager's experience that showed that their permanent administrative support member of staff felt threatened by the new apprentice: "I had to work closely with my existing admin support to reassure her that this person was not going to replace her as a cheaper option".

ORGANIZATIONAL-LEVEL OUTCOMES

Apprentices are cost effective: apprentices are paid below national minimum wage because they are employed on a training contract for their *potential* to do a job.

For this reason, apprentices are not paid the same wage as permanent members of staff who are expected to work autonomously in a role. The managers reported that during times of austerity the apprenticeship scheme was a cost-effective and much needed resource for their teams. When managers were asked what they thought the main benefit the council would realise as a result of the scheme would be, 65% said apprentices are a cost-effective resource. Further, when asked why they hired an apprentice, 50% said it was a cost-effective resource; "we have no budget for admin support but the team needed it".

SOCIETAL-LEVEL OUTCOMES

The apprenticeship scheme has had a positive impact on the borough: when managers were asked the second benefit the council would realise as a result of the scheme, 45% said employing apprentices supported our corporate theme 'achieving better outcomes for children and young people'; "Getting young people from (London borough) into work".

The next section will discuss these themes, allowing the common threads to become guidelines for good practice.

Discussion – building upon what works

The manager–apprentice relationship is an important one; often the apprenticeship is the young person's first experience of the world of work, influencing not only what they learn (the skills) but how they learn (their behaviours). Helping young people to develop the appropriate work ethic will rely upon the right support and role models. The majority of apprentices who described good line-management support mentioned the words 'trust', 'fun' and 'supportive'. The young people really value the encouragement and words of affirmation they have received from their managers, in addition to being able to 'have a laugh' with them. A critical success factor of the scheme depended upon apprentices reporting good experiences and these encouraging findings are indicative of positive experiences.

Looking at the team level, apprentices added significant value in their ability to challenge the existing state of affairs and provide development opportunities for the wider team of which they are part. However, there is a risk that the job security of some staff is threatened by the apprentice role. As part of the manager briefings and support prior to starting an apprentice, it would be prudent for any organization to encourage an open consultation with all team members to share any thoughts and concerns and mitigate issues of job insecurity prior to the placement commencing. This would serve to ensure that all team members are bought into and are made fully aware of the roles and responsibilities to ensure a good experience for all involved.

Part of the LA's corporate social responsibility is to provide opportunities to help young people into employment and/or education. The apprenticeship scheme has gone some way to achieving this by offering apprenticeship vacancies *only* to local residents (with other LAs offering similar schemes for their residents, avoiding notions of discrimination). During the first year of the scheme 20 apprentices were employed by the LA in a variety of roles and 45% of these apprentices went on to permanent employment or an advanced apprenticeship in the organization. Other campaigns such as the outreach work with local schools and contractual stipulations with LA providers yielded further opportunities within the supply chain, with these opportunities being ring-fenced for local people. Supporting young society in this way is the ultimate success factor and objective for the scheme.

Lowlights of the evaluation

Learning lessons about what works well and building on these is important and, likewise, paying attention to salient themes that point to areas for improvement provides equally important lessons to learn from. This section will take a closer look at these lowlight themes.

INDIVIDUAL-LEVEL OUTCOMES

Apprentices may be unreliable: given that many apprentices are entering full-time work for the first time, or at least early on in their career, it is perhaps unsurprising that managers found them to be unreliable. The most common undesirable behaviours managers reported were apprentices using their personal mobiles at work, lateness and sickness absence. However, it was clear from managers' responses that the majority of these issues were experienced early on in the apprenticeship and, in most cases, they were overcome (see highlight above – apprentices show a willingness to learn). Only 50% of managers reported apprentices to be reliable and 40% of managers said issues were experienced in the first two months of the scheme:

> It's a big step to go from college to an adult environment where nobody is there to hold your hand when it comes to personal responsibilities like sick days and poor punctuality. You need the initiative to develop your own maturity to become successful in your role.
>
> (Comment from an apprentice)

Requirement for good role models: coaching the apprentices and setting boundaries early on is an integral part of the apprenticeship scheme. It is the role of managers, peers, mentors, assessors and all LA employees to role-model the required organizational behaviours, work ethic and personal accountability. Indeed, there is the potential for apprentices to pick up bad habits and a poor work ethic from their own teams, managers, or indeed anyone they interact with in the organization. For example: "I have spoken to him about it (using phones at work) and he says if others do it why can't I?" This quote highlights one manager's experience; members of the team frequently role-modelled the wrong behaviour (using phones in meetings and at work) that the apprentice picked up.

Disadvantaged young people: managers and HR representatives became aware of various issues and hardships that apprentices had to deal with in their personal life. The issues include, but are sadly not limited to, homelessness, teenage pregnancies, criminal convictions, physical and sexual abuse, court summons and disabilities. These issues can be difficult for anyone to deal with and the evaluation findings indicated that, for some apprentices, their personal issues have affected their resilience, motivation, enthusiasm and attendance at work.

TEAM-LEVEL OUTCOMES

Dissatisfaction with the ATP: the training provider partnered with the LA to deliver the apprenticeship training was unfortunately the focus of dissatisfaction. The provider assigns each apprentice an assessor who takes them through the qualification and they consult with hiring managers to manage the selection process of all apprentice vacancies. The evaluation identified dissatisfaction around the service provided by the ATP from both managers and apprentices. There are a number of potential causes for this; the case-load of apprentices per assessor is high, which means they are stretched and often appear disorganised, cancelling meetings or turning up unannounced. Fifty-five per cent of managers said the service provided by the ATP was poor or marginal. Thirty-eight per cent of apprentices said their experience of working with their assessor was poor or marginal: "Took many months to make contact and this experience matches the reports from the apprentice of cancelled assessor appointments". However, in the interests of providing a balanced view, some managers have had a good or excellent experience of working with the training provider.

ORGANIZATIONAL-LEVEL OUTCOMES

Apprentices may need more support than other members of staff: apprentices will more often than not require extra support compared with other staff, which is because an apprenticeship is effectively a traineeship. Since the launch of the LA's apprenticeship scheme, there have been numerous managers who have shown an interest in taking on an apprentice only to change their mind at a later time. During these discussions, managers cited not having enough time to dedicate to the apprentice as the main reason for their change of heart. The evaluation findings reinforce the fact that many apprentices will require more support than other members of staff. Seventy per cent of managers affirmed this: "I was unsure when my manager informed me that our team was going to have an apprentice; having time to manage them with my own workload? However, it has proven to be a good scheme and I would recommend apprenticeships within any department".

SOCIETAL-LEVEL OUTCOMES

Long-term retention: one of the biggest anxieties apprentices have is whether they will have a permanent role at the end of the scheme as they understand that this is not a guaranteed outcome of their placement. There have been a number of apprentices the LA could not retain for the reasons of 'no vacant post' or 'no budget'. But this is an issue because the aim of the scheme is to grow skills and talent internally, encouraging young people into work with the obvious benefits for the local NEET population and addressing the ageing workforce issue of the LA. For those managers who were not satisfied with their apprentice's performance, moving them on at the end of the apprenticeship (with feedback) was the next step and would enable another apprentice opportunity to begin. Some managers were able to offer their apprentice progression and moved them to a higher qualification for a second year. Sixty-seven per cent of apprentices said they would like a permanent job working for the council in the same department as they did for their apprenticeship, and 40% of managers said they would like to keep them on if they have the budget.

Discussion – areas for improvement

Apprentices need support and feedback to develop the required attitude and approach to their work, which is, in part, one of the benefits of enrolling on such a scheme. Many managers recognise that there is a period of adjustment or transition at the beginning of most placements where the apprentice will need to adapt to a new environment, ethic and discipline. The evaluation data highlights the importance of managing the expectations of managers and raising awareness of transition behaviours associated with young people entering the workplace for the first time. Helping managers to anticipate and mitigate potential issues is important. It is also worth remembering though that no two apprentices will be the same. This may seem an obvious point to make but it is an important one to bear in mind; where there is an example of poor behaviour with one apprentice, an example of exemplary behaviour was reported in another. But, clearly, early impressions count. Managers and their teams must be aware that while it is the apprentice's responsibility to learn, it is the manager's responsibility to role-model desirable behaviours and to consider the impact of their own work styles on new apprentices seeking a blueprint for work behaviours.

Important themes arising from the evaluation enabled more robust manager briefings and awareness sessions, picking up the detail of what apprentices and managers were finding difficult. The scheme has been modified so that now every apprentice has a mentor for at least the first three months and lasting for the full year if they find it useful. The monthly Apprentice Forums have been adapted to include sessions on the LA's Code of Conduct as well as providing information on where apprentices can seek support and professional advice should they need it (e.g., Employee Assistance Programmes).

To address the feedback surrounding the ATP provision, the LA decided to work with a second provider based in the borough to mitigate some of the issues such as geographical location of assessors, availability and reliability. The quality and delivery of both providers continues to be monitored regularly by HR.

To improve the long-term retention of apprentices, HR worked hard to encourage new hiring managers to consider taking an apprentice who had completed the scheme in another department, particularly if the apprentice wanted to stay on and progress to the next level of apprenticeship. This model worked well for several apprentices. The LA also adapted their redeployment process so that, as an apprentice reaches the end of their contract, if managers cannot offer them a progression opportunity (a permanent role or an advanced apprenticeship) then the apprentice may request to be placed onto the redeployment register, secondary to statutory redeployees. This means that after the staff who are *at risk* of redundancy have been considered for new vacancies, *at risk* apprentices will then be considered before vacancies are advertised to other LA staff or outside the organization.

The rich information gathered from the evaluation allowed the LA to build upon what works well and to address areas for improvement with the scheme. The next section will focus on the endorsed recommendations to address these areas for improvement as the next evolution of LA apprenticeship scheme.

Recommendations for change

To address the lowlight themes a number of recommendations were endorsed and taken forward by the LA. These were as follows.

Develop a Code of Conduct booklet to ensure apprentices behave appropriately in the workplace

This was a strong theme from the evaluation analysis and it is supported by the psychological literature (Kloep & Hendry, 1999; Erikson, 1968), which suggests that young people can display risk-taking behaviour as part of their self-development and the formation of their social identity. Development of acceptable workplace behaviours will require support and feedback from mentors (and role models) to embed these behaviours. The LA had a Code of Conduct for permanent members of staff but the terminology used was not appropriate for apprentices. Two high-performing apprentices worked with stakeholders to design and publish a more contemporary Code of Conduct for new apprentices.

Introduce a work experience scheme to ensure apprentices are work-ready

Evidence shows that there is a need for pre-apprenticeship training and skills development to ensure that apprentices are 'work-ready' when they start an apprenticeship, thereby increasing the likelihood of a successful apprenticeship and translating to long-term retention (Harris, Simons & Clayton, 2005; Spielhofer & Sims, 2004). A work experience scheme was later introduced by the LA.

Source new ATPs to deliver apprenticeship qualifications and improve service delivery

Training providers are critical to the success of any apprenticeship and the lesson learnt was that the LA should have a number of preferred suppliers that meet with required service standards and who undergo regular evaluation. Other training partners were sought and invited to tender resulting in a second provider being appointed.

Aspiring managers to be given the opportunity to supervise/manage apprentices

Offering the opportunity to support an apprentice to aspiring managers was an opportunity to develop further resource. This tactic reduced the workload on busy managers and offered new and exciting developmental opportunities to those employees seeking further professional development while ensuring apprentices got the appropriate level of day-to-day support. This opportunity became an integral part of the LA's managerial development programme.

Change the redeployment policy to improve long-term retention of good apprentices

Changes were made to the redeployment policy by keeping apprentices in the redeployment pool (secondary to statutory redeployees), allowing them to be considered for future roles matched to their skills and abilities before these were offered for internal and external recruitment. This approach significantly increased the number of apprentices receiving permanent employment, with post-apprenticeship retention increasing from 16% in February 2012 to 45% in October 2012.

Summary and conclusions

By 2012, two years after the launch of the LA AS, 101 apprentices had been supported into work by the LA, exceeding the target set by the government through the Backing Young Britain Campaign. The evidence gathered through the evaluation reflects the mostly positive impact the scheme has had on those who have been involved with it. In the subsequent years after the establishment of the LA apprenticeship scheme, the LA went on to leverage further opportunities for local young people through the supply chain via a public–private partnership and contractual obligations for LA providers. In addition to an in-house scheme, the LA apprenticeship strategy included outreach work with local schools and contractors to ensure that they too would reflect the LA values and commit to taking on young people through apprenticeships. This partnership model will enable a far greater impact on youth employment in the borough than any standalone LA scheme.

This detailed case study of an apprenticeship solution has described a number of strategic and operational steps that have been taken to develop and enhance the scheme. The authority continues to offer a working start to young people. Hopefully the lessons learned can help others to introduce similar schemes.

References

Backing Young Britain (2009). Downloaded on 23/01/2016 from: http://webarchive. nationalarchives.gov.uk/20100222072559/interactive.bis.gov.uk/backingyoungbritain/ campaign-updates/success.

Birdi, K. (2006). Evaluating effectiveness: the taxonomy of training and development outcomes (TOTADO). Presented at CBPOT 2 Conference, Brasilia, Brazil.

Birdi, K. (2010). The taxonomy of training and development outcomes (TOTADO): a new model of training evaluation. Paper to be presented at the annual BPS Division of Occupational Psychology Conference, Brighton.

Braun, V. & Clarke, V. (2006). Using thematic analysis in psychology. *Qualitative Research in Psychology*, 3(2), 77–101.

Capsley, I., Pallot, J. & Levy, V. (2002). *From bureaucracy to responsive management: a comparative study of Local Government change*. Edinburgh: The Institute of Chartered Accountants.

Carter, A. J. (2015). Youth employment – the missing facts. *The Psychologist*, 28(6), 462–465.

Coles, B., Godfrey, C., Keung, A., Parrot, S. & Bradshaw, J. (2010). *Estimating the life-time cost of NEET 16–18 year olds not in education, employment or training*. Research undertaken for the Audit Commission, Department of Social Policy and Social Work and Department of Health Sciences.

Connexions Annual Report (2001 to 2002). *Putting young people first*. Downloaded on 23/01/2016 from: http://dera.ioe.ac.uk/10199.

Dearing Report (1997). *Higher education in the learning society*. London: HMSO. Downloaded on 23/01/2016 from: www.educationengland.org.uk/documents/dearing 1997/dearing1997.html.

Delebarre, J. (2016). *Apprenticeships policy, England 2015*, briefing paper. London: House of Commons.

Department for Children, Education, Life-long Learning and Skills (2000). *Numeracy learning pack*. Learning Wales. Report downloaded on 22/03/2016 from: http://learning. gov.wales/resources/learningpacks/mep/numeracy/numeracy-and-society/numeracy- in-education-the-uk-context/?lang=en.

Erikson, E. H. (1968). *Identity, youth and crisis*. New York, NY: W.W. Norton.

Harris, R., Simons, M. & Clayton, B. (2005). *Shifting mindsets: the changing work roles of vocational education and training practitioners*. Adelaide: Australian National Training Authority.

King, N. (2004). Using templates in the thematic analysis of text. In C. Cassell and G. Symon (Eds), *Essential guide to qualitative methods in organizational research*. London: Sage Publications Ltd.

Kirkpatrick, D. (1959). Techniques for evaluation training programmes. *Journal for the American Society for Training and Development*, 13(1), 3–9.

Kloep, M. & Hendry, L. B. (1999). Challenges, risks and coping in adolescence. In D. Messer & S. Millar (Eds), *Exploring developmental psychology*, 400–416. London: Arnold.

Macleod, D. & Hughes, M. (2006). *Apprenticeships: a review of recent policy and practice.* Coventry: The Learning and Skills Council.

Mirza-Davies, J. (2015). *Apprenticeship statistics: England.* London: House of Commons Library.

Rudd, M., Henderson, R., Usher, D. & Hawtin, M. (2008). *Rapid review of research on apprenticeships.* Coventry: The Learning and Skills Council.

Smeaton, D., Hudson, M., Radu, D. & Vowden, K. (2010). *Developing the employment evidence base.* The EHRC Triennial Review. London: Policy Studies Institute.

Spielhofer, T. & Sims, D. (2004). Modern Apprenticeships in the retail sector: stresses, strains and support. *Journal of Vocational Education and Training*, 56(4), 539–558.

Trust for London (2015). *London's poverty profile, 2009 to 2011.* Downloaded on 22/03/2016 from: www.londonspovertyprofile.org.uk/indicators/topics/work-and-worklessness/unemployment-by-borough.

8 Facilitating job search and employment opportunities for young people

Sue Gould and David Carew

Introduction

Young people come into contact with the United Kingdom (UK) government-run employment services usually because of a need for financial support while looking for employment, but also to access job-search support and advice about the labour market to help them in decisions they have to make in their journey towards work. In the course of this early experience the young person's views are being shaped by a number of factors that in time will determine their entry into the labour market and their subsequent success in work. The purpose of this chapter is to outline how young job seekers interact with the government's job-broking system, provided directly by the Department for Work and Pensions (DWP) or its contract providers. We will describe the type of support on offer from the DWP including an overview of psychology provision deployed through its network of work psychologists. The chapter also provides a discussion on the advantages of providing structure to the job search and application processes, including assessment of employment strengths and job entry. Before concluding, a description of support to disabled job seekers is provided. Finally, we will suggest how employment outcomes for young people might be further improved, looking towards future policy and how to advance the prospects for young people looking for work.

For the young person who is in the process of working out who they are, when they are also trying to gain a foothold in the job market, it can be a bewildering time. Exposure to work and the workplace is an important staging point in helping the individual begin a journey that not only defines many aspects of their future life but also provides an outlet for expression of interests, talent, skills and personality. Commonly, however, the young person may struggle with the question 'what can I do?' or, in a labour market context, 'who will employ me?' These questions in themselves are natural for the young person to ask as they represent the early stages of the decision-making that they will face in the context of their wider development. In this relatively early phase the young person has little available information on which to base their decisions so, essentially, it is a time of exploration and experimentation. These are the necessary steps in the formation of the young person's occupational identity.

Department for Work and Pensions and job seeker support

The DWP is responsible for welfare, labour market policy, pensions and child maintenance policy. It is the biggest UK public service department and administers the state pension and a range of working age, disability and ill health benefits to over 22 million people. Through Jobcentre Plus, the department provides job-search and employability-skills coaching, referral to work-focussed skills training and a range of programmes of support to help unemployed individuals into work. For those still in secondary school, the DWP aims to help young people make an effective transition to work, training or further study through the Jobcentre Plus Support for Schools initiative. Young people looking for work and wishing to claim a benefit can contact the department through a number of channels in order to speak with an employment adviser or to make a job search. Increasingly the department is developing its digital capability to enable more job seekers to access services online, including Universal Credit (an in- and out-of-work benefit) and Universal Jobmatch.

Jobcentre Plus employs work coaches, work psychologists, disability employment advisers and employment advisers helping individuals to find employment. Universal Credit (UC) was introduced in 2012. Universal Credit is a significant change programme and is being implemented in a phased way before full implementation in view of its scale. The implementation represents a significant development in helping people to make the transition to employment and, for those in work, to increase their prospects to earn more. The work coach delivery support model aligns with UC and is designed to support the Government's welfare reform agenda to reduce poverty by making work pay. Universal Credit promotes individual personal responsibility to actively seek work and increase earnings, while continuing to support those who need it. This support aims to help the individual to prepare better for work, to move more quickly into paid work and to support those in work to progress, increase hours and earn more. Those claiming UC have a Claimant Commitment. The work coach agrees a tailored set of activities in the Claimant Commitment with each job seeker. This commitment describes the job seeker's availability for work and their job-search objectives for securing work. The job seeker produces evidence of job search and the work coach takes into account each job seeker's individual circumstances and job-search needs to tailor the plan with the aim of increasing the likelihood of securing employment as quickly as possible.

The principle of UC is to provide a system that removes the risks of moving off social security benefit by helping to support the individual to make a successful transition to employment and make progress when in the labour market. A central tenet of UC is the concept that it should always be better to be in employment rather than receiving benefits. In other words, it should always be financially better for a person to earn an income than access financial support through the benefit system. One of the policy drivers for UC is to redefine access where obtaining benefits should be viewed as a temporary staging point and not a long-term situation for the individual or their family. Similarly, as the individual's income increases, either through higher hourly pay rates, the number of hours worked, or both, UC has the scope to taper the rate of benefit received. This has a number of advantages but, most importantly, it provides the possibility for the individual to increase their earnings with support whilst making employment transitions, either within their current job or to a new job. For young people this could be helpful support as they are perhaps more likely to make a number of job changes in relatively brief periods of time.

Employment policy and young people

Employment policy initiatives aim to offer opportunities to gain a deeper under-standing of self and personal preferences, interests and abilities in order to lay important foundations for future participation in the job market. While voli-tion and self-motivation are important to recognising and engaging with such opportunities, these processes are highly influenced by social, economic, and psy-chological factors. Furthermore, the presence of a health and disability issue and the timely access to employment advice, social and financial support will also play an influential role in determination of individual prospects in the labour market. Employment policies are designed to integrate the support available to a young person as they begin to make various life and institutional transitions contributing to a successful employment journey.

The youth employment situation in the UK improved significantly in 2015 and now is favourable in comparison with the European average (European Commission, 2016). Although youth unemployment is actually lower today when compared with the situation before the recession, concerns remain about young people who are not in education, employment or training (NEET). The age of compulsory participation in education and training has increased to 18 years in England. In Scotland and Wales, a scheme exists to incentivise 16 to 19 year olds from low-income families to stay on in education. The Developing the Young Workforce in Scotland also aims to better prepare young people aged 13 to 18 years for work.

In April 2017 the DWP introduced the new Youth Obligation. This provides support, tailored to the individual's situation, for young unemployed people (aged 18–21 years) making a new claim for UC. Where intensive support is appropriate this will include coaching and encouragement to take up an apprenticeship or other job offers quickly, and an opportunity to improve job search, job applica-tion and interview skills. Work coaches may also refer claimants to a range of interventions to address their specific barriers to work, including budgeting sup-port, basic skills, employability skills, sector-based work academies, traineeships, work experience and other initiatives and local provision. Progress and job goals are reviewed for those who remain unemployed with support provided through traineeships, sector-based work academies or work experience opportunities.

Additional support is also provided by DWP for young claimants aged 18–24 years who have a health condition or disability to include supported intern-ships and traineeships, access to work funding (for those aged 16–24 years) and a supported voluntary work experience programme for young people requiring additional support to work. There is also funding through the European Social Fund to help young people aged 14–17 years who are disadvantaged, or at risk of disadvantage, to enable them to participate and succeed in education or training with the aim of improving their employability. The Youth Employment Initiative (YEI) funding supports additional provision that complements existing government programmes to tackle youth unemployment and reduce the number of young people who are NEET, including innovative approaches, customised training, support and volunteering activities. Further, the Youth Engagement Fund Social Impact Bond investment is provided jointly by the DWP and other government bodies for specific target groups such as young lone parents, looked-after children and care leavers, carers, ex-offenders, those involved in gangs, and young people with learning difficulties and disabilities. Social impact bond projects include interventions and support that addresses the needs of these specific groups. One project, for example, is aimed at addressing barriers to participation in education and training for young ex-offenders or those at risk of offending, those in care or care leavers, and those with high levels of school absence.

Work psychology and Jobcentre Plus

Simply defined, work psychology in the context of Jobcentre Plus is about people and work, employment and the labour market. Work psychology and work psychologists play essential roles in helping Jobcentre Plus to be an effective organization in helping people who are looking for work or who are already in work and want to increase their earnings. Work psychologists in the DWP support work coaches, employers and job seekers, as well as service providers and employers, to facilitate employment progression for those wishing to enter or remain in work. This might include working with employees who require identification of work solutions to enable people to retain employment or to progress within work. The role involves helping job seekers with opportunities across the employment spectrum ranging from entry-level jobs to professional and leadership positions. Work psychologists may work with job seekers who are socially excluded, vulnerable or otherwise disadvantaged in terms of job finding, job getting and job keeping, and this can include customers with health conditions and disabilities.

The DWP work psychologists have a first degree in Psychology and/or a Master's degree in Occupational Psychology. All DWP work psychologists adhere to the rules, regulations and ethics of the British Psychological Society (BPS) and, as practitioner psychologists, they are expected to meet the conditions of registration set by the Health and Care Professions Council (HCPC), the statutory regulator for applied psychologists in the UK.

In the next section we look at how work psychology is applied in Jobcentre Plus to help meet the needs of young people looking for work, but first we examine some of the challenges facing the young job seekers as they begin the search for employment.

Young people's employment challenges

Young people who access Jobcentre Plus for employment support can have a variety of work-related needs and issues around health, disadvantage and vulnerability that may influence their ability to find and retain work. Work psychologists focus on offering support within complex employment situations (we offer a case study of this work later in the chapter). These circumstances will be explored before going on to highlight the tools and techniques employed to secure good employment outcomes for young people.

Different groups of young people face different challenges. Most policy initiatives focus on young people between the ages of 15 and 25 years (the so-called NEETs). However, the NEET group is heterogeneous as these young people all have differing backgrounds, ethnicities and skill levels, and a range of reasons for falling into the NEET category (Eurofound, 2012). Although, generally, the lower skilled are more likely to be NEET, graduates can also fall into this category.

The Prince's Trust *Youth Index* annually surveys over 2,000 young people aged between 16 to 25 years. The 2015 survey found that more than half of the unemployed young people were feeling anxious about everyday situations, with many avoiding meeting new people and struggling to make eye contact with those that they do meet. Those out of work or NEET are far more likely to demonstrate anxious behaviour, with 20% of all young people claiming that they regularly fall apart emotionally, rising to 33% if the young person is NEET. Being unemployed has a detrimental effect on a person's overall well-being, with anxious, stressful thoughts increasing significantly. Fifty-one per cent of jobless young people (The Prince's Trust Youth Index, 2015) say that anxiety has impacted on them being able to look for or find work, compared with 25% of all young people reporting anxiety. The ability to bounce back from a setback is a key attribute for young people as they make their transitions in life. This research shows that many young people often struggle to deal with issues arising from negative events, including losing a job. A third of young people in the survey note that being taught how to cope with setbacks helps them manage their anxiety.

The children's communication charity I CAN estimated that as many as one in ten young people leaving education may struggle to find employment and form relationships because of speech, language and communication difficulties that may have gone unrecognised in secondary education (I CAN, 2012). There is an established link between undetected communication difficulties, emotional and social difficulties that might result in a young person failing to use the unspoken rules of social communication (e.g., using inappropriate language, difficulty in asking for clarification and difficulty organising information). Young people with general or specific learning difficulties or social communication disorders (such as autism), or with mental health conditions, may also communicate in an unusual way. These communication difficulties can present specific challenges during the job selection process, especially if staff involved in the assessment of these young people are not fully aware of or are unfamiliar with the implications of some of these hidden disabilities.

In recent times there has been growing recognition that young people need to be ready for work when they leave education. In 2012, the Commission into Youth Unemployment by the Association of Chief Executives of Voluntary Organisations (ACEVO, the UK's leading network for Charity and Social Enterprise Leaders) highlighted the importance of young people acquiring the non-cognitive skills needed for work. This included developing communication skills, learning to relate to and to empathise with others and building self-confidence as critical skills to enable employment (including self-employment and enterprise). It is crucial that when young people are making choices and decisions about work they are supported by accurate advice and realistic previews about work. For example, if they are thinking of setting up in business this can mean long hours, initial low income and isolation from others, whilst it also may bring benefits of autonomy and control. All of these factors may have an impact on individual well-being.

The youth experience is recognised as an uncertain time when the young person is making decisions that may have long-term consequences in their lives. This can be a stressful time too. Pressures to meet expectations from various sources can place additional demands on young people, on their well-being and on their need for additional support. So the importance of guidance and opportunities to explore a number of options are essential to help job seekers make informed decisions affecting their futures. Some young people who come into contact with the Job Centre may initially be unsure about their employment options and have little or no experience of work. Others may have more knowledge of the job-search process or may have already worked, but now need to consider other opportunities due to job loss, end of a contract, or because they wish to pursue other employment opportunities with better pay and prospects. Whatever their reason, each individual may be at a different starting point. There may be underlying concerns about individual skills including job-search skills, the absence of work experience, uncertainty about employer expectations or a lack of knowledge about the kind of jobs available in their area. For some young people the transition to work or gaining another job may be a relatively smooth experience. However, for a number of young job seekers the process may require more support from the Jobcentre Plus work coach or other specialist staff such as a work psychologist. If a person has a disability or a health condition they may require specialist employment advice to enable access to employment opportunities.

In an ever-changing labour market the task of equipping young people with the necessary skills to enable them to fulfil their employment potential is critical. All too often the young person may struggle to get a foothold in the job market, placing them at risk of unemployment. Without the necessary support early on this risk increases, leaving them vulnerable to being left behind by their contemporaries and not fulfilling their labour market potential. The importance of making a successful transition through life stages is essential to gaining, remaining and advancing in employment. Any interruption at critical points in these stages risks eroding the life chances of the individual, affecting not just employment opportunities but savings and financial security in the longer term.

For young people a period of unemployment early in their working lives can have a long-term scarring effect, influencing future employment, life prospects, lifetime income, health status and job prospects (Bell & Blanchflower, 2009). It is important that career advice and guidance takes place before young people enter the labour market. Research shows that career indecision or a lack of realism at the age of 16 years frequently leads to NEET status later, with consequently lower earnings. Although educational systems differ around the world, Akkermans and colleagues (Akkermans, Nykanen & Vouri, 2015) highlight that young people who are more adaptable, better prepared and more competent with regard to their work and career are more likely to be successful in their School to Work Transitions (STWT). They propose that antecedents such as positive family influences, relevant education and work experience, and high core self-evaluations (such as self-efficacy) are important predictors of successful transitions regardless of context. Perceptions of efficacy are even more important when combined with active personal goal-setting (Nurmi, Salmela-Aro & Koivisto, 2002). These authors point out that personal goals can help focus energy and resources and develop strategies for dealing with this transition.

Mann (2012) highlights the importance of young people having early contact with employers, commenting that exposure to prospective employers at school can make a difference to the employment prospects of young adults. Just as early guidance and discussion about careers is important, so too is the necessity of gaining work experience; without this job searches can be inhibited, weakening progression to employment. Within this context, the Jobcentre Plus Support for Schools initiative aims to provide young people in secondary education with information and advice about the labour market, employer expectations, vocational routes into employment and work experience, allowing them to make well-informed decisions about their future career paths. In the next section we turn our attention to address the role and importance of work experience in the journey to employment.

The importance of work experience in job search success

A Chartered Institute of Personnel and Development report (CIPD, 2012) looking at how employers could be engaged in tackling youth employment highlighted that young people might need time to find their first job and might try different occupations and sectors before settling into a career. A further report, *Employers are from Mars young people are from Venus* (CIPD, 2013), highlighted that too many young people have a scattergun approach to applying for jobs (p. 23) rather than taking time to research where they want to work. These findings respond to the high volume of applications employers are required to process in response to a job vacancy, and the demotivating response for young people when they find that they are unsuccessful in gaining the job role. Lack of confidence was identified as an issue for many young people who find interview situations particularly stressful, as they have no prior knowledge of the workplace and often don't know how to talk about their skills or how to market themselves to a potential employer.

Gaining work experience fulfils the important function of validating the application of developing job search skills. The experience of looking for work experience and early job roles is a rehearsal for what may become a more settled role with an employer or enterprise, yet without effective job search skills this may be a vicarious experience. However, even unsuccessful attempts at work experience can offer a young person positive learning depending on their beliefs, attitudes and self-efficacy. Being present in an organization also provides an opportunity to experience the socialisation effects of the work environment. Experience of this process communicates important cues to the young person about organizational cultures, ways of doing things and developing communication skills through interaction with other workers. While there is no national programme for work experience directly aimed at young people, the positive impact workplace experience can have in increasing the chances of a young person finding a job is nonetheless acknowledged. Many employers (60% in the Higher Education Academy's UK Engagement Survey, UKES, 2015) place work experience as a significant or critical factor when making hiring decisions when there are a range of candidates holding the necessary academic or vocational qualifications. If current trends continue, work experience is likely to continue to rank highly in organizational recruitment decision-making and employment policy makers are likely to consider work experience measures as an important way of improving the employability of young people.

Work psychology interventions and support for young people

Work psychologists undertake activities in a number of areas to support young people to find work, either through direct interventions delivered individually or in group-work sessions. They may also try to build young people's capability in work with coaches, managers and service providers (e.g., case conferencing). Case conferences explore complex employment situations to identify specific interventions or work solutions to help job seekers progress towards employment. Case conferences can be themed and partners or employers invited to share ideas and solutions to help individuals with complex employment scenarios (such as health conditions or disabilities) to make progress towards employment.

Work psychologists work directly with young people using professional skills based on the theory and practice of occupational psychology to assess or clarify work goals. A group-work session for young people might involve helping them to consider more broadly their aspirations for the future and how work can facilitate these outcomes. Exercises using interviewing techniques look at assessing, for themselves and each other, skills, values, interests and work goals to focus on distance travelled and longer-term goals considering a job, a better job and their career (we describe this as *the ABC*). Young people develop action plans over these sessions to focus on the detailed knowledge that has started to emerge. Support involves identifying appropriate work solutions, developing effective job-seeking behaviours or enabling individuals to look ahead to manage their performance, social interaction and the impact of their health or disability in the workplace.

A work psychologist can conduct an in-depth employment assessment to help identify a job seeker's strengths and areas of difficulty in relation to their work goals, and to determine what support or adjustments might be helpful to enable the young person to perform well and sustain appropriate employment. Assessments are designed to offer support to work coaches assisting job seekers who are experiencing difficulty making progress in their job search, helping to identify strategies to help them move forward (e.g., developing an action plan). This could involve employment assessment and occupational guidance and the use of specific interviewing techniques or psychometric assessments to provide an objective view of the young person's capabilities.

Such interventions may involve several face-to-face meetings with a job seeker designed to offer support to move towards work. The work psychologist will help the job seeker to work through the difficulties associated with securing work and identify strategies towards achieving their goals. For example, developing tactics to perform better in an interview situation, to manage anxiety about a work-related issue, to agree realistic work goals and identify ways to manage their health condition or disability in the workplace. Three-way discussions between a work coach, job seeker and work psychologist can enable collaboration to agree workable solutions for the young person.

Identifying young people's employment strengths

Work psychologists in Jobcentre Plus apply a number of approaches and techniques to identify the skills and employment strengths of young people. For successful job search it is critical that the young person receives help to understand what they can offer an employer or an employment opportunity. Work psychologists develop work coaches by upskilling them to coach young people to conduct quality and effective job searches, to introduce them to the workplace or to help them to return more quickly to sustained employment.

In terms of employer assistance, work psychologists support young people to identify their skills and importantly how to demonstrate these skills during interview situations. Work psychologists make business cases to employers about the benefits of recruiting young people by highlighting the skills and motivation they bring to the workplace. For example, a work psychologist working with a service organization highlighted the skills a young person had developed in a series of presentations they delivered on a business course. Other business case examples include emphasising the advantages of building a diverse workforce by helping those with health conditions or disabilities to access employment through job analysis and matching, building talent pipelines, enhancing the employer brand and the cost effectiveness of developing their own staff.

Employment Assessment as a labour market intervention

Employment Assessment (EA) is a skills-based approach to help individuals, groups, organizations and societies with employment progression.

Employment Assessment is also a helpful workforce development tool to help organizations identify and support diverse talent and it therefore forms an important intervention enabling effective access and participation of young people in the labour market.

A key component of EA is the importance of the job–person interaction through an understanding of the job and building on a person's abilities (Birkin et al., 2004). The interaction approach has its roots in occupational psychology and work on conceptual models of disability and health, particularly in the United States of America (US). An important line of discussion in the US followed the introduction of three element analysis by Nagi (1991), identifying the individual, the environment and the individual–environment interaction as a dynamic process. As an interactive approach, EA forms a key role in helping individuals find, sustain, perform and progress well in employment, particularly for individuals with vulnerability, health conditions or employment issues.

Employment Assessment assists job seekers to make an informed decision about an appropriate and specific job (Meehan, Birkin & Snodgrass, 1998, p. 3). This can enable them, where appropriate, to obtain or retain a job, perform a job successfully or to progress or develop within a job. This process involves both helping the job seeker to gain information about the job (e.g., key tasks, responsibilities, competences and interpersonal skills) and assessing their potential to successfully perform in the job (Birkin et al., 2004). Employment Assessment involves a number of steps including interviews, feedback and action planning, and the use of, for example, aptitude tests, work samples and job trials in order to contribute to predicting potential job performance. Further, the EA approach aims to support the job seeker by enabling them to appreciate the assets they bring to a job, while at the same time addressing the challenges hindering them from making progress to sustainable work (Carew, Birkin & Booth, 2010, p. 30). Employment assets are a key concept in EA, referring to any factual information providing evidence about an individual's employability or employment potential.

Employment Assessment is relevant to the experiences of young people who have limited or no work history or experience, or where no job goal has been identified, or where the individual has a negative self-image and feels that employers will not hire them. Employment Assessment helps young people to develop job search skills, to identify and comprehend sources of information about jobs (such as job advertisements) and it also helps them to plan and follow through on activities that support job search (such as gaining feedback from employers). This approach can be particularly helpful to support young people with a disability or health condition requiring a work solution that will enable the individual to perform the job successfully, for example designing a bespoke memory aid for a young person with an attention issue or neurological condition.

A work solution is the minimum change that enables the individual to perform their job successfully. The need for a work solution arises when, for a reason associated with their health condition or disability, an individual is currently unable to perform the tasks of their job or achieve their job goal. Work solutions differ from adjustments as they are not subject to negotiation or based on the employer's perception of what may be reasonable. Work psychologists will work with individuals seeking employment and advise those providing job support to identify potential work solutions, helping them to visualise that it is possible to do the job and to build their belief that they can do the job and manage whatever need or issue that may arise in the workplace (Birkin et al., 2004; Birkin, Meehan & Carew, 2013).

The EA model focusses on identifying a job goal based on the actual demands or requirements of the job (often not evident from the job title). This process of task analysis supports the young person's decision-making process by helping them to decide if they have the skills and abilities to perform the job or what specific gaps they may need to address through skills training. This is also based on the premise that many job seekers do not appear to develop the belief that they can work until they have identified a job goal that is appropriate for them, highlighting the importance of self-efficacy. This belief is described as job search efficacy and is shown to relate to positive job search outcomes (Van Hooft & Born, 2012); work coaches help young people to build this belief.

At the core of EA is the importance of the interaction between the person and the job that is developed through the young person's understanding of the job and their individual abilities and aspirations. The EA approach can help individuals identify and comprehend sources of information about the job that will allow a young person to match what they feel they can and want to do. Useful job information can come from a range of sources (such as job descriptions and advertisements) as well as contacting employers directly to create opportunities to undertake work observations, placements or experience. Thus work psychologists support the young person to build an accurate picture of work by exploring the tasks and behaviours required in that specific job.

Work psychologists may also explore with the young person their work interests, employment assets, issues and needs, with the individual very much at the centre of the employment discussion. The aim of these discussions being to lead to employment progress. Exploring the relationship between the young person and the job will assist in identifying training needs, constraints, work solutions and accommodations. Importantly, the young person's beliefs about how they will manage work tasks and their health in an employment setting will influence their employment decision-making. The EA approach helps the young person develop a sense of self-efficacy by challenging self-defeating beliefs and attitudes about themselves and substituting realistic beliefs about their ability to act and make good decisions. The job seeker is helped to develop the working knowledge, life skills and resources they need to succeed and help them challenge themselves to take reasonable risks, while supporting them when they do. In this way the young person develops an understanding of their skills and interests through psychological assessment, careers information and discussion about skills developed through previous education, employment or personal pursuits and hobbies. Evidence suggests that job seekers who specifically planned when, where and how to perform their job-search activities report higher job search activities four months later (Van Hooft, Born, Troon, van der Flier & Blonk, 2005).

Job entry rehearsal or visioning is an important aspect of EA enabling the young person to look ahead, prepare and manage themselves effectively in the workplace. Work psychologists help the young person anticipate and predict how they would cope in the workplace and in specific situations. This enables those with a health condition (e.g., anxiety) to consider a previous task they found difficult to complete or stressful and to think through how they could manage the task differently. If an individual is currently unable to perform the tasks of their job or job goal they are helped to identify potential work solutions that would enable them to perform the job successfully by visualising that it is possible to do the job. Through this process the young person is building their belief they can do the job and manage their issues in the workplace.

Work psychologists are skilled practitioners and are an essential element in ensuring the outcomes from the EA approach can be implemented successfully or to guide further decision-making. Skills such as job analysis, building self-efficacy and using psychological assessment techniques are vital to help young people identify their employment strengths and needs.

Jobcentre Plus work psychologists also facilitate workshops with work coaches to help them conduct effective job search with their customers, helping them to enter or return more quickly to sustained employment. Workshops are evidence-based, exploring job search efficacy and other factors contributing to successful re-employment. This includes the principles of the *Act and Learn* approach (Birkin, Meehan & Carew, 2014), addressing job search quality as well as intensity (effort, duration and rate). The principles of Act and Learn aim to improve job search ability by aligning the job seeker closely with the job and employer requirements. This helps the young person investigate their own resources to gain the information needed to understand the jobs they are applying for and how they manage the process, decide priorities and organise their time. Setting goals helps job seekers to self-regulate their activities (Ouellette & Wood, 1998), making them more likely to persevere when setbacks occur (Latham & Locke, 1991). When setting goals, work coaches take account of a job seeker's strengths and development needs, encouraging early job search activities that will help the young person to learn from their interaction with employers. Importantly, these activities provide feedback that can be used in a supportive coaching approach to enhance the job seeker's on-going activities. A key concept in the literature is that job search is a self-regulated process where action and experience will lead to learning (Zimmerman, 2000). For example, job seekers will benefit from feedback about their job applications to help them analyse why these applications may not be successful and what can be done to develop them. It has been found that a higher-quality job-search process, including preparation of job-search tactics, collecting information about the contact, networking, researching the job, company and industry, predict higher follow-up job offers (Caldwell & Burger, 1998).

In the next section we will illustrate the use of some of these support processes in a young person's journey to employment.

Case study

The following case study illustrates an individual employment intervention conducted by a work psychologist.

A young inexperienced job seeker was referred by their work coach for a three-way employment discussion with a work psychologist. The job seeker had not worked since leaving school but was keen to secure paid employment and had undertaken some voluntary work in an office.

The work coach reported that they were finding it difficult to develop rapport and engage with the job seeker. During the interview the young person initially struggled to interact with the work coach and appeared reserved and withdrawn. The work psychologist used active listening skills to build rapport and establish trust with the young person who appeared to be both fearful and anxious. After seeking permission to explore these issues further, the work psychologist employed specific engagement and interviewing techniques to secure more rapid and effective engagement with the young person. For example, the job seeker was asked to consider job search activities where they were coping well and this helped to move things forward.

Subsequently the job seeker became more open, expressing their concern about being unable to secure work despite having had a couple of interviews for administrative jobs. Although they had achieved General Certificate of Secondary Education (GCSE) passes in English and Maths this was a disappointing outcome as they had expected to achieve passes in other subjects but unfortunately this did not happen. Furthermore, their peers had achieved more passes in different subjects and had been able to secure good jobs or had gone on to further study. The young person wasn't sure why the interviews they had undertaken had not resulted in a job offer. They were unsure of what they could do differently at interview that would lead to a successful job outcome. Their anxiety had grown and their self-confidence had decreased leading to an erosion of their belief that they could undertake a successful job search. A decision was made at this meeting that the work psychologist would help the job seeker to explore the nature of their anxiety to begin to identify what additional help they needed to take their job search forward.

Further sessions explored different work options, work values and outlined the challenges the young person was currently facing. The work psychologist helped the job seeker to explore and refine their job goals, identifying employment strengths and areas for development related to these job goals. This work identified the young person's employment interest to work in administration. Interviews highlighted strengths in work organisation, time management, accuracy and attention to detail and, in particular, they were interested in work involving spoken communication with others.

Through this process of occupational guidance, the job seeker was able to give further consideration to their possible career pathways and future plans. They remained interested in administrative work. However, their work values also indicated interest in having contact with people and a desire to do work that supported a community. The work psychologist facilitated further exploration of these specific interests enabling the job seeker to identify a range of opportunities in particular employment sectors. The young job seeker expressed that they would like to work as a receptionist, ideally in a community organization. They also decided to consider undertaking further vocational qualifications to enable them to achieve their longer-term ambition of working as a community worker. This targeted employment intervention helped them to make progress in their immediate job search as well as developing a more informed and realistic understanding of potential career opportunities.

Another session with the work coach and psychologist explored how the young person used their time and specifically how to organise job-search activities over the period of a week. The purpose was to help them to prioritise activities that would identify and describe the skills they had used in past projects at school and during sports activities. This approach was designed to help them to sell their skills to a potential employer in an interview situation. Further coaching over several sessions enabled the young person to plan and prepare for an interview situation. The work psychologist helped the job seeker to align their strengths closely with employer requirements in community organizations and to identify what an employer might be looking for in a successful job applicant.

However, the young person was still experiencing feelings of highs and lows and the work psychologist was able to draw on knowledge of anxiety and cognitive-behavioural techniques in order to support them when setbacks occurred. Specifically, some strategies were identified that could be used to support their job search activity and to build belief that they could retain focus even when feeling low or uncertain. For example, the job seeker could focus best on activity during the afternoon so they ensured that they built in regular slots to focus on job searching at the time when they were most effective.

These sessions continued over several months and the job seeker had several job interviews. After the interviews the work coach encouraged the young person to reflect on what went well and not so well in the assessment process to enable them to learn and develop their interview skills. The outcome of this process was that the job seeker managed to secure a job as a receptionist in a local business. It was explained to the job seeker that the work coach would be available for on-going support to help them retain the job and ensure sustainability of employment outcomes.

In the next section we outline the specific support available to young people with disabilities or chronic health conditions.

Supporting young job seekers with health conditions or disabilities

Specialist support is delivered to job seekers with disability or health conditions looking to find work, and to employers, helping them to retain individuals who are experiencing difficulties within their job due to a health condition or disability. Advice is also given to employers wishing to engage in recruiting job seekers that have particular issues to enable entry to employment. The help provided to employers might include training or other interventions to engage them in recruiting individuals who have complex problems and enable them to support young people's well-being at work. The next section will describe in more detail some of these interventions delivered by work psychologists and the approaches in these situations.

Working in partnership with work coaches

Work psychologists and work coaches working together are well placed to help the young job-seeker to identify and promote their employment strengths to a prospective employer. The work coach assesses each job seeker's needs and support requirements through a personalised coaching relationship, with the work coach retaining responsibility for the individual during their journey. This involves identifying challenges and offering advice and support to underpin the job-search process and helping to develop the skills the young person requires to find and retain work. The work coach role focusses on mentoring and setting job-search activities with job seekers to help them to plan and focus their job search as well as agreeing actions that will give them the best chance of finding work.

Work coaches undertake a range of interventions depending on job seekers' needs and at an appropriate time on their personalised journey. Interventions can include group information sessions, face-to-face interventions, action learning sets led by work coaches, or employer support with specific activities. Work coaches will have mixed case-loads of job seekers, supporting individuals across all age groups including young people. Specialist advisers will continue to support 16–17 year olds and there are specific initiatives for young people including work experience apprenticeships and the Youth Obligation (see pp. 132–133 of this chapter).

Recent developments have expanded the role of the work coach enabling them to tailor support based on each job seeker's needs. Thus work coaches are required to develop skills that will challenge, engage and support job seekers through delivering quality interventions to move them closer to or into work. Work coaches are supported in their role by a central learning and development team, which includes tailored support from the Department's work psychologists who offer a specialist service to support claimants, work coaches and their managers as well as employers and third-party external service providers. Work psychologists play a key role in building workforce capability, provision of quality assurance for training interventions, coaching and development, providing training and co-delivering training with work coaches to build their skills. All these activities aim to build job seekers' skills and task performance to achieve positive work outcomes. For example, skill development sessions for work coaches may include customer engagement and developing awareness of hidden disabilities that may be impacting on job-search activities (e.g., communication difficulties as mentioned on p. 134). Training will also help work coaches to be vigilant to individuals who may be struggling with job search because of a mental health issue such as anxiety and depression and who may need facilitated access to specific support. Learning, training and development aims to increase the competence and confidence of work coaches with the purpose of improving employment outcomes for young people.

Having looked in depth at the support that can be provided to young people to enter and maintain employment we will now consider the future focus of employment policy.

Future directions for youth employment policy

Countries wishing to make sustained economic progress rely heavily on high employment rates including the engagement of individuals considered economically inactive for whatever reason. Central to this objective is the availability of a skilled, productive and engaged workforce. As the fortunes of market sectors change so too does the availability of job opportunities. Therefore, employability skills become a key ingredient for workers wishing to remain in or progress in work, or, in the case of young people, to secure their first or next job.

Policies designed to address the needs of young people present choices that are informed by a number of important factors relating to the prevailing economic climate such as the need for particular skills where skills gaps exist in particular sectors, and the opportunity cost of pursuing a particular employment direction (e.g., educational and training costs). In general, labour market policy is concerned with driving up the skill levels and capabilities of all workers in order to give the country a competitive advantage through having a workforce that is highly skilled enabling competition with others in the world market.

A recognised challenge in youth employment policy is the task to increase young people's skills to enable entry and progression in the labour market. However, young people can face the age-old dilemma of not being able to gain entry to the job market as they may not have the necessary skills and experience, even if this is on the journey to finding a job that matches all of the individual's requirements for the future. In the context of change arising from transformations of the support available to young people there is an emerging focus on either taking steps to build skills, or taking up employment opportunities to gain useful work experience. This presents a choice to young people as there are really only two routes if state support is to be accessed, namely, take a job opportunity or commit to a structured programme of learning to build skills to enable entry into employment. In a rebalancing of welfare support for young people, the UK government is essentially contracting with young people through specifying an obligation whilst providing an offer of support that could combine a blended approach of earning and learning to help improve employment prospects and long-term outcomes. Recent developments in policy encourage young people to take 'Saturday' and summer jobs to build their skills and help develop their employment evidence that they can use when applying to employers in the future.

While the majority of young people in receipt of *Jobseeker's Allowance* (an out-of-work benefit for unemployed people) leave the benefit at around six months, approximately 15% do not, with an increased risk of experiencing long-term unemployment. Of course, a policy that does not address the root causes of youth unemployment is likely to have limited impact. Active measures that address and develop specific skills for employment and skills development strategies are worthy of consideration in labour market policy development for the UK and other countries if they are to help more young people into, and progress in, employment. Akin to what would be the equivalent in disease prevention in public health, employment policy measures aimed at young people need to reduce missed transitions from education to a successful entry to the labour market. In recent times the policy focus has shifted to early intervention from the age of 12 years in order to reduce the risk of worklessness taking hold. This is work that has recently started through engagement with the school system (the Jobcentre Plus Support for Schools Initiative), with employment advisers going into schools to help young people understand the available range of employment and training opportunities and to better appreciate what is expected of them from employers as they enter the world of work. Whilst a number of factors can influence young people, the principle of reducing risk of unemployment at an early age is intuitively logical, provided the approach is underpinned by appropriate support and interventions.

Fostering enterprise and self-employment

Economic growth is essential for job creation and, while government and industry can act as a stimulus, the individual can also play a vital part in bringing forward their own ideas, contributing to generating new businesses and job creation. Young people are an important resource for any economy and encouragement to be enterprising is essential to drive current and future economic performance. In the UK efforts to encourage young people to start businesses are an important feature in the task of diversifying the economy to broaden the base of economic activity and to promote job growth. Therefore, helping young people early in the formative phase of their education is an ideal place to start by enabling young people to develop the skills for enterprise. While self-employment may not be an option or even a preference for every young person, for those who show a desire to create new business opportunities employment policy should do what it can to enable this to happen.

Recession-proofing future careers

The occurrence of economic recessions or downturns is a recognised feature of the economic cycle that has significant consequences for labour markets. The impact on young people can be disproportionately severe, particularly in circumstances where unemployment rates rise. Economic recovery may take time and where some jobs permanently disappear this will cut-off entry points for young people. With lower skills and experience compared with other workers seeking employment, young people are vulnerable to the risk of not getting started in the job market. The net impact on the economy is the loss of a potential workforce with migration a common response in times of high unemployment as young workers look elsewhere to secure employment.

The underutilisation of young people in the labour market can lead to increased poverty, higher social costs, social exclusion and a cycle of intergenerational worklessness (ILO, 2009). Many young people attempting to enter the job market during times of a recession where labour demand is low are well aware of the challenges they face. Consequently, this can limit the individual's scope for longer-term planning as the immediate choices may limit options for career exploration, with young people perhaps having to take on less secure work roles or types of jobs they would not have chosen if other opportunities were available. However, the latency effect of having to defer important career planning and development is often not seen until years later after a recession. Early choices will have implications for individuals' employability and earnings potential leading to diminished opportunities to build up savings for independence, housing and financial security in retirement. Youth employment policies must therefore be a key consideration in the broader economic and workforce planning efforts to ensure the needs of young people are taken into account if their future careers are not to be put in jeopardy.

Summary and conclusions

In this chapter we have introduced a number of concepts that impact and influence the job search process and outcomes for young people. Critical to whether young people get a foothold in the labour market is the importance of early access to employment assessment, advice and tailored support to help the job seeker to carry out job search independently (or with support where necessary). Successful navigation of the labour market and the achievement of a position where the job seeker can become self-sufficient are clear goals in this process. However, crucially, the ability to adapt as changes occur in the macro-economic situation and prevailing labour market conditions will depend on the employment strengths the young person can offer the employer. Without recognition and attention to these factors there is a risk that the young person has a maladaptive working experience. The consequences for their life chances and risk of long-term unemployment and economic inactivity increases the longer they are detached from the job market. For young people with low skills or for those who have disabilities or health conditions the risk is greater and requires active policy measures to help ensure these risks are diminished. Interventions derived from the science and practice of work psychology and psychologists in the DWP provide an important resource to young people who are beginning the process of job searching.

Labour markets are not static entities, and as conditions change the rise and fall of economic fortunes affect the supply and demand for labour. For the young job seeker, getting to grips with the job-search process early is essential, as is having access to good employment advice to inform the young person's decision-making. Also of importance is access to social and peer support that can help protect against setbacks and build effective coping strategies. The possession of effective job-search skills as well as the ability to use them is recognised in the success individuals have in gaining work, or not. In the area of policy development future labour market strategy will undoubtedly reflect lessons from current and planned policy responses. Adaptive responses at the individual level are likely to have more success but only if we are able to equip the individual with the prerequisite knowledge, skills and attributes. Above all is the importance of belief in the job seeker and those who help them that employment is possible, and without this policy measures are likely to have low impact. The design of future employment programmes needs to take account of the need to build belief and employment strengths to give individuals the best possible chance of being successful in work and to progress in the labour market over the life course.

References

Akkermans, J., Nykanen, M. & Vouri, J. (2015). Practice makes perfect? Antecedents and consequences of an adaptive school-to-work transition. In J. Vuori, R. Blonk and R. H. Price (Eds), *Sustainable working lives. Managing work transitions and health throughout the life course*. Dordrecht: Springer.

Association of Chief Executives of Voluntary Organisations (ACEVO) (2012). *Commission into Youth Unemployment*. London: Association of Chief Executives of Voluntary Organisations. Downloaded on 14/07/2016 from: www.acevo.org.uk/publications/youth-unemployment-crisis-we-cannot-afford.

Bell, D. N. F. & Blanchflower, D. G. (2009). *What should be done about rising unemployment in the UK?* Stirling Economies Discussion Paper 2009-06. Stirling: University of Stirling. Downloaded on 11/10/2016 from: http://dspace.stir.ac.uk/bitstream/1893/856/1/SEDP-2009-06-Bell-Blanchflower.pdf.

Birkin, R., Haines, V., Hitchcock, D., Fox, D., Edwards, N., Duckworth, S., Gleeson, R., Navarro, T., Hondroudakis, A., Foy, T. & Meehan, M. (2004). *Can the activity matching ability system contribute to employment assessment? An initial discussion of job performance and a survey of work psychologists' views*. Loughborough: Loughborough University Institutional Repository. Downloaded on 03/10/2017 from: https://dspace.lboro.ac.uk/dspace-jspui/bitstream/2134/908/1/PUB207.pdf.

Birkin, R., Meehan, M. & Carew, D. (2013). *Employment and wellbeing: a toolkit for work coaches and employment advisers*. London: Department for Work and Pensions.

Birkin, R., Meehan, M. & Carew, D. (2014). *Maximising employment outcomes in Universal Credit*. London: Department for Work and Pensions.

Caldwell, D. F. & Burger, J. M. (1998). Personality characteristics of job applicants and success in screening interviews. *Personnel Psychology, 51*(1), 119–136.

Carew, D., Birkin, R. & Booth, D. (2010). Employment, policy and social inclusion. *The Psychologist, 23*, 28–31.

Chartered Institute of Personnel and Development (CIPD) (2012, May). *Engaging employers in tackling youth unemployment: discussion paper*. London: Chartered Institute of Personnel and Development. Downloaded on 21/04/2016 from: www.cipd.co.uk/knowledge/work/youth/unemployment-report.

Chartered Institute of Personnel and Development (CIPD) (2013, April). *Employers are from Mars young people are from Venus: addressing the young people/jobs mismatch*. London: Chartered Institute of Personnel and Development. Downloaded on 21/04/2016 from: www.cipd.co.uk/knowledge/work/skills/jobs-mismatch-report.

European Commission (2016). *Country Report United Kingdom*. Brussels: European Commission. Downloaded on 10/07/2016 from: http://ec.europa.eu/europe2020/pdf/csr2016/cr2016_uk_en.pdf.

European Foundation for the Improvement of Living and Working Conditions (Eurofound) (2012). *NEETs, young people not in employment, education or training: characteristics, costs and policy responses in Europe*. Loughlinstown: European Foundation for the Improvement of Living and Working Conditions. Downloaded on 21/04/2016 from: www.eurofound.europa.eu/publications/report/2012/labour-market-social-policies/neets-young-people-not-in-employment-education-or-training-characteristics-costs-and-policy.

I CAN (2012). *Speech, language and communication in secondary age pupils*. London: I CAN. Downloaded on 18/04/2016 from: www.ican.org.uk.

International Labour Organization (ILO) (2009). *World of work report: the global crisis and beyond*. Geneva: International Institute for Labour Studies.

Latham, G. P. & Locke, E. A. (1991). Self-regulation through goal setting. *Organisational Behaviour and Human Decision Processes, 50*(2), 212–247.

Mann, A. (2012). *It's who you meet: why employer contacts at school make a difference to the employment prospects of young adults*. London: Education and Employers Taskforce. Downloaded on 21/04/2016 from: www.educationandemployers.org/media/15052/its_who_you_meet_final_report.pdf.

Meehan, M., Birkin, R. & Snodgrass, R. (1998). Employment, disability and equal opportunities. *Psychologist, 11*(2), 56.

Nagi, S. Z. (1991). Disability concepts revised: implications for prevention. In A. M. Pope & A. R. Tarlov (Eds), *Disability in America: toward a national agenda for prevention*. Washington, DC: National Academy Press.

Nurmi, J., Salmela-Aro, K. & Koivisto, P. (2002). Goal importance and related achievement beliefs and emotions during the transition from vocational school to work: antecedents and consequences. *Journal of Vocational Behavior, 60*(2), 241–261.

Ouellette, J. A. & Wood. W. (1998). Habit and intention in everyday life: the multiple processes by which past behaviour predicts future behaviour. *Psychological Bulletin, 125*(1), 54–74.

The Prince's Trust Youth Index (2015). *The Prince's Trust Macquarie Youth Index*. Downloaded on 18/04/2016 from: www.princes-trust.org.uk/Youth-Index-2015.pdf.

UK Engagement Survey (UKES) (2015). *Students' perceptions of skill development.* York: UK Engagement Survey, Higher Education Academy.

Van Hooft, E. A. J. & Born, M. Ph. (2012). Intentional response distortion on personality tests: using eye-tracking to understand response processes when faking. *Journal of Applied Psychology*, 97(2), 301–316.

Van Hooft, E. A. J., Born, M. Ph., Troon, W. T., van der Flier, H. & Blonk, R. W. D. (2005). Bridging the gap between intentions and behavior: implementation intentions, action control, and procrastination. *Journal of Vocational Behavior*, 66(2), 238–256.

Zimmerman, B. J. (2000). Attaining self-regulation: a social cognitive perspective. In M. Boekaerts, P. R. Pintrich & M. Zeidner (Eds), *Handbook of self-regulation*. San Diego, CA: Academic Press.

9 Focussing on young people's future work

Angela J Carter

Youth employment is a real social issue

Today, it is difficult for young people to get a good job and youth employment remains an issue in most developing countries around the world. This book has explored the issues of youth employment from multiple perspectives: national and international labour information, the voices of young people themselves, government agencies, educational and organizational views. There is agreement that young people's futures in the workplace are uncertain and, unless steps are taken to resolve these issues, the result will be severe national skills shortages in the future. The long transitions from education to work currently experienced by many young people lengthens their adolescence by delaying any notion of independence when they are able to build their own futures. Being unable to secure work during these transitions brings strain to families, often leading young people into unhappy and dependent relationships with family or the state, all of which has a high cost to society (see Chapter 1 for more information). Therefore, youth unemployment (and underemployment) is a serious issue of our time requiring urgent attention as it affects every part of our society.

As we end our enquiry there are 476,000 young people (aged between 16 and 24 years) unemployed in the UK (ONS, November 2018) and 783,000 not in education, employment or training (NEET) (ONS, August 2018). These are difficult figures to understand in comparison with previous data as the school leaving age has been raised and the numbers in higher education (many of whom are in or seeking part-time work) continue to grow. More instructive are the estimates of the value of human capital (from 2004 to 2017) (ONS, October 2018) accounting for people's skills, qualifications and earning over a working lifetime. In cash terms the stock of human capital in the UK grew by 1.8%, but by removing the effects of inflation human capital actually fell by 0.8%, reflecting slower growth in earnings relative to inflation. Usually, the value of human capital is higher in younger workers as they have more working years ahead of them. However, recent data (2011 to 2017) confirms young people's inequities of employment and development with the average stock of human capital for individuals aged over 35 years growing by 7.0% compared with only 3.6% for those under 35 years. These facts were validated by an ONS Forum (2018, October) held to explore *Young people and intergenerational fairness* and discussing policy related to earnings, housing, employment, skills, career progression and poverty, and how they relate to older generations.

It is interesting to compare reactions to levels of youth unemployment in different countries. National economies benchmark themselves with each other and the UK position is that youth unemployment is no better or worse than that in other European countries (see Chapter 8). However, there is recognition that the number of young people not in work is worse now than in the pre-recession (2008) period, with particular concern for young people who are not in employment, education or training (NEET). Therefore, youth employment would be best explored by examining both unemployed and NEET populations together, giving a truer picture of the issues facing young people in their transitions from education to work. However, it is important to note that by using these descriptions young people are being classified into groups with perceived undesirable characteristics, many of which are quickly picked up by employers resulting in their continued exclusion from job-selection processes.

The human capital data revealing the under-representation of young people in the workplace are rarely acknowledged or discussed, even in the diversity literature. Even the term *journey from education to work* implies there is an endpoint; that everyone will gain a job. But, with the world unemployment rate standing at around 8%, this may not be a realistic goal for everyone unless society finds ways of increasing employment opportunities specifically for young people. While some attention has been given to address issues facing young people in the UK, Europe and the US, there are significant issues for young people finding work in the Middle East, North Africa and Asia (the MENA counties). Chapter 2 offers a more detailed description of the global issues of youth unemployment.

Early chapters of this book (specifically Chapters 3 and 4) explore the issues young people are facing trying to gain employment after leaving education. We hear the voices of young people looking for work. These studies clarify that it is not a minority of young people who are finding it difficult to transition into work but a majority. It is not only those who are NEET or have few educational qualifications that are experiencing difficult transitions, students with postgraduate qualifications both within the UK, Europe and Asia find it difficult to move into employment. Therefore, an extended education no longer offers young people protection against unemployment and serves to create mismatches between young people's work aspirations and the knowledge, skills and abilities (KSAs) employers are seeking. Further, the longer separation between education and work leaves teachers, and sometimes parents, lacking clear understanding of the needs of the workplace.

While these problems are frequently treated as an individual issue (focussing in on what is wrong with the young person), the larger issues of succession planning in organizations and skill loss to national economies likely to hamper future growth and development are rarely considered. In fact, what is remarkable is the lack of attention youth unemployment (and underemployment) receives in daily life, and in discussion and debate in the media and political spheres. For example, a slight increase in the overall employment figures (16 to 64 years) is often heralded by politicians and the media as economic growth, with little concern given to the disadvantages young people are facing in the workplace that will influence everyone's futures (see *BBC News*, 2018).

So why is the important matter of excluding young people from the workplace so rarely discussed? First, this is not a new issue that has just been discovered and, while many commentators describe the rise in youth unemployment having occurred since the recession in 2008, evidence presented in Chapter 1 (p. 23) suggests that, in the UK at least, this has been a growing trend over several decades. Second, getting sufficient young people into the workplace is a complex problem to explore, investigate and to which to apply appropriate interventions, involving issues of population change, education and economic prosperity, along with significant societal, cultural and attitudinal differences that vary between nations. This a complex and multi-faceted problem (often described as a wicked problem) (Blackman, Greene, Hunter, McKee et al., 2006) and therefore unlikely to have a single or simple solution. Further, the persistent issues of youth employment are a shared problem across most developed countries of the world. Sadly, the international commonality of youth unemployment tends to downgrade the importance attached to finding workable solutions. Governments (and employers) look at benchmarking data comparing their situation with that of others, concluding that if their position is much the same as others it is not such a big issue and hence the reporting, awareness-raising and significance of the problem decreases.

But the effects of unemployment are more severe for younger people who are more likely to suffer from poor well-being than those in other age groups (see Chapter 4 for a more detailed discussion). Some are unable to complete their journey from education to work or are taking high-risk atypical job roles being unable to find full-time work. Unemployed and underemployed young people face a double disadvantage when unable to use or continue to develop the KSAs gained during their education. Without work, or with only limited skilled work, these abilities will decline and will eventually be lost. Further, the young person's self-esteem, identity formation and resilience are challenged by unemployment and underemployment, leaving them less able to cope with uncertain futures. Employers meeting young people at this stage will be unsure of what they can offer their company and, in a majority of cases, are likely to choose to employ a more experienced worker. Therefore, many young people find it hard to get a job where they can flourish and grow, and this experience may scar them for life.

The aim of this book is to keep the debate fresh about the issues young people are facing to find good work, thus maintaining the need to develop solutions on the national agenda. Further, it is critical to highlight the important role employing organizations have in enabling young people to maintain and develop their skills by offering good quality work experiences. This chapter will build on the positive interventions described in Chapters 5 to 8, exploring actions needed to address youth unemployment, describing research identifying the benefits of employing young people, providing an overview of useful psychological concepts that will aid interventions to get more young people into good work roles and offering some simple advice to employers and young people and their families.

Actions to improve youth unemployment and underemployment

As previously mentioned, the issues young people are facing gaining access to good work are unlikely to have one clear solution. A key feature of this book has been to explain the complexity of the issues young people face from educational, economic, political and social perspectives. Therefore, any intervention must be multi-faceted, involving integrated actions by all key stakeholders who do not see the root cause of the problem being the failings of one party (e.g., young people, education or government). It is particularly important that policy makers encourage employers to ensure young people are well represented in the workforce by generating more entry-level work roles and developmental pathways enabling young people to gain more skills and experience to develop their human capital.

Taking a world view of the varying national labour markets, the first major step that will support youth employment is the move from an informal to a formal work economy. Those working in the informal economy will "fail to adhere to the established institutional rules or are denied their protection" (Feige, 1990, p. 990), often being self-employed or earning money from casual work rather than being paid a wage by an employer. Such work is associated with emerging economies and is unregulated, offering poor working conditions, little stability for the worker (Gereffi, 1999) or growth. However, with goods and service supply chains crossing country borders, products (such as clothing or computers) are often produced first in informal economies before being imported into more regulated economies. Further, while young people wish to secure work within a formal economy, it is clear from our earlier discussion that globalisation and mobile technologies are encouraging the emergence of informal economies (for example, using zero-hours contracts or the gig economy) within established formal economies, continuing to sustain these less stable forms of employment. Therefore, with a majority of employers preferring experienced workers, this pushes young job seekers into risky atypical work that uses only a few of their KSAs. While in these job roles the young people are gaining work experience but employers often consider these skills to be unsuitable for their work sector and this continues young people's exclusion from more stable and developmental work roles. Evidence suggests (Calvard, Carter & Axtell, 2008) that atypical work enables the development of valuable transferable skills and abilities associated with self-reliance, flexibility, change orientation and resilience. Therefore, it is important to present evidence to employers of the benefits of atypical work experience and how this can translate into valuable strategic organizational development when employing young people.

The debate about access to the labour market is often referred to as the notion of *employability* (see CIPD, 2016), i.e., the overall success of an individual in the labour market, spanning different job roles, modes of employment and even multiple careers (p. 2). The CIPD study (2016) surveyed 1,014 line managers and 1,078 Human Resource practitioners, gathering opinions from a range of people in employment and unemployment. Findings suggest employers have a narrow conception of employability, being a feature of individual characteristics rather than a result of external factors (such as macro-economic changes) in the supply and demand for skills. This conception emphasises the power employers hold as gatekeepers of employment and opportunities for career enhancement, while at the same time limiting the range of skills available to their organization.

The CIPD researchers conclude that both employers and workers need to appreciate the dynamic interplay of employability where both parties should be working together to develop competitive advantage. Evidence such as that presented by the CIPD is vital to change hearts and minds of employers to increase entry-level job roles. But the disadvantage of distilling research findings to simple take-home messages tends to encourage the categorisation of "young people" into a perceived homogenous group. Young people are certainly not all alike, differing on dimensions such as age, education and socio-economic background, with different experiences of life events, migration, parental and social support. These factors will lead the young person to have varying levels of self-esteem and resilience and to be at different stages of identity (personal and occupational) formation. However, one thing all young people share is a wish to have the chance to be treated as individuals and to develop and thrive. Next, we will look at some of the facilitators of work for young people.

What helps young people to get a job?

There are some solutions and interventions that can assist young people with job seeking and building their self-esteem, enabling them to be more successful in their transition from education into work. Chapters 4 to 8 explore interventions by schools, employers and national agencies, offering insights into how the tide of youth unemployment can begin to be arrested.

Summarising from these chapters, several facilitating factors emerge, often working in combination, that will help young people to make a successful transition into good employment.

Building a longer-term perspective of work

A critical factor supporting youth employment is employers who are looking ahead to the needs of their future workplace (e.g., 10 years from now) and are considering the changes that need to happen now in order to sustain productivity and service over time. Evidence presented in Chapter 7 (and in the next section) suggests that enlightened employers, appreciating the need for a diverse workforce including young people, are taking a long-term view of developing KSAs within their workforce. Such strategies will encourage the employment of young people and challenge practices of employing "more of the same" when it comes to recruiting new workers. Critical for the success of such activities is the provision of support and development for staff and management who will be supporting the young workers.

Bringing education closer to work

Young people are more likely to be successful in securing work when there is greater connection between their education and the workplace; both in terms of specific skills being taught and direct links between employers and education (Breen, 2005). Countries with low youth unemployment (e.g., Austria, Denmark, Japan and Switzerland) have close relationships between education and work, encouraging greater clarity in career planning, goal setting and proactive career behaviours. This trend is noted in Chapters 6 and 7, reinforcing the need for young people to have early contact with the workplace and employers, beginning as early as 12 years of age.

Why so young? Transitions from education to work start well before job search begins with young people making complex choices of educational subjects and pathways while they themselves are undergoing immense personal development. Should these choices be based on matching or liking for the educational subject, their ability to work with these concepts, or the availability of work in these areas? How young people make these decisions and who supports them in this process is critical to this dilemma because the young people themselves have little or no prior information about the workplace to base their decisions upon. Hence young people need to receive workplace information, as young as possible and from a number of different sources but, principally, from employers. Such information, suitably interpreted (by work coaches or government advisers, see Chapters 6 and 8) will enable young people to develop educational choices and focussed job-search activities more likely to produce actual jobs. Such developmental activities could become regular activities within the school curriculum if there were close contacts with employers willing to engage with young people and act as coaches, mentors and role models.

A strong example of bringing education closer to work was described in Chapter 6, with a strategic activity of a community college to engage their pupils from an early age with local business, not just through occasional talks and visits but to embed these activities within an on-going coaching framework, bringing young learners and workers together to explore what work is really like and how decisions being made at school can open (and close) career pathways in the future. For example, talking through a visit to a law firm and discussing the training commitment of such work with a worker (rather than an educator) can inspire a young person to see such a career as a preferred future or to disregard the idea completely. Either way, valuable decisions are being taken that will provide the motivation for the young person to work hard to follow their chosen path.

In particular, for those living outside cities, it is important to be aware of local work opportunities and this is an area that schools could well invest in to develop more work-experience opportunities for pupils. This is critically important for those in rural areas where the number of work opportunities are fewer and longer distances need to be travelled to gain experience. Strengthening social networks to bring young people into contact with work opportunities is another important factor that will assist young people into rewarding jobs. Further, the ability of young people to appreciate their value in the workplace and an awareness of the KSAs they bring are vital for every young person regardless of their educational background. But, too often the development of employability skills has featured in the education of academic achievers and Chapter 3 describes how important it is that those with minimal education and skills appreciate job search and job information in order to make informed choices about the work that they are seeking, while also stopping them falling into the insecurities of the informal economy.

Key to these activities are enlightened employers keen to engage with young people who do not see work readiness as an educational activity. Companies have much to gain from meeting young people early in their transitional journey. They get a feel for the young person's KSAs, seeing if they match the company culture. Evidence suggests that some employers 'get' the value of working with young people and others do not (e.g., Carter, 2016). With only 25% of organizations in the UK (SKOPE, 2012) employing under 24 year olds, many more companies need to appreciate the value young people can bring to the workplace. Clearly it is necessary to reinforce the business case for employing a diverse workforce including young people, emphasising how this develops the company image or brand to be attractive to young job seekers and consumers and to reinforce the economic value of developing an internal workforce as opposed to attracting expensive experienced workers.

Offering feedback to develop effective job-search strategies

Employers play a vital developmental role by giving feedback to young job seekers about what they did well, and not so well, in their job-application process. Accurate feedback about how a young person is perceived by others in the workplace allows individuals to change and adapt their behaviours and develop more successful strategies in the future. Chapter 8 outlined the specialist work that work coaches and work psychologists do to assist unemployed young people to gain access to work. However, this support work is needed because employers don't offer sufficient or appropriate feedback. In a busy workplace some employers may feel there is no time to offer feedback to young people and, with a large number of applicants usually applying to any advertised job role, this is often considered an unnecessary activity. However, recruiters frequently note how many unsuitable applications are received or, increasingly over the last years, they ask professionals like myself to help them to attract young applicants as "young people no longer apply for our jobs anymore". With today's young people being well networked and connected they will often avoid applications to employers where their peers have had poor recruitment experiences or no feedback. So, while feedback can be considered a time-consuming activity, there are positive benefits of feedback for employers who want to recruit suitable applicants for entry-level roles. Further, companies with a strategy to recruit and develop young workers often have specialist recruitment staff with expertise in working with young people to achieve successful recruitment.

Providing support for young people

A number of agencies have described support activities to enable young job seekers to gain work. Youth workers, work coaches, work psychologists and educators are all seeking ways to enable individual young people to appreciate their strengths and career competencies (e.g., see Chapter 6 for more detail) while developing resilience and adaptability in the face of setbacks in their job-search activities. The level of support offered to young people will vary according to their needs (see Chapters 3 and 8 for examples), however most agencies agree it is critical to have the young person centrally involved in decision-making and to focus on their preferred job role rather than the vaguer approach of "just finding a job". With specific focus on job roles the young person can imagine for their future motivation to continue with education and skills development, which will be maintained to purposely achieve their goal. Further, such attention will reduce unfocussed job applications that are unlikely to be successful.

Developing specific work roles for young people

Enlightened employers offering young people early work experience will see individual aspirations grow through holiday job roles and work secondments during higher education. This saves companies thousands of pounds in advertising and recruitment costs, maintaining a pipeline of new talent that can be called upon as company needs change and growth rises. This also means that employers are much more aware of what young people have to offer at the various stages of their educational journey and are able to match work opportunities at the right level to utilise young people's KSAs. Such activities will build young people's confidence and self-esteem as they are doing a job that they feel is a good fit with their abilities.

Changing attitudes and offering role models for young people to talk to is one thing, but without actual entry-level job roles there will be no vacancies for young people to take. Chapter 7 describes the intensive work undertaken within a local authority where managers had little resource to develop new work roles but were desperate for additional resource to get things done. By carefully analysing apprenticeship roles that would provide additional support to departments with high workloads and provide additional support for busy managers to introduce new work roles changes were made and roles created. However, there was further work required before such roles were advertised, both within the organization and with the local community, to support staff and attract suitable applications. Such communication processes are detailed and time-intensive, involving activities designed to change ways of working and attitudes towards the work of the organization. Therefore, not only must companies develop new entry-level roles and developmental activities to support skill growth within those roles, but there must also be an understanding of the need to expand these roles for young people. Organizations successful in their recruitment of young people will have a strategy for growth and development that is adequately resourced and regularly evaluated in order to maintain and develop activities that will continue to provide suitable young talent.

Adopting a psychological focus to increase work roles for young people

There is a developing understanding that aspects of work psychology such as coaching, goal-setting, development of career-related competencies and resilience can increase the effectiveness of these transitional interventions to bring young people into entry-level roles. Work psychologists and other professionals need to assist employers to understand what constitutes a good work role. Jobs that provide variety, challenge and skill use along with support and development will be fulfilling for the young person; rather than simple repetitive roles that will result in underemployment of their skills leading to eventual skill loss.

Successful interventions like those described in Chapters 6 and 7 are multi-facetted, involving changes in the way people work and attitudes associated with work. In order to drive and maintain change successfully these interventions had strong psychological focus in their planning, execution and evaluation. There are two critical aspects to young people's successful transition from education to employment. First, and most crucial, are employers who are willing to engage with young people and work with them to develop their potential skills and abilities to deliver developmental and fulfilling work experiences. Second, greater attention needs to be paid to the support work psychology can offer to tailor job design, selection, assessment and individual and organizational development to bring out the best work from young people.

Critical among psychological skills is the ability to thoroughly evaluate an activity or intervention from multiple perspectives, feeding back this information to the various stakeholders so that activities are modified, changed and developed. This was shown clearly in Chapter 7 when the local authority realised that a re-employment strategy was required to enable young workers to be offered further job roles at the end of their apprenticeship programme. Evaluation revealed this was something concerning supervisors and managers as well as the young people themselves. Such an approach is more likely to sustain an intervention and avoid a short-term response like "we tried this and it did not work".

With ageing workforces and a reducing number of young skilled workers to support growing retirement populations these activities make good economic sense. But at present there is disconnection between industry's focus on short-term gains and building for longer-term futures with young people playing a significant part. Broader culture-change interventions are required to encourage organizations to change their recruitment strategies. For example, policies encouraging employment quotas of young people (e.g., the apprenticeship pledge, Chapter 7, p. 111) and awareness raising and media attention about success stories of young people in the workplace will encourage further organizations and agencies to work together to improve young people's futures.

In summary, critical to the improvement of young people's futures in the workplace are:

- awareness of the value a diverse work force including young people brings to an organization;
- a strategic approach towards the development of entry-level roles for young people that are suitably resourced by the organization;
- activities that bring education and work closer together;
- multi-agency activities where education, government agencies and organizations work together to shorten and simplify young people's journey from education to work;
- encouragement for employers to offer feedback on young people's job-search behaviours;
- adopting a psychological approach to sustain successful activities that encourage the employment and development of young people.

This section presents important messages for educators, employment advisors and employers not to overlook the importance of partnership working between education, industry and government support agencies to develop effective work roles for young people. Awareness of the transitional journey young people are undertaking is critical for employers to understand in order to reap the benefits that young people can bring to an organization. However, without an awareness of the benefits young people bring to the workplace few of these changes are likely to occur. The next section explores research designed to identify these benefits.

The benefits of employing young people

"Hiring and developing young people is not only the right thing to do but the smart thing to do with wide-ranging benefits for all involved" (Hannah Matta, personal communication, 2018), but how many organizations are aware of these benefits? This section will outline research exploring what young people bring to the workplace.

In order to access employers' views I used in-depth unstructured interviews to provide insights and explanations about the issues young people face transitioning into work. Open-ended questions asked "What advantages do you find in employing young people?" and "Why do you think organizations choose not to employ young people?" to gain a balanced view. In total, 21 participants from 19 organizations (11 private, five charities, two public and one research) volunteered to be interviewed. Of these participants 16 were routinely employing young people.

During the interview participants' comments were summarised and repeated back to ensure understanding and to validate the emerging themes (Bryman & Bell, 2003). Interviews mainly took place in participants' offices lasting 60 to 90 minutes. Written notes and audio-tapes were transcribed and analysed using template (King, 2004) and thematic analyses (Braun & Clarke, 2006) exploring similarities and differences in content and perspective (see Table 9.1 below).

Table 9.1 Summary of research findings (source: the author).

Themes	Participant employers' themes	Perceptions of others not employing young people
What young people bring to the workplace	*They are*: proactive and engaged; flexible and willing to take on responsibility and be moulded into work; energetic, passionate and enthusiastic; and are loyal to those who support them. *They bring*: fresh approaches; new ideas; different perspectives. *They want to*: work hard, make a difference and contribute to greater good. *They will*: improve productivity and encourage transfer of knowledge.	*They are*: hard work, requiring effort; have poor work behaviours; not loyal. *They bring*: difficulties, as they are more likely to be off sick; more interested in their social life and want lots of money. *They will*: cause fall out and their attitudes can threaten people (making them feel uncomfortable); work their own way.
Reactions to young people in the workplace	Positive feelings they bring pass on to others, invigorating departments, teams, staff and customers. They create a more diverse workplace; reducing stereotypes.	Other employers want *experienced staff* and have *an ageing workforce because they*: are playing safe; have preconceived ideas; assume there are no challenges with older workers; lack understanding of their transferable skills.
Organizational processes that support young workers	*Design work that*: motivates them (i.e., not boring); gives responsibility and has set targets. *When working with them be*: flexible to their needs; take time to appreciate their behaviour and training and development needs. *Give training and development*: to understand work processes and planning; and customer service. *Mentorship*: they should have mentors that are recognised and rewarded by the organization. *Organizational strategy*: to employ them and create a diverse workforce.	*Training and development*: they have issues requiring more training that needs to be provided by specialists and will come at a cost. *Misconceptions of training*: not expensive and does not need to be provided by specialists as their needs are no greater than others. *Lacking in organizational strategy*: not seeing the need for diverse workforce and have a poor business case for their employment.

(continued)

Table 9.1 (continued)

Themes	Participant employers' themes	Perceptions of others not employing young people
Social, cultural and educational issues	*Disadvantaged group in UK*: given negative image by media contributing to negative assumptions about employment. *Little being done* to help them into work so they have to take on short-term jobs; there needs to be an industry-wide strategy to employ more young people. *Many have difficult home circumstances*: with a background of long-term unemployment lacking soft skill development and employment networks; or having "pushy" or over-protective parents. *Poorly informed*: lacking up-to-date careers information.	*Educational issues*: poor educational standards create scepticism about what they can actually do; UK education is out of touch with the modern workplace. Education is inflating expectations of possible entry-level roles. *Education is improving*: some can achieve managerial roles on entry; now noting positive changes in education with increased graduate work experience and specialised coaching offered in schools.
Notes	'They', 'their' and 'them' refer to young people.	

Participants offered insight into what young people bring to the workplace and how other workers react to them. In addition, as many participants had worked in organizations not employing young people, they presented the opposing perspective of issues perceived by these employers. Participants described organizational processes helpful and supportive for young people and their transition to work and contrasted this with the perceived issues those with little experience of young people believed. Finally, participants highlighted the complexity of understanding youth employment by identifying social, cultural and educational issues making it difficult for young people to transition into work.

What young people bring to work and how others react to them in the workplace

Employers agreed that young people are proactive and engaged at work, bringing new ideas and fresh approaches, for example: "We noticed crazy ideas were no longer out of the question; some of those crazy ideas were actually fantastic ideas". They are energetic, passionate, enthusiastic and willing to take on responsibility and be moulded into work, for example: "They are often fearless and will step-up to take responsibility".

Critically participants noted young people wanted to work hard and make a difference. One company was examining the return on investment with their young workers noting "they (20 to 30 year olds) were outperforming other age cohorts".

Importantly, employers noticed that young people invigorate others, passing on their positive feelings to teams, staff and customers. For example, they: "Refresh others that they work with (who have been in the company a while) and help them to remember their enthusiasm". Further, young people can increase others' resilience: "They help me (business owner) cope and offer me lots of ideas". These factors further contributed to productivity and encouraged transfer of knowledge among workers, demonstrating the value of a diverse workforce.

What those not employing young people perceive young people have to offer

The differing perspective was that young people would be hard work, requiring much effort and attention from managers, supervisors and staff. Further, they would exhibit poor behaviours at work (e.g., being on their phone all the time, having superior attitudes) and would want to work in their own way (rather than how they are told). The belief was that the impact of these difficulties would cause "fall out" or bad feelings with other workers and that their attitudes and behaviours may threaten some staff and managers who were used to more subservient workers. The outcome of these perceptions was that these employers would rather offer jobs to experienced staff, assuming they will "slot into job roles" and offer little challenge to other workers.

Balancing perspectives

Study participants commented on these varying perspectives, for example describing managing young workers: "It can be hard work; but it is very enjoyable as a manager. This is a passion of mine and now we have got a business going with young people it can be so fulfilling". They also noted that employers with little experience of young people lack understanding of their transferable skills (e.g., with information technology) and that young workers were loyal to employers who gave them a break or trained them.

Further: "We had an ageing workforce (with an) average age of 45 years, four to five years ago, and now we have seen this change (employing young people) with our early career strategy". However, one participant noted that employing young people required careful stakeholder management: "We need to explain . . . that they may not be 'ready to go' to enable them to develop for future roles".

Supportive organizational processes and attitudes

Participants described a number of supportive processes helping young people transition into work. While there was less agreement as to the process, valuable advice was given about designing work that motivates (and not "mind-numbing"), offers responsibility and has set targets; taking time to be flexible to young people's needs, for example "Don't use (their need for feedback) as a reason for not giving them responsibility".

Job roles needed to be supported by training and development helping young workers to understand work processes, planning and customer service. Participants were keen to develop young people for future roles rather than to fit them to a specific role. These activities helped young people to develop confidence, soft skills (such as communication, influencing and commercial awareness), life skills and managerial skills.

Importantly, participants felt young people should have formal mentors who were recognised and rewarded by the organization. Mentorship and support went hand in hand with quiet listening and supportive leadership. For example:

> Command and control management styles will not be successful (they will not respond to tactics of fear or 'we are doing you a favour giving you a job'). Young people take leadership quietly; you need to earn their respect and you do this by understanding how to channel their energy.

Insightfully, eight participants described strategic organizational choices made to employ young people to create a diverse workforce, for example: "We are prepared to spread our resources to develop young people for the longer-term benefits they will bring to the company; we think of it as an investment". Or, noting active competition with other organizations (role anonymised):

To compete in the graduate market we have to position ourselves well to attract the best graduate xxxx. We know there is competition to employ xxxx graduates and we need to make sure we are positioned as an employer of choice. We have good jobs to offer and there is a lot of competition for these roles.

Perceived concern of those not employing young people

The differing perspective was that young people would require considerable training and development to be able to transition into a work role and that they had many issues (such as emotional problems) that would require training to be provided by specialists. The overriding concern was that such training would be expensive and is not required by experienced workers.

Balancing perspectives

Participant employers felt that there were misconceptions that young people's training was expensive or required specialist skills, suggesting there were no differences in young people's training needs compared with those of other workers. The key issue was that these employers lacked an organizational strategy to develop a diverse workforce and thus were putting forward a poor business case for employing young people as they did not see any of the benefits.

Social, cultural and educational issues surrounding youth employment

Participant employers agreed that young people were a disadvantaged group in UK society that was being given a negative image by the media causing young people's work to be undervalued. These views were seen to contribute to negative assumptions being made about young people in certain organizations. For example: "no-one really believes that they can do anything, or at least not until they are 30 years old". Little was being done to help young people into work and this caused them to have to take on short-term job roles to gain any employment. A more positive response would be to have an industry-wide strategy to employ young people, possibly using quotas.

Several participants felt many young people had difficult home circumstances. These issues may be associated with long-term unemployment in the family, reducing the young person's opportunities to develop soft skills associated with work or to develop social networks aiding employment. They described experiences of parents either being over-protective or "pushy", prospecting for work on their behalf. Their main experience was that young people were lacking in up-to-date careers information, not knowing where to look for work and what job roles were available.

It was felt that poor educational standards contributed to youth unemployment making employers sceptical about what the young person could actually do. Further, educators were felt to be out of touch with the workplace, particularly in the UK, as some had found young people from the European Union more aware of the KSAs needed in the workplace. Further, education was thought to be inflating young people's expectations of work roles they could achieve at entry-level. However, some employers had seen positive changes in education with practical placements during degree courses.

In summary, this research highlights that young people are proactive within the workplace, with their actions and behaviours invigorating the work of others and having an overall effect of improving productivity. They bring energy and enthusiasm to the workplace and are quick, willing to learn and to be moulded to organizational needs. Moreover, those not employing young people lacked experience of young workers, believing in stereotypes and assumptions about behaviours and the effort needed to support young workers. Valuable advice is given in relation to policy and the development of entry-level roles.

Future research

Studies like this are needed to raise employers' awareness of the benefits of a diverse workforce and to encourage strategic development towards employing young people. However, youth employment is an under-researched topic often seen as an "add-on" to adult employment enquiries when, in fact, young people are going through different processes transitioning from education into the workplace. We particularly need to understand more about identity threat to young people who can't get into work or who are trapped in underemployment. Not being able to find work or gain work appropriate to their human capital is likely to have a lifetime effect for young people. However, there are few studies of young people's progression from education to work examining the impact of their education on future experiences of work, work progression, unemployment and underemployment.

It is important that future research exploring young people's journey from education to work examines both the supply aspects (the young people themselves) and the demand aspect (the organizations employing young people). Indeed, it is the organizational understanding that requires most attention, particularly to guide employers to get the best from their potential and new employees and to safeguard their development into experienced workers.

Valuable work psychology concepts that can inform interventions to address issues of youth employment

Young people will transition more easily into work when employers recognise their need for the human and social capital that young people possess. Currently there is a lack of understanding that aspects of work psychology can successfully facilitate these transitions. Through this book we have emphasised the need to appreciate both the supply and demand aspects of youth employment and we have suggested a number of pivotal theories and models of work psychology that could enable more young people to successfully gain and maintain employment (see Figure 9.1 below). This section will explore the evidence presented in this book to encourage further use and development of models to increase our understanding of youth employment.

Identity concepts

We began looking at *Social Identity Theory* and have noted how many of the categorisations of youth employment place young people in groups with negative meanings. Groupings of unemployed, NEETs, contingent workers, and those seeking work experience suggest negative attributes of these groups when compared with experienced workers. This places young people in *out* groups compared with those who are *in* because they have perceived experience of the workplace. These attributes reinforce young people's exclusion from the workplace and leave them experiencing the demotivating consequences of *stereotype threat*.

Young job seekers suffer greatly from social categorisation and, once part of an 'out group', other demographic differences become salient such as nationality and educational attainment. Chapter 3 showed postgraduate students being negatively labelled as they had studied abroad for their degree. Hence social grouping has impact across many different populations. Further, the most disadvantaged group of young people in the labour market are those with few educational qualifications and skills, described as NEETs. Sadly, this group is often excluded from career or employability education while in school and are seen as a group of young

PIVOTAL THEORIES OF WORK PSYCHOLOGY
Underpinned by *Human Capital Theory*

➤ Identity Concepts: Social Identity Theory (identifying in and out groups, negative attribution), Stereotype Threat, Possible Selves (including Feared for Selves), Occupational Identity Formation, Future Work Self
➤ Person–Environment Fit (considering power and politics of organizational decision-making)
➤ Work Role Transitions (considering autonomy), Career Adaptability (considering reflection), Career Competencies (considering workplace development)
➤ Goal Setting (setting targets in entry-level roles, providing feedback)
➤ Organizational Culture (youth friendly, led by strategy, managerial choice, and shared beliefs)
➤ Job Characteristics Model and Vitamin Model to design and develop entry-level roles providing *good work*.

Figure 9.1 Pivotal theories of supply and demand issues of youth employment.

people who 'just need a job' rather than work in which they show interest. This lack of individual focus during job-search support identified in Chapter 3 was particularly demotivating for these young people, posing both stereotype threat and lack of opportunity to build their *future work self.*

Managers, being *in group* members, are often tasked with employment decisions about who makes up the future workforce. Faced with the negative dialogue about young people's attributes, they may perceive them as a threat to the dominant group of experienced workers that could disrupt working relationships and productivity (see employers' comments on p. 163 of this chapter). But, in reality, those who employ young people see this difference playing out in a very different way, with the energy and new ideas of young people invigorating the behaviours and attitudes of more experienced workers with positive benefits to both relationships and productivity. Whatever the outcome, the perspective of *social identity* is clearly a powerful concept requiring specific attention when developing a diverse workforce.

Activities that see 'in' and 'out' group members sharing together are the way forward to reduce Stereotype threat. Chapter 6 described experienced workers as role models offering knowledge building, coaching and support for young people both during their schooling and after they leave education. This support enables young people to become aware of the attributes of experienced workers and how they can describe their KSAs in ways that will be recognised by the in group. Further, Chapter 7 described how managers aware of the strategic objective to employ more young people learnt to develop an understanding of applicants' potential work competencies when assessing them for work roles. Once in a job role managers continued to guide young people's workplace behaviours by role modelling and behavioural direction. The authority provided opportunities for managers, workers and young people to come together to explore differences and similarities in projects and forums. These activities replaced previous perceptions of out group characteristics with more realistic understandings. In addition, young people (out group members) need support with their early work experiences. The local authority provided apprentice forums for young people to share their feelings and concerns (possibly of Stereotype threat) as a group. Apprentices were introduced to the workplace as a cohort with peers to support them in their early experiences of work (this successful tactic was also mentioned by employers participating in the research presented earlier in this chapter). Therefore, social identity theory applied to the workplace is a valuable model to assist the understanding of group difference, but requires additional concepts such as awareness of strategy, potential work competencies, provision of feedback, behavioural modelling and coaching in order to develop meaningful interventions to successfully introduce young people into the workplace.

Activities bringing the workplace closer to education mentioned in Chapters 6, 7 and 8 increase young people's understanding of the work roles they can see themselves performing in the future, thus building an image of their *future work self.* Therefore, young people gaining work in the industry of their choice, before venturing into higher education, are more likely to be successful after achieving their education goals and to move into that industry. Employers are attracted to young people who understand their working culture, appreciate the language used in their industry and have shown commitment to this type of work from a young age. There are examples of large employers in industries such as engineering and telecommunications (e.g., Carter, 2016) sponsoring young people who have undertaken work experience in their company through their time in higher education, with a job role for them when they leave education. With many young people today being aware of the dangers of getting into major debt during their educational journey this is an attractive way to pace education with work opportunities.

However, young people need time and opportunities to build up a picture of their *future work self* in order to inform their inquiries about the workplace and to drive their decision-making about the type of work that they wish to pursue. Sadly, as we see from Chapters 3 and 4, opportunities to create a *future work self* often depend on educational achievement and socio-economic status. It is important that exclusion from career development activities is not interpreted as lack of interest and opportunities to explore work experience are offered to all young people within education. Further, it is the reflection process and assimilation of these work experiences ('can I see myself doing this job or not') that are useful. Therefore, it is likely that those with lower educational attainment may require more support to make the best use of these experiences, although it is these young people who receive the least work-related support in education.

While the *future work self* is a useful device to explore what is possible for young people to achieve in coaching and work experience situations, it does appear overly optimistic in the current economic climate. Further development of how to work with concepts that cause young people to feel anxious about their possible selves (their *feared-for selves*, Markus & Nurius, 1986) and to deal with negative images and overcome anxieties would be useful developments of this model.

The development of young people's social identities into various occupational identities can be further supported after leaving education within the community. Less attention is paid to these informal activities occurring within families, friends and those in the local community, but they are useful in unstable work environments. Chapter 2 described developing evidence of community involvement in the socialisation of young people into work, for example in Greece and Spain, where the sharing of occupational networks has proved particularly helpful in gaining employment for young people (e.g., Vakola, Nikolaou & Kyriakou, 2015).

In summary, the identity concepts derived from social psychology and applied to the workplace have valuable explanatory power to assist young people in their transitions into work. Awareness of the perceptions associated with in and out groupings suggests useful interventions. But young people are not a homogenous group and vary in their stage of individual and occupational identity formation. So, while individual coaching interventions are time-intensive these are strong examples of how differences can be acknowledged.

Person–Environment Fit (PE)

Principles of *PE Fit* are fundamental to the way people are recruited into organizations and the gateway to work that young people have to pass through to achieve their first job role. The hiring manager is the gatekeeper to entry-level roles, making decisions about who will join the workforce. However, we assume hiring decisions to be rational with minimal political influence on decision-making. This over-optimistic approach ignores notions of power and politics fundamental to organizational life and the role decision-makers play in developing shared meaning within organizations (Ferris & Judge, 1991). The authors argue that many decision-makers, in the absence of defined standards of fit, are most likely to use the "like me" decision-making bias as they believe themselves to be successful employees and that those they appoint should be like them. But young job seekers are not like decision-makers and, without policy, strategy or quotas to assist their appointment, young people will be seen as not "fitting" with an individual job or with the organizational culture. Further, Ferris and Judge (1991) contend that hiring standards (and promotions making way for entry-level roles) are based on the competing interests of dominant groups within organizations. Therefore, if there are no, or few, young people in an organization there is no group supporting their interests in obtaining employment. Not only do young people not have a voice within such an organization but employing one or two young people would appear to be going against the organizational culture.

The notion of fit has become popular and is used in a general form by many people. However, it is possible to do work with which you do not feel a "fit" and probably many people do, particularly young people seeking any employment role. This suggests many are not happy or satisfied in their work and, again, this is likely to be true. Work, in its broadest sense, generates income enabling independent living and so is craved by many young people. Chapter 3 saw descriptions from young people who were cycling in and out of insecure work and looking forward to achieving more fulfilled job roles. This research suggests an expansion of the notion of fit into atypical work. This would be beneficial in a number of ways; to inform employers of the progression from insecure to secure work as a legitimate pathway and to look at the advantages employees from atypical work roles can bring to employers (e.g., being flexible and resilient). Further, education about the issues of lack of fit will help young job seekers see the perils of the insecure economy, encouraging them to seek or push to progress to more secure forms of work.

Difficulties facing young job seekers are sensitively explored in Chapter 5. All job seekers are facing complex decision-making processes about their futures in the workplace, an area they have little or limited information about and will feel anxious about discussing with future employers. This is an important difference to acknowledge about young job seekers (in comparison with those who have some work experience) and requires tolerance on behalf of employers when meeting this group. Training and increased contact with young people will enable organizational decision-makers to distinguish between future and current competence when assessing young people in the workplace (see Chapter 6 for more information).

In summary, while the notion of *PE Fit* is useful in our understanding of employment decisions it is incomplete, requiring complex understanding of the drivers of organizational decision-making. Further, with many now having to work in jobs lacking fit, some reconceptualisation of the concept is required. However, as a popular and flexible concept, it is a useful vehicle to begin conversations about the value of employing young people and to debate what they bring to an organization working towards a strategic decision to employ young people. This is a huge step forward as hiring managers will now have a benchmark against which to measure 'fit' and a dominant group of senior managers championing young people's employment. This will particularly be the case with changing job roles in the future, enabling the potential of young people's KSAs to be utilised.

Role transition, career adaptability and career competencies

Moving into work is a huge transition and we referred to *Work Role Transitions* (Nicholson, 1984) in Chapter 1 as a useful model to assist these changes. Fundamental to coping with the encounter of a new work role is adaptation, either by developing new KSAs and building experience or by proactively changing the role (role innovation) to benefit from their KSAs. But this process depends on the new employee having autonomy to make these changes and this may not be the case with entry-level roles. Employers on p. 164 of this chapter (Table 9.1) referred to "careful job design" for entry-level roles that may consider the young person's KSAs, values and experience, but there is no reference to autonomy in the adaption process. While these changes may occur through the mentorship process, input from the young person bringing new ideas and different perspectives may be lost. Using the role transition model with new employees offers a simple model to enable co-creation of job roles that can be innovative and developmental rather than assuming there is one best way to do things.

Career adaptability and career competencies

The education-to-work transition expects young people not only to have hard skills to perform the job role but also a wide range of soft skills suitable for the workplace. The point of debate explored in this book is how much these hard and soft skills should be developed in education and how much in the workplace. Employers with a strategy to bring young people into entry-level roles see themselves involved in this skills development (for example, by role-modelling and providing feedback, see p. 164). There are also employers offering early 'tasters' of work to young people during education breaks so both they and young job seekers can see career skills develop in working alongside education.

Young people developing *career competencies* (of reflection, communication and action behaviours) are learning to appreciate their own KSAs, to set targets and to reflect on their ability to achieve these targets. These are valuable skills and, if appreciated by employers, would enable the co-creation of entry-level roles. But reflection is not a simple skill to master, requiring support from a range of developers, mentors, teachers, friends and family members. There is growing evidence that reflection is an important part of building an occupational identity in the bridge between education and work. An interesting study (Get Mobile) used reflective tools and action learning in small group settings to support unemployed (or underemployed) female business and science graduates (from the UK, the Netherlands and Iceland) to enhance their work experience (Parry, 2013). This study revealed reflection as a planned activity enabling learning from experience, but this is not always a comfortable process and therefore requires support and coaching. Cycles of feedback and reflection were found helpful to select or reject appropriate aspects of participants' concepts of their *future work selves* that would motivate proactive job-seeking behaviours. This project encourages broad reflection on knowledge, skills and abilities, including consideration of things that are difficult such as moving to work in another country, in order to break down barriers to job-seeking activities that may be successful to achieve work.

However, missing from many of these studies is an awareness of how *career competencies* and behaviours play out in organizations and what role employers have in their development. A career theory of many years ago (Schein, 1971) is one of few to consider individual life career development alongside organizational processes of recruitment, promotion and succession. Coaching and mentoring are suggested as positive processes to bring diverse age groups of workers together for organizational benefit. This theory has been well supported by employers' comments earlier in this chapter, both within and outside organizations. More recent notions of *career adaptability* and *career competencies* are applied to young people during their education-to-work transitions, but their impact on workplace behaviours is rarely explored. For example, Chapter 6 developed a competency-based approach for school pupils to enable educational choice and early transitions from education to further study or work. Following through on how well these competencies equip young people in the workplace would broaden this understanding, particularly if employers took an active part in the research, with the added benefit of developing employers' appreciation of what young people can offer in the workplace. Exploring the synergy between work psychology theory and practice leads to a greater understanding of how and why young people are included within the workplace. It is important that this work speaks to organization practices to enable business to appreciate the advantages young people can bring and the practices that will enhance and grow future capability.

Goal setting

Goal setting forms a major role in the development of *career competencies* and the workplace transition of entry-level roles. The value of *goal setting* was particularly mentioned in activities supporting young people not to drop out of Youth

Guarantee Programmes (in Chapter 4), developing apprentices (see Chapter 7), focussing support from work coaches (in Chapter 8) and setting targets for entry-level employees (p. 164 of this chapter). But it is interesting to note that while young people are encouraged to seek feedback during their job-search process, this same behaviour may be interpreted less positively by employers (see p. 164 this chapter) as it suggests lack of self-confidence. Therefore, when goals or targets are being set with young people in entry-level roles these need to be supported by sensitive feedback and coaching to enable the young person to adapt their behaviours to the new work environment. However, there is a cost to providing a coaching resource to young people and employers were keen to raise awareness that such work should be rewarded within the organization and not be a hidden cost to individuals wishing to support young workers.

Organizational culture

Key to successfully recruiting young people to entry-level roles are youth-friendly *organizational cultures*. We have seen evidence of what this looks like in the intervention chapters of this book. Fundamentally, a culture welcoming young workers has people who appreciate the value of a diverse workforce and has a strategy to support the recruitment of young people. These organizations put in place measures to assist the recruitment of young people, to appreciate that their work competence is developing and to support young workers with feedback, mentoring, training and development. Further, they will engage in workplace activities to remove barriers to socialisation with the dominant groups within the organization (e.g., inviting a young worker to be involved in selection decisions). While this may appear a long list, once assimilated into organization practice employers express that young people are really no different to other workers (e.g., "have no different training needs compared to other workers", see p. 165 of this chapter).

Employers familiar with young workers suggest working and leadership styles that are flexible to their needs, taking time to appreciate their behaviours and offering quiet leadership (rather than a command and control style, see p. 164 of this chapter). Looking at the evaluation of the new apprentices in Chapter 7, young people are developing their work behaviours, testing out what they can and can't do. Risk-taking is a natural part of this process and an *organizational culture* that is not quickly dismissive of these behaviours is essential to enable productive work behaviours to emerge. Reassuringly, employers commented that mature working behaviours took only a few months to be in place.

Taken together, these activities support and develop the values and beliefs of people working in the company as common behaviours that get things done in the organization (Eldridge & Crombie, 1974). While such a youth-friendly culture is led by strategy and managerial choice, these are shared beliefs held by workers throughout the company. In the early stages of developing entry-level roles Handy's (1979) typology of *power, role, task* and *people* offers a simple model to evaluate where further intervention may be needed.

Good work

Two influential models of good work were described in Chapter 1 (the *Job Characteristics Model* and the *Vitamin Model*, see pp. 17–18) enabling people to develop and thrive in the workplace. Sadly, in many cases, these models only suggest work most young people can aspire to do, being far from the reality of atypical work. However, this suggests a major contribution that work psychology can make in the application of these models to the design and development of entry-level roles. We saw this opportunity used in Chapter 7 when an Occupational Psychologist worked with busy managers to design entry-level roles that would benefit both apprentices and hard-working local authority departments.

Employers describing entry-level roles designed for young people (see p. 164 in this chapter) were aware of some of the Vitamin Model characteristics (work offering variety, responsibility and challenge) along with the need for supportive supervision. Further, many were aware these job roles were the first steps for these young people to achieve independence in society. However, employers were uncertain what skills the young people had to offer and this made them cautious of offering opportunities for autonomy. Suitable interventions would be to recruit young people to generic roles (see Chapter 7) and to spend time exploring skills use and skills acquisition with the new worker in order to co-create a role benefitting from new ideas and perspectives. In a traditional work setting it is unlikely that a hard-pressed manager would have time to do this but support from specialist teams familiar with principles of work psychology and experience of working with young people could facilitate such growth. There is evidence of such activities in some work sectors (energy, engineering and telecommunication).

Summary

It is evident that theories from social and work psychology have much to offer in our understanding and assimilation of young people into today's workforce. Hopefully this book will be an advocate for developing this application to practice and disseminating examples of good practice. Summarising this material, it is clear that there is considerable energy spent in both preparing (some) young people for work and developing (some) entry-level roles for young people. However, this work is rarely joined up or followed through to useful evaluation of benefit. Once education and industry can work more closely together alongside work psychology these benefits will be more easily realised.

Advice to employers, young people and their families

Employers are able to shape youth employment to a great extent and there are benefits in developing a diverse workforce, both in terms of productivity and organizational development. The following key points will help employers to effectively introduce young people into their workforce:

- Build a strong business case to bring young people into the organization and develop an employment strategy considering what these young people will contribute to the workforce of the future.
- Take a work psychology approach using the principles of good work when designing entry-level roles to include variety, responsibility and some autonomy. Set targets and goals to challenge young workers and offer feedback on their achievement and developing skills.
- Develop and support young workers with feedback, mentoring, training and development based on their needs. Build a mentorship programme that recognises the time mentors spend with young people as part of their job role. Consider peer mentoring with successive cohorts of young people to build managerial skills.
- Begin entry-level roles in two or three areas with groups of new employees. Monitor changes and disseminate good practice before offering further opportunities.
- Offer support to both the young people and their managers and supervisors, particularly in the first years of employing young people, enabling mentorship and discussion forums to explore changing attitudes to working with young people.
- Build and develop an organizational culture supportive of young people. Construct activities bringing together new and experienced workers to share projects and develop new initiatives. Offer staff training to appreciate the transitional process young workers are experiencing.
- Encourage workstyles and leadership supportive to young people reinforced by role modelling and feedback through the performance appraisal process.
- Assist the recruitment of young people with selection and assessment processes that appreciate developing competences and skills that may have been learnt in differing contexts (such as atypical working). Ensure all applicants receive acknowledgement of their job application and brief feedback as to their performance. Offer young employees involvement in decision-making roles within the selection process.
- Evaluate activities regularly with multiple stakeholders to modify and change policy and practice refining changes. Disseminate good practice through the industry sector, learning from others' experiences.
- Work within the community with local education suppliers and support agencies enabling young people to gain knowledge of the workplace such as: what jobs are available, what people do at work, the intrinsic benefits to be gained in employment and what a good job looks like. Develop holiday-job roles and placements introducing part-time work opportunities.
- Introduce young workers into ambassadorial roles outside the organization to aid future recruitment.

The following points will be of benefit to young people (and their families) in their journey from education to work:

- Take every opportunity to find out about work. What do your parents, teachers, family members and their friends do at work? Visit their workplace if you can.
- Identify four or five work roles that interest you and find out as much as you can about the job and training needed to access these roles. Present this information to your teachers, friends and family to discuss your thoughts and potential choices of role.
- Find a mentor (your school may help with this) to discuss your work ideas with and see how subject choices and length of time in education may affect those ideas. But, be careful when selecting an adult to talk to about work. Be sure they have been introduced by your family or school and are known to them. Tell family or your school when you are meeting your mentor and where. You may like to take someone with you for your first mentor meeting.
- Work alongside your education in part-time or voluntary roles to explore what certain jobs are like. Reflect on what it feels like to be in the workplace, how it is different from education and on what is expected of you. What skills, knowledge and attitudes are you learning?
- Any experience of work is useful even if it is not positive (you may not like a job or the training may be long and difficult), but this all helps you to make decisions.
- Build and continue to build knowledge of the things that you do well (your strengths) and learn how to describe your strengths to others.
- Plan your job-search process by being selective and focussing on a specific set of work roles and employers. Set targets and review your progress and modify goals as you find out more. Talk to your mentor about what you are learning.
- When considering higher education, are you able to work alongside the course? Are there any placements or secondments that help you to experience work during the programme?
- Accept that there will be setbacks in your job search activities; ask for feedback and look at what you could do differently in the next application. You don't need to do this alone. Share experiences with your peers, offering them support and learning from their experiences.
- Getting your first job may not be the one that you want but it will offer experience to develop workplace skills. Continue the job-search process by seeking opportunities with companies with youth-friendly cultures.

Concluding remarks

Youth unemployment is a serious issue of our society and this book aims to raise awareness of the consequence of this issue for current and future generations. Useful frameworks from work psychology have been put forward to guide interventions and solutions to get more young people into good work roles. However, the issues of youth unemployment are complex, requiring multi-agency approaches to bridge disciplines to affect change. Too often employers are seen as passive entities in this situation whereas, in fact, they have important roles enabling young people to gain their first steps into the labour market. Further recognition is required by employers of the benefits young people bring to the workplace and the value they will contribute to on-going organizational growth, development and sustainability.

References

BBC News (2018). UK unemployment at lowest since 1975. *BBC News*, August. Downloaded on 28/11/19 from: www.bbc.co.uk/news/business-45181079.

Blackman, T., Greene, A., Hunter, D. J., McKee, L. et al. (2006). Performance assessment and wicked problems; the case of health inequities. *Public Policy and Administration*, 21(2), 66–80.

Braun, V. & Clarke, V. (2006). Using thematic analysis in psychology. *Qualitative Research in Psychology*, 3(2), 77–101.

Breen, R. (2005). Explaining cross-national variation in youth unemployment: market and institutional factors. *European Sociological Review*, 21(2), 125–134.

Bryman, A. & Bell, E. (2003). *Business research methods*. Oxford: Oxford University Press.

Calvard, T. S., Carter, A. J. & Axtell, C. A. (2008). The tenuous link: psychological contracts and perspective taking between a promotion agency and its workers. *European Work and Organizational Psychology In Practice*, 2, 3–13.

Carter, A. J. (2016, April). *Creating more jobs for young people*. Invited presentation for the British Psychological Society North East England Branch, Psychology in the Pub, York.

Chartered Institute of Personnel and Development (CIPD) (2016, September). *Attitudes to employability and talent*. London: Chartered Institute of Personnel and Development. Downloaded on 18/12/2016 from: www.cipd.co.uk/search?q=employability+talent.

Eldridge, J. E. T. & Crombie, A. D. (1974). *A sociology of organizations*. London: George Allen and Unwin.

Feige, E. L. (1990). Defining and estimating underground and informal economies: the new institutional economics approach. *World Development*, 18(7), 989–1002.

Ferris, G. R. & Judge, T. A. (1991). Personnel/human resources management: a political influence perspective. *Journal of Management*, 17(2), 447–488.

Gereffi, G. (1999). International trade and industrial upgrading in apparel commodity chain. *Journal of International Economy*, 48(1), 37–70.

Handy, C. (1979). *Gods of management*. London: Pan.

King, N. (2004). Using templates in the thematic analyses of text. In C. Cassell and G. Symon (Eds), *Essential guide to qualitative methods in organizational research*. London: Sage.

Markus, H. R. & Nurius, P. (1986). Possible selves. *American Psychologist*, 41, 954–969.

Nicholson, N. (1984). A theory of work role transitions. *Administrative Science Quarterly*, 29(2), 172–191.

Office for National Statistics (ONS) (2018, August). *Young people not in education, employment or training (NEET) UK*. Newport: Office for National Statistics. Downloaded on 19/11/18 from: www.ons.gov.uk/employmentandlabourmarket/peoplenotinwork/unemployment/bulletins/youngpeoplenotineducationemploymentortrainingneet/latest.

Office for National Statistics (ONS) (2018, October). *Human capital workplan: 2018*. Newport: Office for National Statistics. Downloaded on 19/11/18 from: www.ons.gov.uk/peoplepopulationandcommunity/wellbeing/articles/humancapital workplan/2018?utm_source=govdelivery&utm_medium=email.

Office for National Statistics (ONS) (2018, November). *Educational status and labour market status for people aged from 16 to 24 (seasonally adjusted)*. Newport: Office for National Statistics. Downloaded on 19/11/18 from: www.ons.gov.uk/employment andlabourmarket/peopleinwork/employmentandemployeetypes/datasets/educational statusandlabourmarketstatusforpeopleagedfrom16to24seasonallyadjusteda06sa.

Office for National Statistics (ONS) Forum (2018, October). *Young people and intergenerational fairness*. Newport: Office for National Statistics. Details downloaded from: www.eventbrite.co.uk/e/ons-forum-young-people-and-intergenerational-fairness-tickets-51509142231#.

Parry, E. (2013). *Final report for Get Mobile*. Project funded by the European Commission Lifelong Learning Programme. Sheffield: Inova.

Schein, E. H. (1971). The individual, the organization, and the career. *Journal of Applied Behavioral Science, 7*(4), 401–426.

SKOPE: ESRC Centre on Skills, Knowledge and Organisational Performance (2012, May). *Youth transitions, the labour market and entry into employment: some reflections and questions*. Research Paper no. 108. Oxford: ESRC Centre on Skills, Knowledge and Organisational Performance, the University of Oxford.

Vakola, M., Nikolaou, I. & Kyriakou, O. (2015). Dealing with unemployment through job pairing. Paper given as part of a symposium, A. J. Carter (Chair). *We need to tackle youth employment in other ways*. European Association of Work and Organizational Psychology Congress, 20–23 May, Oslo, Norway.

Index